Pax Democratica

Also by James Robert Huntley

EUROPE AND AMERICA: The Next Ten Years (*with W. R. Burgess*)

MAN'S ENVIRONMENT AND THE ATLANTIC ALLIANCE

THE NATO STORY

UNITING THE DEMOCRACIES: Institutions of the Emerging Atlantic–Pacific System

Pax Democratica

A Strategy for the 21st Century

James Robert Huntley

Foreword by Lawrence S. Eagleburger

First published in hardcover 1998

First published in paperback 2001 by
PALGRAVE
Houndmills, Basingstoke, Hampshire RG21 6XS and
175 Fifth Avenue, New York, N. Y. 10010
Companies and representatives throughout the world

PALGRAVE is the new global academic imprint of
St. Martin's Press LLC Scholarly and Reference Division and
Palgrave Publishers Ltd (formerly Macmillan Press Ltd).

ISBN 0–333–71767–8 hardback (*outside North America*)
ISBN 0–312–21326–3 hardback (*in North America*)
ISBN 0–333–94598–0 paperback (*worldwide*)

This book is printed on paper suitable for recycling and
made from fully managed and sustained forest sources.

A catalogue record for this book is available
from the British Library.

The Library of Congress has cataloged the hardcover edition as follows:
Huntley, James Robert.
    Pax democratica : a strategy for the 21st century / James Robert
Huntley ; foreword by Lawrence S. Eagleburger.
        p. cm.
    Includes bibliographical references and index.
    ISBN 0–312–21326–3
    1. Peace. 2. Security, International. 3. Democracy. I. Title.
    JZ5538.H86 1998
    327.1'7—dc21
                                                    97–49331
                                                        CIP

10   9   8   7   6   5   4   3   2   1
10   09 08 07 06 05 04 03 02 01

Printed in Great Britain by Antony Rowe Ltd, Chippenham, Wiltshire

Dedicated to the Memory

of
Clarence K. Streit (1896–1986)
whose 1939 book *Union Now* ushered
in the era of
unifying the democracies
in the pursuit of peace

and of
Jean Monnet (1888–1979)
who showed Europe
how to begin

Contents

Foreword

This is a book which looks at the world differently – differently from the way the policy pundits, media denizens and foreign policy experts are wont to do. The author, James Huntley, rests his case on a fundamental truth, often overlooked: that the 'foreign' relations of the United States and its highly-developed partners are no longer 'foreign' in the old sense. Over the past half-century, we have become thoroughly enmeshed in one another's economies, societies and political networks. Interdependence is no longer a convenient slogan, it is an inescapable fact of modern life for Americans and all others who aspire to keep up with a transparently interconnected world.

Our interdependence has grown out of the inexorable interlocking of modern scientific and technological development, instant communication (the Internet and Worldwide Web are merely the latest manifestations) and rapid transport of people and goods. Borders have become increasingly less relevant.

The United States has exercised world leadership since 1945 because no other nation was able to do so, nor would be accepted by the other powers. Successive US administrations used this leadership for the most part wisely by promoting, as a first priority, the institutionalization of joint effort among the democratic allies. The reason is simple: the other democracies' views of the world and their aims and interests most closely approximated ours, and our leaders understood this. We worked together well and, in the process, began to form a series of communities of interest and joint endeavour which have stood us – and the entire world, for that matter – in good stead. The most important ties have been institutionalized and made more or less permanent in such bodies as NATO, the OECD, the European Union and their ancillaries. Moreover, much of the way the democratic allies conduct themselves in more universal bodies, such as the United Nations, reflects their open, democratic, free market goals and methods and – increasingly – world sentiment as a whole.

Now, Mr Huntley contends, it is time to take stock of what we have wrought in these historic years, to survey the greatly changed world scene since the Cold War's end, to reassess the interests and goals of the great democracies, and to plan anew for a future which will continue to be more and more interdependent. For this new era, which might become the Era of the Democracies if we wish it, the democracies will require a group global perspective, they will need to re-define and re-state the principles of the democratic way of life, and they must develop improved common methods for attacking common problems.

But what we have won, often with great difficulty, must however not be thrown away during a deceptive lull in world affairs. No overriding great Crisis of Survival currently threatens us, but I believe one will surely come, sometime in the next few years, to tax and strain this half-built international system. It is time *now*, not just when we think we can afford to shift our focus from pressing national concerns, to undertake the reassessment and renovation of the international system. Back to the drawing boards. Mr Huntley suggests how we should begin.

After years of service – in diplomacy, thinktanks, and what we today are calling 'international civil society' – James Huntley retired to the western edge of the American continent to set down what he believed he had learned about war and peace and the importance of democracy. His geographic and intellectual vantage point is unusual. However, it is not on the margins but at the very centre of what ought to be a forthcoming great debate on the future of world order.

My friendship with James Huntley goes back a quarter-century. We have laboured in different institutional vineyards, but our paths have crossed many times as we worked to consolidate and build the Atlantic alliance and the larger Atlantic–Pacific community of democracies. I urge readers of *Pax Democratica* to ponder carefully what Mr Huntley has to say, because it is based on long experience and careful analysis, and provides a fresh – even rare – perspective on our future. There may be other, or additional, ways to accomplish the goals which he proposes, but the aims and the principles seem to me incontestable.

The wars, hot and cold, and the obscene dictatorships of this century have taught us much. While survival is always an ultimate goal, democrats – and Americans in particular – have persistently asked, 'Survival for what?' And the fundamental answer returns persistently: for the liberty without which life can have little meaning. We now see the United States, as a new millennium begins, poised at the centre of two interlocking communities, based on liberty, which it has laboured for years to create. These are an Atlantic and a Pacific community. In building this new kind of international institution, democracy and human rights have been central concerns. If the great allied democracies had any fundamental reason to unite as they have, it was for these indispensable and precious principles.

First principles, however necessary, are insufficient. Principles must be embedded in policies and structures that abet action. Absent the requisite 'political will', resting on publics that are at least moderately agitated about the international system, many will ask how major changes in policy can possibly be undertaken? Our present leaders, and even more the electorates in all the great democracies, seem disinclined to put a priority on their closest foreign entanglements. Domestic concerns can always seem more urgent. But this current prevailing 'wisdom' argues strongly for leaders to launch just such an appeal as James Huntley makes. The better-informed, better-educated, more-concerned and most authoritative people in every corner of our democratic societies need to put this case for fundamental change to their publics.

History suggests that strong leadership *can* on occasion generate political will. It has been my own experience that the profoundly good things of this century did not just happen. They were created through the unremitting work of individuals – leading democrats in several countries – who harnessed themselves together in the service of ideals and a vision. Such ideas are embodied in this book. Read on.

The Honorable LAWRENCE S. EAGLEBURGER
Charlottesville, Virginia
2000

Preface to the Paperback Edition

As a returned soldier . . . I cannot escape the feeling that in this partisan dallying with the League of Nation's [*sic*] Covenant, this country is being trifled with, and all the mighty sacrifice of millions held a light thing.

Veteran of the Great War, 1919[1]

My father was one of 4.3 million US 'doughboys' mobilized in World War I. In World War II, three times that many young Americans – including myself – were called to the colours to preserve democracy.

Of the 65 million mobilized by 16 belligerents in the 1914–18 war, around 8.5 million died; millions more were wounded and missing; more civilians died than did military. The 1939–45 figures dwarf these: the *Encyclopædia Britannica* (1995) estimates total deaths ('inexactly') at from 35 to 60 million; nearly half were civilians. Especially in World War II, a large number of the civilian dead were not collateral war casualties, but executed illegally by the aggressors in the course of 'occupation duties'.

The dead of the two world wars died needlessly. A better international system could have saved them. Leaders and peoples, however, in 1914 and 1939 were caught under the measureless burdens of their national myths and histories, in the grip of their own ignorance.

Apart from the staggering war deaths in the 20th century, an additional multiple of three to five times more civilians were exterminated illegally by governments. Only a tiny fraction of these executions – for that is what they were – is attributable to democratic governments; the vast majority were perpetrated by the Communist regimes, the Nazi tyranny, the Japanese before 1945 and, in not inconsiderable numbers, by smaller but still vicious despotisms. Chapter 1 discusses both this phenomenon and war.

Out of both world wars and the unspeakable mass cruelties of modern totalitarianism came a widespread sense of public outrage and determination that things *must* change. Some changes came, but such waves of resolution inevitably fade.

'Back to normalcy' was the cry in 1919. With a vengeance after 1929 came general economic and political disaster. After World War II, the victors did a better job by setting up the UN system. When the Cold War intervened, the West – this time led by the United States – combined resources and energies to convince the Communist powers that they could not dominate the world by either war or intimidation. By 1990 what has been called loosely 'the international community', depending mainly on such bodies as the astounding European Union and the equally amazing North Atlantic Treaty Organization, had begun to make a big difference in the way the world's affairs were run. The West's record from 1945 to 1990 was far different from its pitiful performance in the two decades after 1919; Chapter 2 tells this tale.

Nevertheless, despite major improvements, as the new millennium began, humans and their institutions were challenged again. It is not all certain that we can hold on to the beginnings of a world community that we began to build from 1945–90. Through the 1990s, various crises around the world cried for action. The Persian Gulf war elicited a powerful, immediate response from the UN, NATO countries and at least temporary allies in the Middle East; the aftermath a decade later was not yet satisfactorily resolved. Various wars broke out in Africa, where the response of neighbours and sometimes of distant powers was either too late or inadequate to contain conflict. Several countries in Latin America were destabilized by the deterioration of fledgling democratic regimes or internal conflicts touched off, for example, by the impact of the international drug trade. A few states in Asia and North Africa, widely characterized as 'rogues', endangered their neighbours, and in some cases world peace, through the combined threats of despotic and unpredictable regimes plus possession of weapons of mass destruction. In 1997, a sudden financial collapse in East Asia brought fears of a regional or even world-wide 'economic meltdown', which fortunately was averted through prompt and decisive action by international institutions and leading powers. The announcement in 1999 that both Pakistan and India possessed presumably usable nuclear weapons puzzled and frightened the world community.

Beginning in the early 1990s, conflict and severe ethnic strife broke out as the jerry-built Yugoslavia – a creation of the peace settlement of 1919 – began to come apart. The United Nations and finally NATO and other European regional institutions intervened belatedly, first in Bosnia and in 1999 in the Serbian province of Kosovo, to try to prevent still more bloodshed and displacement of whole populations on a vast scale. In the Russian province of Chechnya, a civil war broke out twice in the last decade of the 20th century; rebellion and disorder were quelled mainly by extreme military measures that brought great suffering and world condemnation of the Russian government. The new century promises no quick or easy end to these and other threats to stability and progress in various parts of the world.

This is by no means a full catalogue of the world's crisis points – political, military, economic, environmental, or otherwise – as the new millennium begins. But this sobering experience, at a time when thinking people had felt that, with the end of the Cold War and the collapse of the Soviet superstate, a new peaceful era was beginning to unfold, rudely shattered such hopes.

Despite the great progress, in advancing prosperity for many, in introducing and nurturing democratic government and respect for human rights in many former dictatorial states, in learning how to settle conflicts in new and peaceful ways, and in bringing nations and peoples closer together to confront global dangers, such as environmental deterioration and international crime, the record of the 20th century and the beginnings of the 21st century, did little to reassure the world's peoples that a new day had in truth arrived.

Thus, despite major improvements from 1945 to 1990 in the way the world runs its peoples' common affairs, humans and their institutions are challenged yet again. It is not at all certain that we can hold on to the beginnings of a world community that we have built in the past half century. And even if we can hold this now-old, thin line, post-1945 visions and institutions are insufficient for the days ahead. The resolve of 'never again' is once more fading. But more than ever, we require still greater changes in the way nations and peoples conduct their common business. If we wait too long to do this, the world could revert to the greatest excesses of the century just past . . . or worse.

To make sure that we do not lose the foundations of community so laboriously laid down, and to energize more changes, good men and women everywhere will have to team up. This book is about things that democratic governments and peoples should do, in concert, to give our successors a decent framework for managing world change long term. Our priority should be to strengthen a new fragile Community of Democracies, which can bring about *Pax Democratica* – a Democratic Peace. This will be a new kind of order, based on democracy, not on hegemony of some over others.

Fortunately, there are signs in the new century that give rise to hope that the world might reorganize itself sufficiently, modifying international institutions and methods and placing much more reliance on democracy – the theme of this book – as the cement of the global community. In the summer of 2000, the Polish government invited the foreign ministers of several score democracies from around the world to begin, in Warsaw, a Community of Democracies. Many of the principles set out in this book, especially the definition of good democratic government and practices and some of the ways in which co-operation among democracies might be better institutionalized, were discussed or at least broached. Nongovernmental groups and individuals working for democracy and peace have also begun to discuss how the world might be reorganized on democratic principles by the peoples and governments who have everything to gain, that is, those who already live under democratic regimes or who aspire to do so.

But the international dialogue begun in Warsaw in 2000 can be only a small beginning. Individual nations will have to change the way they manage their involvement in world affairs, and this will mean not only (at least in democracies) serious and prolonged public debates about the purpose and direction of foreign policies, but if the outcome is to be successful and lead to a far better framework for peace and all other good things, considerable changes must take place in the attitudes and understandings of political leaders, educators and other leaders of the complicated societies which make up modern nations. And ultimately, publics will have to learn new ways to think about their own goals in an ineluctably interdependent world.

Experts in government, diplomacy, the media and academia may be interested in this book; they influence the course of affairs and mould public opinion. Some of these specialists believe that we are locked into a world system based on the balance of power, that *Realpolitik* will for a long time remain the only practical way to organize a world animated pre-eminently, as they see it, by nations and their interests.

But other specialists and concerned citizens might be ready to consider an alternative model for world order and to be persuaded that the prevailing paradigm could be improved. Together, their changed views could have a powerful influence in democracies.

Because the United States, with all its faults, remains the best hope of the world for some time to come, this book is addressed especially to Americans. Between 1941 and 1945, the vast majority of US citizens came to share a fresh view of our world responsibilities. But now, the novel concept of the 1940s, that if their great nation acted in the best interests of mankind it would best serve its own interests, is fading. Since the euphoric end of the Cold War, the American people and their political classes are paying less and less attention to the great long-term issues of world order.

No US administration since the Cold War ended has offered Americans a coherent, long-range international vision. There were glimmers in 2000, and off-stage noises during the run-up to the elections of that year, but generally speaking neither major US party has competed to show the people how to meet the tremendous world challenges ahead, to put forward a compelling concept that would entitle us to continue to deserve Lincoln's encomium, 'the last best hope of mankind'. To help bring about *Pax Democratica*, a world order based ultimately on federal principles that we Americans invented, is our true vocation. Chapter 3 explains this, telling the tale of how the world system arrived at the present day.

However, this book is addressed not only to Americans, but also especially to British, German, French and Japanese citizens, because – along with Americans – they comprise the strongest, richest and most stable democracies in the world. Over the past few decades, these five countries have shown themselves more capable than others of providing the leadership and the resources for accomplishing demanding international tasks. Their democratic credentials are tested. They are a good group to bring about *Pax Democratica*.

Other tested democracies – largely the members of NATO and the OECD – have shared in building the present Euro-Atlantic system. They too have helped set the foundations for the new Intercontinental Democratic Community that is required for the next century. They have a continuing role to play, and this book is for them too.

The experienced democratic peoples are more of one mind about essentials than other groups in the world. They not only share strong common interests, but they *know* that they do. They have already developed sophisticated ways of working together that do not characterize other international groupings; this is historical fact, not bias or wishful thinking. It is with these likeminded peoples that we must begin to re-fashion world politics.

Finally, this book is also for *all* democrats, anywhere, who believe that a decent future can only be achieved within a free civic order. Some live in societies (such as the former Soviet empire) newly liberated from autocracy, but aspiring to 'join the Club' of stable, prosperous democracies. Some are just now constructing, or reconstructing, a democratic order.

Still other democrats-in-their-hearts unfortunately live in iron dictatorships; individually they may be modern-thinking people but the societies around them sleep, in terms of politics or economics or human rights. Their future is problematical; we who live in experienced constitutional democracies need to reach out to these isolated democrats and create new links between today's likeminded nations so that non-democracies, once liberated, will have a community to join. The challenges posed by pre-modern nations are outlined in Chapter 4; succeeding chapters outline a vision, and plans and problems in creating a new world system.

The editor of a journal of international affairs recently rejected a friend's article: ' . . . as you know my views are different from yours in some respects. You tend to focus on what *should* be done; I, more on what *can* be done. . . '. Readers will see that I fall into the 'what *should* be done' category. I believe, if the stakes are high enough and we understand that, then we *can* do what we *should* do. If not tomorrow, then the day after. At least we can try.

JAMES ROBERT HUNTLEY
Bainbridge Island, Washington
2000

Acknowledgements

This book could not have been written without the patience, encouragement, dedication and infinite common sense of my wife, Colleen Grounds Huntley.

Over many years, I also owe a large debt of gratitude to many friends and colleagues for wisdom, fresh insights, helpful criticism and unflagging support in my quest to do something difficult that they and I all thought was important. Chief among these I must mention, and thank especially: Amelia Augustus, Beatrice Bazar, David Barton, Georges Berthoin, John Brademas, Robert Brand, Peter F. Brescia, Bill Brock, Dean Claussen, Richard N. Cooper, Peter Corterier, John M. Davis, Jonathan Davidson, Brewster C. Denny, Samuel De Palma, François Duchêne, Lawrence S. Eagleburger, Herbert Ellison, Pierre Emanuelli, Robert Foulon, Malcolm Fraser, Raymond D. Gastil, Reinhard and Hildegard Geimer, Carl Gershman, Elliot Goodman, Albert Hamilton, Charles Heck, Arthur Hoffman, J. Allan Hovey, Robert Hunter, G. John Ikenberry, Masamichi Inoki, Christopher Jones, Erasmus Kloman, John Leech, H. W. Lessing, James V. Martin, James Moceri, George Modelski, Frank Munk, Leslie Lipson, Hisahiko Okazaki, Richard Olson, Robert K. Olson, William C. Olson, Misashi Owada, Charles Patrick, Ancil Payne, John Richardson, Ray Raymond, Walter R. Raymond, Sir Frank Roberts, Brent Scowcroft, Adolph W. Schmidt, Melvin Small, Robert Strausz-Hupé, George Taylor, Lars Uhrdin, R. W. Van Wagenen, Donald Vollmer, Alan Lee Williams and A. E. Younger.

Joseph A. Bulger is the unsung hero of the Appendixes' graphics. I must also thank Dave Thompson for assistance and advice in computerizing manuscripts.

Special gratitude goes to Sherwood L. Fawcett, Ron Paul and James M. McDonald of the Battelle Memorial Institute. They encouraged and enabled me to undertake research on which a good deal of this book is based. The decade I spent as a Battelle Fellow was invaluable.

Others, now passed away, deserve mention but the roll is too long to call.

JAMES R. HUNTLEY

An ABC of Key International Organizations

UNIVERSAL OR WIDELY-INCLUSIVE INSTITUTIONS

IBRD	World Bank (1945)	Development loans
IMF	International Monetary Fund (1945)	Loans to troubled economies, coordination
UN	The United Nations (1945)	World forum, deals with all questions
WTO	World Trade Organization (1995) formerly GATT (1948)	Global trade issues, reduction of barriers, adjudication of trade disputes

SELECTED REGIONAL AND SPECIAL-PURPOSE BODIES

ANZUS	Tripartite Security Treaty (1952)	Defence pact, along NATO lines, binding Australia-New Zealand-US
APEC	Asia-Pacific Economic Cooperation forum (1989)	Pacific Rim market economies' planning group, trade stimulator
ASEAN	Association of Southeast Asian Nations (1967)	Promotes economic growth, development in region
CofE	Council of Europe (1949)	Defends human rights, promotes democracy and European cooperation
EU	European Union (1993); united ECSC (1952), ECE, Euratom (1958)	Engine for economic and political unity of Europe; guardian of the single market and currency
Mercosur	Southern Cone Common Market (1991)	Links six big South American economies in future union
NATO	North Atlantic Treaty Organization (1949)	Mutual defence, security, crisis planning

OECD	Organization for Economic Cooperation & Development (1961)	Industrial democracies' joint economic clearinghouse, statistical agency, development aid planner, critic
OSCE	Organization on Security and Cooperation in Europe (1975) (formerly CSCE)	Discusses and monitors security from Atlantic to Urals; mediates conflict
WEU	Western European Union (1955)	Defence union for W. Europe, NATO link
C of D	Community of Democracies (2000)	The key proposition of this book, tentatively begun in Warsaw on a global basis

EVOLVING A DEM

Composite extracted from:
Huntley, James Robert, Pax Democratica: A Strategy for the 21st Century
(London Macmillan; and New York St. Martin's Press, 1998).

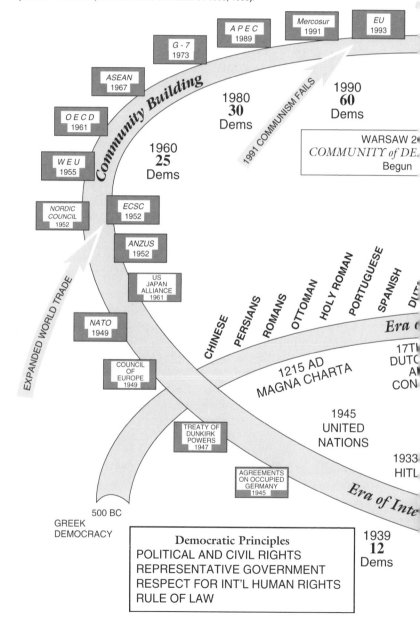

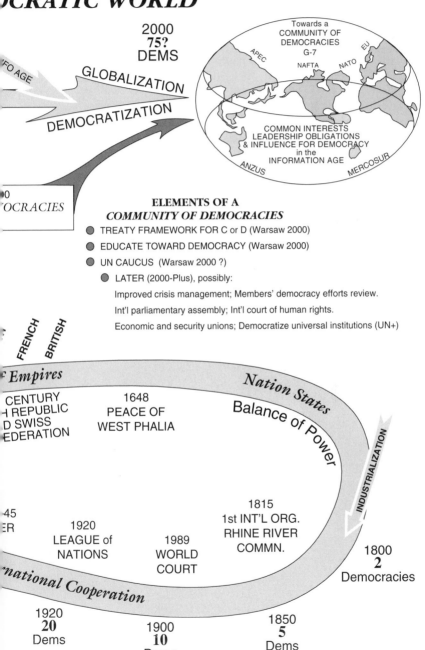

CRATIC WORLD

2000
75?
DEMS

FO AGE

GLOBALIZATION

DEMOCRATIZATION

Towards a
COMMUNITY OF
DEMOCRACIES
G-7

APEC   EU

NAFTA   NATO

COMMON INTERESTS
LEADERSHIP OBLIGATIONS
& INFLUENCE FOR DEMOCRACY
in the
INFORMATION AGE

ANZUS   MERCOSUR

0
OCRACIES

ELEMENTS OF A
COMMUNITY OF DEMOCRACIES

- TREATY FRAMEWORK FOR C or D (Warsaw 2000)
- EDUCATE TOWARD DEMOCRACY (Warsaw 2000)
- UN CAUCUS (Warsaw 2000 ?)
  - LATER (2000-Plus), possibly:
    Improved crisis management; Members' democracy efforts review.
    Int'l parliamentary assembly; Int'l court of human rights.
    Economic and security unions; Democratize universal institutions (UN+)

FRENCH   *BRITISH*

Empires   *Nation States*

CENTURY
REPUBLIC
D SWISS
EDERATION

1648
PEACE OF
WEST PHALIA

Balance of Power

INDUSTRIALIZATION

-45
ER

1920
LEAGUE of
NATIONS

1989
WORLD
COURT

1815
1st INT'L ORG.
RHINE RIVER
COMMN.

1800
2
Democracies

national Cooperation

1920
20
Dems

1900
10
Dems

1850
5
Dems

1 War, Demographic Cleansing and Democracy

The 20th has been a terrible century. Both war and demographic cleansing became much more efficient. Between 170,000,000 and 230,000,000 human beings lost their lives in the wars and the arbitrary illegal killings of our era.

But paradoxically, this has also been a century of hope. Overall, people treat each other better and care more. Humanitarianism is a worldwide, well-organized trend, thanks in part to unprecedented communication and interaction among all peoples. And almost unnoticed, the greatest political invention of this century – the European Union – represents an historic advance on every form of international togetherness that went before, creating zones of peace where before, war was always just around the corner.

We must learn how to strengthen further the brotherly impulses of our world, to suppress the propensities for war and mass murder, and to create ever-larger zones of peace and freedom ... a state of affairs that would be worth calling 'a new world order'. The principles of democracy applied within nations, plus groups of nations organized around democratic principles, give us the best chance to capitalize on the hopes and successes of mankind and to control the terrors of the future.

This is not an impossible task. We *can* bring about a *Pax Democratica* because we have already begun well to lay its foundations, in the European Union, the Atlantic community, some key Pacific arrangements and larger webs of cooperation. What we have built is not enough for the future, but it is a good beginning. We are on the way to inventing a new political pattern for the world. We must finish the job, because the alternatives are too grim.

DICTATORSHIP VS DEMOCRACY

Hitler had been in power four years and the Great Depression was on when Anne Morrow, wife of the misguided hero Charles Lindbergh, wrote *The Wave of the Future*.[1] She argued, 'better Fascist

1

than dead'. Her central proposition: Democracy is working badly. Hitler and other dictators are showing how we can have full dinner pails and peaceful societies by putting order before liberty. Relax, she wrote, and let the wave of the fascist future wash over you.

Lenin's and Stalin's apologists in the West said the same things from the 1920s to the 1980s. The Communist arguments were, in the eyes of many softheaded intellectuals and the downtrodden, more noble than those of Hitler and his racists; Soviet Communism, they said, held a wide swathe of the world in a sort of trust for the goodly working man, whose kind formed the great majority. Social justice would eventuate everywhere if people would simply endure the Dictatorship of the Proletariat for a while ... well, maybe for several decades ... or as long as it had to take.

The confrontation between Communist dictatorship and the Western democracies – the Cold War – really began in 1917, ending only in 1990. The standoff with fascist nationalist dictatorships began in the 1920s, gathered force in the 1930s, and culminated in World War II.

The advent of nuclear weapons (1945) and the war-born power of the Soviet Union introduced sinister elements into the Cold War. A peace movement composed of Western intellectuals, frightened people and the immature mouthed the proposition, 'Better Red than dead'.

But the big dictators lost out. As the last half of the century wore on, it became evident to all who could see – Germans, Japanese and others who had survived fascist dictatorship, as well as Russians and satellite peoples who suffered under Communist dictatorship – that the supposed gains of totalitarian control were at best ephemeral, entailed ultimate catastrophe and in the end were not worth the sacrifice of liberty. They, as had others before them, learned that only liberty, accountable government and the rule of law give humans the only real chance to create their own future. A vast number of peoples began to see that with democracy, if things didn't go well, one could always start over again ... and yet again, if necessary. Without the knout or firing squad.

If Hitler and the Japanese militarists hadn't been opposed by force and defeated, after millions of deaths ... and if a goodly portion of the world's democracies hadn't stood up for four decades after 1945 to Stalin and his successors, saying, in effect, 'Better *dead* than Red' – despite the enormous risks of a third, nuclear World War, then the world might well have had to say 'Goodbye, Democracy' for a very long time to come.

The future of civilization itself has been at stake at least thrice in this century. It could be challenged again in the next. Why is democracy the best bet for meeting this challenge?

WAR, DEMOCIDE AND DEMOCRACY

My early thinking life began with a simple proposition: Wars have killed millions, for insufficient reason. War is humankind's greatest evil. Good people should make a system to eliminate war.

Not yet out of school, I came to believe that the democracies must make war impossible. To get peace and preserve freedom, however, they must be prepared to go to war to stop aggressive dictatorships, because these breed wars. Those were the simple messages I believed in, worked for. Those ideas won World War II and the Cold War. But in thinking today about the political future of humankind, these propositions for me, although still valid and powerful, are no longer sufficient.

Authoritarian regimes, answerable to no one but a single strongman or handful of bosses, are largely responsible not only for the atrocious slaughter of modern wars but also for the illegal and arbitrary murder of defenceless civilians on a vast scale under government authority. This kind of killing is *democide*, which has taken even more lives in this century than war. Priority should now go not just to stopping dictatorships but to their replacement by democratic regimes.

To banish both war and democide by promoting democracy is the central task of the coming century, perhaps of the next millennium.

THE SOURCES OF DEMOCIDE AND WAR

R. J. Rummel wrote *Death by Government*[2] after years of study of perhaps the world's most grisly phenomenon: the arbitrary, unlawful, organized murder by governments – overwhelmingly, the non-democracies – of *170,000,000* defenceless people in the first nine decades of this century. Rummel has coined a new word for this kind of death: democide, which includes genocide (e.g. the Nazi killing of Jews or Gypsies) but also 'politicide' (Hitler's 1934 purge of the SA; the Viet Minh murder of nationalists), 'mass murder/

massacre' (such as Nazi reprisals in Lidice and Malmedy or on a vast scale in Yugoslavia; the Japanese rape of Nanking), elimination of whole classes (Stalin's annihilation of the Kulaks) and government-authorized terror (Guatemala death squads; Argentina's 'disappearances').[3]

These democide figures do not include military deaths in warfare, or noncombatants killed in attacks on clearly military targets. Because of the primitive state of civilization and international law, war deaths are still considered 'legitimate killing'. But democide deaths – arbitrary and illegal killings, by government agents acting under authority – have no legitimacy. The distinction may be repulsive, but it is real.

Battle deaths in this century (in both domestic and civil wars) Rummel calculates at about 38,000,000. This is only about one-fifth as many as the 170 million killed through democide by governments, the vast majority of them dictatorial non-democracies, since 1900.

Together, democidal deaths and war dead total 210 million humans, give or take some millions, who have died in the 20th century from the barbarism of war plus democide.

In *Out of Control: Global Turmoil on the Eve of the 21st Century*,[4] Zbigniew Brzezinski analyses roughly the same phenomena, although defining terms a bit differently, and calculates a combined total of 170,000,000 'megadeaths', including war dead. Both Rummel and Brzezinski concede that it will never be possible to arrive at exact figures. Most dictatorships, by their nature, want to obscure such grisly facts; many simply are incapable of keeping accurate records. Rummel has invested years of scholarship in his macabre calculations; his final estimates seem generally cautious. He (and Brzezinski) may have erred, if at all, on the conservative side; the total deaths by democide in this century could well be much greater, especially if one adds in figures for the 1990s, estimated in 1997 at 9 million more.[5] The ultimate statistics will remain for ever unknowable. But how much is enough to make such a ghastly point?

From his grim accounting, Rummel draws these conclusions:

- The deaths by democide in this century were perpetrated overwhelmingly by dictatorships, not by democracies which, by their built-in safeguards for life and the rule of law, severely limit the numbers of atrocities their leaders could authorize, even if they would.

- The vast bulk of these 20th century megadeaths by democide (Rummel: around 170 million) were committed by just five regimes. Top billing goes to the USSR (61m!); next in order come the People's Republic of China (35m), Nazi Germany (20m), the Kuomintang regime in China (10m), Japan between 1936 and 1945 (6m), and the Chinese Communists before coming to power in 1949 (3.5m). Five other regimes committed megamurders exceeding 1 million: the Khmer Rouge in Cambodia, Turkey (from 1900 to 1918, mainly Armenians), Vietnam (1945–87), Poland (1945–48, extinguishing civilian Germans in Silesia), Pakistan (1958–87) and Tito's Yugoslavia (1944–87). Many other murderous regimes, each with records of less than one million democides, bring the overall total to about 170 million for the first nine decades of this century.

- Those who think killing is wrong must face this evidence and acknowledge that while organized warfare is an abomination and a top requirement for elimination in any peaceful, orderly world of the future, war on defenceless people by democide has been much more vicious. Simply put, democide has eliminated nearly five times as many human beings arbitrarily and unjustly from the face of the earth in this century, than has war. The regimes which perpetrate democide know no rules; their crimes are even more difficult to contain than war: 'sovereignty' usually protects them. Democide has been the ultimate and most significant violation of human rights in this century, and probably in all others.

- Replacing arbitrary and autocratic regimes with democratic governments is the best route to curb drastically, if not eliminate, democide.

But what of the connection between war and democracy? This has also been made clear.[6] While fledgling democracies may sometimes war on each other or democracies war on non-democracies, stable democracies rarely if ever war on each other. There is little chance now, for example, that France and Germany will again go to war. But this is not only because they are mature democracies. A second factor in maintaining no-war relationships is a system to bind likeminded nations securely together. Such bodies as the European Union, NATO, the OECD and the Council of Europe have been indispensable to the construction of peace in Europe.

SOME CONCLUSIONS FOR THE DEMOCRACIES

Given the historical record, we can conclude that:

1. Well-established democracies, tied together in cooperative webs, are most unlikely to make war on one another.
2. Well-established democracies are highly unlikely to perpetrate democide on their own peoples, or on others.

Therefore:

3. Democrats everywhere should regard it as their first duty to help extend the realm of democracy in the world, as the best insurance that eventually, at some unknowable time in the future, both democide and wars will become relics of a gloomy past.[7]

This should be the top international priority of every humane government. But in order to promote democracy effectively, and to build global conditions in which all nations and peoples can prosper and be reasonably secure:

4. The democracies should form a permanent, strong intercontinental community among themselves, open to others when they are ready, able and willing.

Begun in timely fashion and executed effectively, such a combined policy will result in *Pax Democratica* ... the Peace of the Democracies.[8]

BUT WHAT IS DEMOCRACY?

There will always be disputation about this, because by its very nature democracy promotes change and protects those very differences of opinion its practitioners cherish. It is a broad, all-encompassing 'church', with room for all who revere freedom, and for virtually all ways of doing things, except for ways which would destroy democracy itself. Democracy is a set of general principles and a do-it-yourself kit of tools. But there can be no one-size-fits-all model.

The forms and practices of democracy are enormously pliant: Canadian democracy, for instance, is a good deal different from that of South Korea or Greece or Germany or Botswana ... or even (sometimes especially) different in crucial respects from that of Canada's great neighbour to the south.

Modern democracies embody these principles:

1. Political freedoms, including free periodic elections, universal suffrage, plural party systems with majority votes leading to changes of government, elected free parliaments with the right of legislation, taxation, budgetary control, and deliberation of (including opposition to) the government's measures.

2. Guaranteed civil rights, including freedom against arbitrary imprisonment, freedom of speech and assembly, freedom of the press, freedom of petition and association, freedom of movement, freedom of religion and education.

3. An independent judiciary and courts to which everyone can have access.[9]

These are the basics. Alone, they will not guarantee social or economic goals or national survival, but they are the best and surest framework for attaining whatever a particular people want. Societies' objectives and structures may change; adherence to the principles should not.

No democratic nation in practice honours these rules fully and consistently. But with time, the ideals and practices of democracy tend to become second nature and increasingly durable. It is fair to say that virtually all western European countries, Japan, the United States and Canada, Australia and New Zealand, plus a score or more (usually very small) countries in other corners of the world, have strong records in the protection of civil rights, the rule of law, and the exercise of political liberties.[10] By the time a nation has reached a stage of advanced democracy, 'the ship tends to right itself' when excesses or backsliding occur; this is one of democracy's great strengths.

A word too about democracy's 'tool kit', the social infrastructure without which it is virtually impossible to make the principles operative. Such seemingly minor behaviour as the conduct of citizens' meetings, the civility of political debates, the acquiescence to majority votes but respect for the concerns of minorities, the willingness to compromise, the respect for duly constituted authority, obedience to constitutionally established rules and laws coupled with a knowledge of how these can be changed without violence, and the practice of free speech (e.g. London's Hyde Park) are some of the essential tools.

A frequent mistake is to equate democracy with capitalism. They often go together but are not the same. Capitalism is another name for a free market economy in which business is largely in private hands. This book emphasizes the superiority of democracy as a way of organizing political life, including making decisions about the framework within which the economy operates, but also about many other matters.

Some commentators make a distinction between 'republics' and 'democracies', defining the latter as direct rule by the people and identifying 'republics' with a system in which citizens elect representatives who work on their behalf in a parliamentary body. This distinction, however, is today largely irrelevant. In a modern democracy, the people are sovereign, whether citizens vote in a town meeting or elect representatives who act for them at various levels.

Federalism is a method of organizing states, particularly useful for large or multi-ethnic countries. A dictatorship may on paper be a 'federation', but in practice it is virtually impossible to have a true federation, with various levels of self-government, without democracy as its organizing principle. Democracies may or may not be federations; federalism tends to enhance self-government but it is not necessarily appropriate for every society. Federal principles can be extremely useful in organizing multi-state relations, as the European Union is showing.

In the heyday of the Soviet and Nazi empires, the word 'totalitarianism' was coined to describe iron forms of total control over individuals and society. Unchecked domination by a single individual or group of the levers of government, no matter what the guiding ideology (if any), constitutes dictatorship, the antithesis of the open society. Today a few states, such as China, Iran, North Korea, Cuba or Iraq, still struggle to maintain this extreme mode of all-encompassing government. Leaders in many other countries exercise authoritarian control, but are usually less efficient or bloodthirsty.

Who knows what the future might bring by way of new justifications for control by a few? But as things now stand, the question is fundamentally simple: either you are a democracy – an open society – or on the way to it, or you are some form of dictatorship, or on the way to *that.*

If you live in a democracy, you constantly face choices: different avenues beckon, various sets of civic tools can be used to get where you want to go. But all roads lead essentially in the same general direction . . . freedom. *Or,* there is the *big* choice, if one despairs of democracy: to revert to dictatorship. This is what Germans did in 1933, when their democratically-elected parliament voted Hitler dictatorial powers. It can still happen.

Once in, dictators are hard to remove. There are a few cases of peaceful turnover, including the collapse of the entire Soviet system after more than seven decades. Kemal Atatürk, Turkey's dictator from 1923 to 1938, aid the foundations for democratic change and relinquished power peacefully. South Korea and Thailand have both in recent times moved from autocracy towards democracy with minimal bloodshed. But the passage to sanity and freedom can also be a long and bloody one.

Democracy is the only system of government that keeps choices open. All other systems are inadequate; the longer they run, the more ruinous they become. Depending on a society's traditions and makeup, it can be easier or harder to practise democracy. Sometimes a failed democracy can be recreated, sometimes not. But in the long run, the establishment of democratic ideals, practices and institutions is the only safe system, domestic *or* international . . . and not just for any particular people under the microscope of political science, but for all humankind. Everyone, everywhere has a great stake in the evolution towards democracy of all states and peoples in the world.

This does not mean that every society could readily become a stable, functioning, mature democracy. Nor should we believe that all societies will inevitably be democratic. On the other hand, any society *could* conceivably become democratic, someday. It is often said that democracy is suitable just for Westerners; however, democracy can be – and has been already – adapted to many non-Western cultures. Of the 79 countries listed in Freedom House's most recent survey as 'free', more than half did not stem from Western cultural roots. A worldwide trend, irrespective of cultures or continents, is accelerating.

Think of democracy as the *modern* way, not just the Western way.[11]

THE EVOLUTION OF WORLD ORDER

World order in our times has come to depend on democracy and its combined defenders. But this was not always the case.

The international system based on a 'concert' of nation-states ultimately could not prevent the Great War (1914–18) and was replaced with the League of Nations (1919). Although its charter professed new principles of international responsibility, the League proved incapable of coping with war, world depression or the fascist totalitarians.

At the end of World War II, the United Nations was launched to try to prevent or stop wars, and undertake world housekeeping. Unfortunately, the UN is not a sufficient answer to the problems of either war or democide. It performs other useful tasks; the world cannot do without it. But any international body hoping to resolve profound issues such as war or democide requires a certain degree of mutual trust among its members; by its very nature, the UN's trust quotient is low. Today's 184-nation UN, representing the most watered-down common denominator of 'likemindedness', cannot provide *the* basis for managing an age of unprecedented global interdependence ... now, soon, or perhaps ever at all.

Another scheme, parallel to the UN but more effective, has developed since 1945 to handle the toughest issues. It comprises a growing partnership of likeminded democracies in the North Atlantic area, which form a 'security community'.[12] There is little chance that these countries will ever again make war on one another. This community, reflected in NATO, in turn is tied to Japan, Australia and New Zealand by shared political values and defence links with the United States. These twenty or so democracies also enjoy the closest economic ties, reflected in their Organization for Economic Cooperation and Development. This is today's working nucleus – an extended Atlantic system – on which to build an *Intercontinental Community of Democracies* (ICD). These countries belong to this evolving security and economic community because none of them any longer, on its own, can truly defend its most substantial national interests and make its sovereignty prevail in crucial cases – the core attribute of the classic nation-state – without unacceptable costs. And they *know* this to be true.

To make this new system work in the future, however, even the biggest and most modern democratic nations – Britain, France, the United States, Japan and Germany – will have to reassess their attitudes towards their own nationalisms, the prerogatives and interests of their nations and the limits of their sovereignty. They will have to share more decisions, pool more functions. And the system will have to expand.

But ... one cautionary note: while in the West nationalism has begun to wane, deferring gradually to such concepts as European and Atlantic–Pacific union, in much of east Asia and elsewhere the age of nationalism is just dawning. Can former colonies, such as Malaysia, Indonesia or South Korea, despite the rapid pace of modernization, be expected to merge their immature sovereignties into visionary collectivities along the lines, say, of a European Union? The needs of countries – or at least their *perceptions* of their needs – vary greatly. This is the main reason why an ICD must begin with a receptive, capable and likeminded nucleus, involving less ready democracies gradually, at varying speeds and depths of participation.

THE COMMON INTERESTS OF THE DEMOCRACIES

It will be possible for an effective international system – an ICD – to be constructed by the experienced democracies because they began some years ago to realize that their common interests are greater than their so-called national interests. These overriding common interests might be defined, more or less in order of priority, as follows:

1. Promotion and consolidation of the spread of democratic ideals and practices, including the protection of human rights and the Rule of Law, among the peoples and nations of the world.

2. Extension of the community of democracies, viz., bringing all democracies into a common system of mutual help.

3. Opposition to inter-state aggression; resistance to tyranny; damping down violent conflict within states; reducing the spread of weapons of mass destruction and armaments generally; containing states endangering international order and their own peoples; making democide impossible; resisting international terrorism and crime; and supporting other measures conducive to international stability, security and world order.

4. Giving better form and rules to the global economy: furthering free market systems, unfettered trade, international investment, monetary integration and harmonized economic policies, with the democracies as the core structure, open to all nations as they are able; mitigating commercial competition among the democracies as necessary to achieve their community's top priorities of promoting democracy and opposing aggression.

5. Protecting the environment, assisting economic development, furthering the broad distribution of prosperity and opportunities globally, encouraging population control, discouraging disruptive

migration, and otherwise promoting the planet's sustainability.

6. Strengthening the Rule of Law in world affairs; introducing democratic forms and practices into international institutions.

The elaboration of common interests will be a consuming, long-term and indeed never-ending process. In a disjointed sort of way, this debate has already begun, but the process, which should lead to a fresh and attractive overall vision for the democracies, should be announced to all peoples and their contributions invited.

SUMMING UP

This book grew out of personal alarm at the needless and continuing loss of life through war and extrajudicial murder in this century, out of a deep concern for the future of freedom in the world, out of an understanding that beginning in 1945 the democratic peoples assumed a major responsibility for that future, and out of an unsettling feeling today that the world as a whole could lose most of the last half-century's gains if the democracies do not redouble their united efforts to bring about a lasting *Pax Democratica.*

For the first time in history, 'might' and 'right' are so wholly on the same side; let us not lose this opportunity, which could prove fleeting. A look at what the democracies were able to do in the recent past, 1940 to 1990, may give us heart; this is reviewed in the next chapter.

2 How the Democracies Saved Democracy: 1940–90

Humankind has just survived one of the most murderous and chaotic centuries in history. Yet incredibly this same, vile era has also brought unprecedented prosperity and – near its end – relative peace, with democracy, free markets and humanitarianism pushing the frontiers for humanity. From a long period of night puctuated with solid progress, we confront finally – as the 20th century closes – broad prospects for a much more hopeful future.

How could we have fallen so low, yet still moved so far ahead? The short answer is that beginning around 1940 the democratic peoples took an uncompromising lead:

- they determined that democracy *must* survive, that it is worth our lives, if necessary, to preserve;
- they envisioned a world order based on common action by the democracies, the liberating forces of free enquiry and free markets, and a continuing expansion of their community;
- they created an interlocking web of international institutions to smooth the transition to a new phase in the advance of civilization.

In short, humankind was saved by the creativity, resilience and inherent humanity of democracy. These qualities surfaced increasingly during and after World War II as it became clear that old forms of international relations, such as empire and the balance of power system, would have to be replaced. The transformation which followed is largely the story of the efforts of the great democracies from 1940 to 1990. But its antecedents are important.

COMMANDING VISIONS

In the 1920s and 1930s, it was common to ridicule the high-minded slogans of the Allied side in the 1914–18 War: 'the war to end all wars', 'make the world safe for democracy', and so on. Looking back on four long years of vast slaughter, it was later easy to call this butchery 'useless', to damn both sides and their leaders equally,

13

to attribute war to the greed of capitalists, and to aver that all the sacrifices had really been for nothing.

Perhaps a better international system and better leaders on both sides could have avoided the Great War, but probably not. At bottom, the overriding issue in 1914 was, as it became again two decades later: would Western civilization be ruled by democratic or by autocratic principles? By the will of the peoples, or by militarism? By competing nationalisms, or by cooperation?

World War I did not finally settle these questions, but it gave the democracies a new chance.

In 1900, only a handful of nations deserved the term 'democracy', even by the rudimentary standards of that day: Britain, France, the USA, the Low Countries, Scandinavia, Switzerland and the British Dominions. Italy and a couple of Latin American countries could be counted 'aspiring democracies'. By 1920, democracy had become more fashionable; there were starts (most later aborted) in a dozen more nations.

Under the impact of the Great Depression and the rise of dictatorships, democracy by the summer of 1940 was truly beleaguered: only Britain, Sweden, Switzerland, the United States and the Dominions of Australia, Canada and New Zealand remained free under representative government, and even then most were beset domestically by the totalitarian temptation. Fascism was fashionable in Latin America. Asia, locked in struggle, had never known democracy. The Soviet Union was the furthest thing from a democracy. The failure of the democracies over two decades to stand united against non-democracy and together to mend a fractured world economy had brought on World War II.

Churchill and Roosevelt, in their historic meeting at sea (August 1941), outlined a new vision, an 'Atlantic Charter' that committed both nations to a democratic world regime of cooperation once the War was won. The Charter embraced Roosevelt's simple but profound 'Four Freedoms'... of worship, of speech and expression, and from want and fear. The Charter had a powerful effect worldwide. With these aims, plus integrated political direction and combined chiefs of staff – precursors of NATO – the Allies went on to win the War.

Roosevelt and Churchill also set in motion plans for the postwar

United Nations, replacing the old League. But the UN machinery could not cope with the titanic pressures of the Cold War, which became evident by 1947. The USSR had never subscribed to Atlantic ideals; Stalin had his own agenda for the liberation of mankind, beginning with a Soviet empire in eastern Europe. What Henry Adams in 1906 had called 'the Atlantic System'[1] was again in danger, even though Nazism and the Japanese autocrats had been thoroughly vanquished.

THE DEMOCRACIES GALVANIZED INTO ACTION

The years 1947–49 were a watershed. To contain the USSR and to rebuild Europe, it was necessary for the democracies to think through their common aims and develop new ways of pursuing them together. Thus were born the Marshall Plan, NATO, the European Communities and other initiatives and institutions which re-made the world and gave democracy yet another lease on life. Taken together, these measures amounted to a Western vision and plan of action for humanity's broad democratic future, in scope and aims unprecedented in history.

Marshall aid rebuilt Europe economically; Japan enjoyed comparable American help. US security guarantees for Europe and for Japan and other Pacific allies provided the shield to enable recovery. Canada played her part.

The United States conditioned Marshall aid on moves towards a united Europe; this ultimately changed the political and economic face of the Old Continent. European leaders themselves, sick of centuries of bloody feuding, wanted unity. To have brought about the peaceful, voluntary near-unification of first six, today fifteen, and – by the early years of the next century – probably as many as two dozen European nations, is a momentous event in world history. The consequences for Europe and for world peace are virtually incalculable; such developments could never have been dreamed of in 1900, 1917, 1929 or 1940.

The European Union is the greatest political invention of the 20th century, even though the process is not complete.

But the unification of Europe has depended for its great success on even more than the Marshall Plan, NATO and the political inventiveness of its progenitors: there has been a quiet but profound revolution in the German mind and heart.

Perhaps the greatest gift that the United States, Great Britain and France made to the German people (and to the world) was the opportunity and active encouragement to embrace democracy as the surest road to self-respect and comity with other peoples. Japan was tutored comparably. Both countries, once bastions of militarism, today are functioning democracies.[2] Without their firm commitment to a free way of life, and without active German and Japanese participation in the powerful coalition of democracies, the world could not have survived the Cold War nor put together today's vibrant global economy, nor could the recent astounding turn of events in the former Soviet empire ever have taken place.

The political climate in western Europe after 1947 was congenial not only to the development of German democracy, but to the growth of free regimes in Austria, Portugal, Spain, Greece and Turkey, to the restoration of democracy in Italy, and to its strengthening in France and other countries. The Atlantic System upgraded democracy, downgraded tyranny and freed economies for a great transformation.

The West's 1947–49 vision, which guided its common affairs for the next four decades, embraced the goals of global (not just European) prosperity, help for developing countries, mutual security guarantees, regional integration in Europe and the spread of democracy itself. Public support for the programmes and enormous expenditures was elicited, however, in large part by appealing to the fear of communism; this was unfortunate, because virtually all the political and economic steps taken were good in and of themselves.[3] However, fear is the most powerful cement of alliances. But because alliances contain the seeds of their own decay, it was imperative to go further and create more durable *supranational communities*, transcending the limitations of conventional alliances.

ACHIEVEMENTS OF THE EXTENDED ATLANTIC SYSTEM

By 1990, this system – a larger version of the Atlantic System conceived early in the century[4] – had 'won' the Cold War, greatly enriched the world, brought about the decolonialization of virtually all subject peoples, made staunch democratic allies of implacable enemies, accelerated the global spread of free markets and democratic practices, transformed Europe's prospects for harmony and well-being and strengthened the fabric of international cooperation generally. As we approach the new century, there is no threat of World War III, the danger of nuclear war has receded, world social conditions have improved and the sustainability of the planet itself has been put high on the world's agenda. These are no mean accomplishments.

Whereas in 1940 there was fear and little hope, today there are opportunities and expectations for a better life generally. The experienced democracies constituted the engine for this momentous global change. They provided the bulk of the material, intellectual, organizational, civic and educational resources for the great transformation after 1945, as well as the primary political and economic leadership.

Today, virtually all countries between the old Iron Curtain and Russia want to join NATO which – along with the European Union – is seen as the ticket to a secure and prosperous membership in the democracies' club. Most of these prospective members of the extended Atlantic community have only a rudimentary, if any, democratic past. Russia's place is more difficult but still hopeful; it is so large and its problems of growing to maturity so great that special partnership arrangements with the Atlantic System are called for. But even with these reservations, the prospects for Europe generally are today amazingly good . . . perhaps better than ever before in recorded history.

This optimistic outlook extends to other parts of the world. East Asian economies which only a few years ago were struggling at low levels are now burgeoning. In some, the power of democracy is growing in tandem with free economies; in others, such as China, great questions shroud the future. Seven states[5] have formed ASEAN, moving towards political and economic entente. Eighteen Asian nations, plus Australia, New Zealand, Canada and the United States, have created APEC (Asia-Pacific Economic Cooperation forum) for trade and general cooperation. Although east Asia is more unstable politically and lacks the cultural coherence of Europe's Union, there is little doubt that the optimism found throughout that region would be far less today without the economic aid, trade openings and security assurances given by the Western democracies (including Japan, Australia and New Zealand) over 40 years. This transformation, too, is a product of the extended Atlantic System.

In other regions, more than two dozen attempts at economic and other forms of togetherness are modelled on the European communities.[6]

None of this existed in 1945; Appendix B delineates this institutional growth. But if international organizations are to be effective, a great deal more is required than the mere signatures of governments on sheets of paper.

At present, the notable intergovernmental and supranational structures are the European Union, NATO, OECD and a few subsidiary bodies which together make up the modern extended Atlantic System. Some bodies with wider membership and global programmes, such as the International Monetary Fund, World Bank and World Trade Organization (formerly GATT), in which Western influence is dominant, are also important. APEC, ASEAN, Mercosur and others are mainly hopes for the future. In this core framework of intercontinental dimensions, the extended Atlantic System, by means of which the serious intentions of the experienced democracies were largely carried out beginning in the 1940s and 1950s, lies the principal hope for averting chaos and bringing about good things in the 21st century.

CAN THE DEMOCRACIES CONTINUE THEIR GREAT WORK?

The extended Atlantic System has, in five short decades, come far. For the first time in history, the democracies have the combined momentum and power to change the world in great and positive ways. There are no ready world class challengers. There are major problems, but also momentous opportunities. This situation is astonishing when one looks back at the dark days of the Depression, two World Wars and the Cold War. The Cold War has ended and the post-Cold War period too. This new age could be the Era of Democracy, *Pax Democratica*. Can the democracies, using what they learned from 1940–90, build anew to fit the age?

So far, the Scottish verdict must apply: 'Not proven'.

By the mid-1990s the democratic peoples, displaying an understandable urge to remove the constraining corsets of the Cold War, had found it more difficult to pull together when economic and political crises, coming piecemeal and individually less than compelling, called for their attention.

To compound the danger, it seems that worldwide there has been an astonishing withdrawal of public support for anyone in a political leadership role. By the late 1990s, of the Cold War generation of Western and Japanese leaders with power to sway their own people, only Chancellor Helmut Kohl had survived. And even he had mounting difficulties, plus waning clout with his neighbours.

Used to a *Pax Americana* and a Cold War, peoples and statesmen alike now have great difficulty in believing that unpleasant situations – such as the Yugoslav civil wars, the increasing power, petulance and unpredictability of huge China, the persistence of rogue-state behaviour, or the pervasive slow growth and increasing social dislocations in Europe and Japan – can grow into major crises. It is much easier to relax under the delusion that conflict and tension are the usual condition of humankind; that most such problems will eventually take care of themselves by the operation of cyclical economics or the growing weariness of combatants or demographic forces; that we shall somehow muddle through. In spurious complacency, we have been living on our accumulated psycho-political capital.

And even if a few worry about some things going wrong in the world, we seem not to agree on the nature of the dangers, or on the degree to which they could disrupt our lives if not dealt with, or on a hierarchy of importance among them. Publics tend to see rolling crises as 'somebody else's problem' – or fault. The Western democracies therefore are not organizing adequately to meet challenges which their elites and their peoples either do not see or do not want to see. But the challenges form a composite threat which can only grow and eventually will have to be met; the bills *will* come due. The forces impelling our interdependence cannot be denied. Chapter 4 deals with the challenges.

The democracies' supportive attitudes and cooperative machinery – built up in prodigious effort over half a century, had become, by the mid-1990s, wasting assets. This is a new and uncertain era, for all its hope. Can the responsible experienced democracies – who will have to lead if anyone does – bring themselves to diagnose the 'world case' adequately, make a serious prognosis and begin the 'cure'? Can they strengthen the rules for the global economy, rework the collective capability to thwart aggression and develop a joint capacity to promote democracy and human rights? Who can know? World history unfortunately suggests that nations and peoples must face obvious, urgent crises before they are moved to act. But now this process of re-tooling world systems, because of the accelerating pace of events, must be done *before* major crises strike. Can the likeminded democracies repeat their stellar performance of the 1940s to 1990s and thereby advance the interests of all peoples?

As we seek the answer, it will be helpful to first review briefly, in the next chapter, the historical record of the search for international order. The past can give us some clues as to what we should avoid, as well as to what we might be capable of in the future. Those familiar with the record will find only a few milestone-reminders; those who wish to delve more deeply will find guides in the footnotes.

3 The Long Search for International Order

Of the gods we believe, and of men we know, that by a necessary law of their nature they rule wherever they can. And it is not as if we were the first to make this law, or to act upon it; we found it existing before, and shall leave it to exist forever after us; all we do is to make use of it, knowing that you and everybody else, having the same power as we have, would do the same as we do.

The Athenians to the Melians
(416 BC, quoted by Thucydides)[1]

FOUR PHASES IN THE SEARCH FOR INTERNATIONAL ORDER

The problem of war and the search for more stable relations between groups of hunters, then tribes, city-states, empires and nations has been with humankind since the beginning. This book divides the search for international order into four phases of development: the first was imposing peace through imperial conquest; the state-based balance-of-power system was the second phase; organized international cooperation constituted a third development; the most recent, which we are now entering, is that of supranational community-building.

These four phases are not, except in the broadest sense, consecutive. Empires co-existed with smaller nation-states and both practised balance-of-power politics. Nation-states have been the building blocks for cooperative international systems. Nations have also pioneered supranationalism. But there is a progression in these phases of human development, and the latest has led powerfully to the advancement of freedom.

FIRST PHASE: ORDER THE OLD-FASHIONED WAY . . . THROUGH EMPIRE

In antiquity, stronger powers such as Persia, Egypt and Rome sought to impose international order by dominating their neighbours. Empire was the surest method; alliances were backups. The Chinese empire has been the longest-lasting, for more than four millennia extending dominion over contiguous peoples. The Holy Roman Empire, the Russian/Soviet empires, the Austro-Hungarian, the French and most recently the Second and Third German Reichs all sought to impose order in Europe. France, Portugal, Spain, Britain and the Netherlands acquired major empires overseas. Japan had a brief fling (1895–1945).

The recipe for imperial order was simple: conquer your neighbours, annex their lands, put down all insurrection. You alone impose order and peace. The task was never-ending, but all great empires except the Chinese eventually broke down.

Not until the second half of the 20th century was a European order comparable in scope to that of the Romans again created. But this time there was a major distinction, a watershed in world history: the new European Union is no empire, but a voluntary amalgamation of powers whose cement is democracy. The historical road from the earliest form of international order – empire, imposed by force – to a union among consenting democracies required two millennia, four stages of international development and accelerating forces peculiar to our time.

SECOND PHASE: PEACE THROUGH A BALANCE OF POWER

As the Athenians knew, power and state sovereignty were considered indivisible. Diplomatic convention and the laws of the interaction of states took centuries to develop. The European age of the modern nation-state dates from the 17th century. The conduct of foreign relations was solidly codified in the Peace of Westphalia (1648), which spurred the widespread exchange of diplomatic envoys, led to the general creation of foreign ministries, established the principles of state sovereignty and relations between states and (most important to the argument of this book) by implication sanctified the idea of *raison d'état* – the unprincipled principle that the state can do whatever it wants when it asserts its 'vital interests' . . . self-defined of course. With Westphalia, '[t]he state became the lodestone of political loyalty'.[2]

Westphalia was a compact between monarchs, but by 1789, impelled by the French and American Revolutions, the concept of 'the nation' began to carry more weight than kings. 'Nation-states' arose. Westphalia's principles remained, but the stakes increased. The 'nation in arms', conscripting the entire male population, was pushed to the limit by Napoleon and copied by other great powers, all promoting their own 'interests'.

The usual nub of trouble between nation-states is this: 'interests' look different depending on which side of a border you sit. And within each country, the politicians, bureaucracies and military classes develop a vested interest in pursuing the 'national interest' and, just incidentally, in protecting their jobs too.

SECOND PHASE SQUARED: NATIONALISM, THE NATION-STATE AND NATIONAL INTERESTS

A nation is a society united by a common error as to its origins and a common aversion to its neighbors.

J. S. Huxley and A. C. Haddon

Patriotism – love of one's country, one's people, one's homeland – is healthy. Nationalism – patriotism carried to extremes – was perhaps a necessary stage in the development of humankind but today it is a menace to a violence-free and orderly world. Nationalism is enshrined in nation-states, which in turn exercise 'sovereignty', i.e. the legitimate claim to rule. Many countries remain in a stage of nation-building, trying to make a cohesive state based on ethnic, religious, linguistic or other forms of exclusiveness, and are therefore more or less dependent on nationalism, and often war.

For modern peoples and for a stable, free, cooperative and prosperous world, nationalism (but not patriotism) has now become a drag on progress. Unbridled nationalism has been the central defect of Phase Two world order systems, dependent on theoretically self-sufficient nations, each propelled by its own nationalism. Nation-states are Phase Two's inherently unstable, ever-changing actors.

In 1992, Turkey's prime minister rejected Syrian claims to a say in dividing the waters of the Euphrates, which rise in Turkey, in these words: 'This is a matter of sovereignty. We have every right to do anything we want.' This expresses to perfection the idolatry with which humans – and especially their governments – in virtually every nation-state, everywhere – still regard their own 'national interests'. When the crunch comes, virtually all governments echo Turkey's: 'We have every right to do anything we want.'

Even though the nation-state has often saved our skins, nationalism and the nation-state undiluted have now become increasingly the source of endless trouble, indeed bringing on the wars that nation-states choose, or are forced by others – or by the system itself – to fight. Extreme nationalism has also led often to dictatorship. Henry Kissinger believes, as did Bismarck, Metternich, Richelieu and others, that great nations are stuck with the balance-of-power system and had better make the best of it. This balancing, or *Realpolitik,* must of course be done, he believes, by defending US interests insofar as possible with allies. But in the last resort, we should act unilaterally when we must.

Kissinger's arguments and those of other 'realists'[3] tend, however, to discount recent developments in international community-building. Largely European but also transatlantic and transpacific in scope, these in effect have downgraded the nation-state and transcended the old dog-eat-dog system. In his book *Diplomacy*, Kissinger never mentions the European Communities, except one that failed. The Council of Europe – home to an extraordinary international tribunal for human rights – earns two fleeting references as a stage for speeches. It is a pity that Kissinger nowhere gives us his views on the larger questions of intergovernmental organizations and supranational integration.

From the 17th century to the present day, the inadequacies of Phase Two world order based on a balance of power have bedevilled us.

SECOND PHASE ORDER, THIRD PHASE BEGINNINGS IN THE 19TH CENTURY

In 1815, sobered by the carnage of the Napoleonic Wars, the four victors and the French losers wished to reorganize the international system. In a great peace congress at Vienna, they re-created a balance-of-power which proved durable for some decades. A distinction was made between great powers who decided things, and all the others. This has carried into our day, with the five victors of World War II holding permanent veto power over decisions of the UN Security Council. A 'Concert of Europe' evolved a code of international conduct based on cooperation and restraint among the great powers. Despite notable but still limited breakdowns, this European system was kept patched together until the outbreak of World War I in 1914.

The 19th century arrangements, while based solidly on the balance-of-power concept,[4] with the great nations combining in different ways at different times to 'balance' powers which threatened order, also adumbrated new forms of institutionalized cooperation. The oldest international organization – the International Commission of the Rhine – was created in 1815 in Vienna.[5] In 1856, a Commission for the Danube and a Universal Telegraph Union were established; in 1874, the General Postal Union was added. As international commerce grew, some agreed rules had become necessary. These small steps inaugurated Phase Three in the search for world order.

Another Third Phase effort began in the 1890s, when other European nations had become fearful of Germany. The powers began to look for new instrumentalities to minimize conflict. The Hague Peace Conferences of 1899 and 1907 discussed disarmament and created the first international court. A Phase Three system had begun, almost imperceptibly, alongside Phase Two realities. But balance-of-power diplomacy, backed by military threats and diplomatic jockeying, remained the norm. The 'great powers' were likened to billiard balls – all were at rest until one ball was sent cracking to strike others and upset the delicate constellations. Such an unstable equilibrium cannot last; the stage was set for 1914.

PHASE THREE: THE SEARCH FOR PEACE THROUGH INTERGOVERNMENTAL ORGANIZATION AND INTERNATIONAL ARBITRATION

The United States, secure behind two oceans and preoccupied with developing a great continent, did not join the club of 'great powers' until the 1890s. It had been content, relying tacitly on the powerful British Navy, for most of the century to simply order the Europeans to stay out of the Western Hemisphere (Monroe Doctrine,

1823), and once (1854), to intervene in the Far East, 'opening' Japan's closed society. But it then retreated to continentalism and civil war. As the 19th century ended, however, the United States moved on to the international stage. Belatedly joining the colonial race, she acquired the Philippines and other small possessions (imperial route, Phase One), began to assert leadership among the great powers in 'opening' China (balance-of-power route, Phase Two) and took part in the new disarmament conferences (Phase Three). In other words, the United States began to ape the other great powers.

Establishmentarians on the US east coast, for a few years at least, were taken with the idea that peace could be secured by means of international arbitration, a narrow but important limitation of sovereignty. Arbitration between nations began with the Jay Treaty of 1794, settling claims arising out of the American Revolution; the US–Canadian border in the Far West was later arbitrated; the settlement of the 'Alabama' case in 1871 was significant. In 1892, the private International Peace Bureau opened in Bern.[6] In 1893, arbitration resolved a dispute between the United States and Great Britain over South American borders. More nations signed arbitration treaties. The first Hague conference (1899) established a Permanent Court of Arbitration.

British intellectuals and politicians had founded a peace movement in the 1880s. Gladstone espoused such ideas. In 1903 a Peace Society was founded in New York. From such beginnings, and from concerted diplomacy as the German danger became apparent, the US–UK axis of perceived shared values and interests arose as the cornerstone of their common effort to build international community throughout this century. France shared these concerns.

Andrew Carnegie, the Scottish-American industrialist, retired in 1900 to devote himself and his vast fortune to philanthropy, and took up international arbitration as a sacred cause. He recruited distinguished Americans, including Theodore Roosevelt, William Howard Taft and Elihu Root. Taft as President signed a sweeping arbitration pact with Britain (1911) – a treaty which among other things would have bound the parties to foreswear 'national honour' as an excuse for not submitting all disputes to binding arbitration. A few months later, France subscribed to a tripartite arbitration treaty.[7]

This was too much for TR, no longer President but still a political power; he wrote that he was 'skeptical . . . about [international arbitration] as a general remedy for the ills of an increasingly fractious international society, or as a substitute for war among nations'.[8]

Carnegie had cajoled and charmed Roosevelt, when he was President, into backing arbitration and a 'world court'. But now TR thought Taft – with Carnegie urging Taft on – had gone too far. TR was right, in one sense, because 'arbitration' would prove to be only a small part of the kind of supranational community that Europe would require, 50 years later, within which war could finally become unthinkable. But TR, essentially a Second Phase man, was more wrong than right, because he helped by his intransigence to entrench the nationalistic forces in the United States which impaired American ability to exercise leadership in supplanting the bankrupt nation-state system with strong Third Phase and, later, even stronger Fourth Phase institutions.

Taft's most far-reaching arbitration treaties were defeated in the Senate in 1912.

MORE PHASE THREE AND VISIONS OF PHASE FOUR: THE LEAGUE OF NATIONS

Theodore Roosevelt was often and publicly of two minds in these fateful years. His personal belief system encompassed all the conflicting ideas of his countrymen in this era – some good, some bad, some unrealistic – about peace. TR had won the Nobel Peace Prize for mediating an end to the Russo–Japanese War; in his acceptance speech at Christiania (1910), he declared that it would be a 'master stroke' if the great powers honestly bent on peace 'would form a League of Peace, not only to keep the peace among themselves, but to prevent, by force if necessary, its being broken by others'.[9] In January 1915, Roosevelt expanded his Christiania statement to include advocacy of an international court, the use of international force and the guarantee of the territorial integrity and independence of nations.[10] These were powerful Fourth Phase ideas. But TR could never reconcile his intense nationalism, especially after America entered the Great War, with his sincere beliefs in conciliation or even implied supranationalism. His repudiation of Third and Fourth Phase concepts helped to torpedo American membership in the League of Nations.

During the War, popular sentiment against the senseless slaughter and in favour of a new international system with the collective power to stop aggressors, mounted.[11] President Woodrow Wilson, who believed fervently that the old ways of secret diplomacy and *Realpolitik* could no longer be tolerated, insisted that the Allies set up a League of Nations for collective security. The victorious powers grudgingly reorganized the world along Wilsonian lines.

But the League of Nations was destined to fail, not least because the United States failed to follow its own President's lead. In the 1918 congressional election campaign, Roosevelt stumped the country against the League of Nations Treaty, despite his earlier advocacy.[12] In 1919, Wilson made 40 speeches in 17 States in just 20 days, arguing for the League, and then collapsed, a broken man. Taft, who had headed the private citizens' movement to promote the League, buckled under pressure from Republican colleagues and withdrew his support. Wilson refused to compromise on changes to the Treaty, the Senate failed to ratify, the United States never became a member of the League, and can – as the nation most destined, even in 1920, for superpower stardom – be held responsible in good measure for the eventual failure of the League, and for the resumption of Armageddon in 1939.

In 1919, the League started bravely nevertheless. It excelled in some kinds of financial rectification, in preventing some small wars, in smoothing world commerce and in setting the stage for decolonization. But as economic dislocations in the 1920s and 1930s became severe, as democratic regimes were threatened and in some cases overturned, and as aggression by dictators went unchecked, the League became more and more helpless. The League of Nations was replaced by the United Nations in 1945.

THIRD PHASE REDUX: A NEW START FOR INTERGOVERNMENTALISM

I'm not one who has the slightest anxiety about the eventual triumph of the things I've stood for. The fight's just begun. You and I may never live to see it finished but that doesn't matter. The ideals of the League are not dead just because some men now in the saddle say they are. The dream of a world united against the awful wastes of war is too deeply embedded in the hearts of men everywhere ... I'll even make this concession ... it may come about in an even better way than we proposed.

Woodow Wilson's farewell to his Cabinet
on the day of President Harding's inauguration, 1921

Determined to create a more durable world order, the United States and the United Kingdom led the victorious powers of World War II in creating the United Nations. The USSR felt compelled to approve the new Charter, but – as events were to prove – had no subsequent hesitation in grinding the new world machinery to a halt. China and France were also invited on to the UN's Security Council as permanent members. The Big Five each held a veto over its proceedings. Constitutionally the new UN security machinery was somewhat better than that of the League. However, the cultural basis for UN cooperation was extremely diluted, an inevitable condition given its aspiration to represent all nations.

Precisely because the UN's members (in 1997, 184) represent such a wide spectrum of values, cultures, historical myths, political beliefs and habits, it is – at this stage in history – impossible to turn the Third Phase UN into a *political community* for the entire world. A few years after the UN's inception, Arnold Toynbee wrote: 'The UN is not, in fact, a political community, it is a political forum . . .'.[13] A forum is useful, indeed indispensable, for a world with close to 200 sovereign states, but it cannot hope to be successful in managing the most crucial requirements of international interdependence, as distinct from peripheral questions. But the UN is still the best encompassing Third Phase institution we have.

Within the UN family, additional universal organizations were established in 1946–48. Some have launched important global programmes to fight disease, provide humanitarian aid, improve food production, and so on. The World Bank and International Monetary Fund (IMF) represented important improvements on pre-World War II economic cooperation. The General Agreement on Tariffs and Trade (in 1994 reconstituted as the World Trade Organization) was born soon after the UN and brought about freer commerce. None of these special economic bodies, however, has embraced all states – as does the UN – but centres membership on nations willing and able to bear the necessary burdens, monetary and otherwise. Both the World Bank and IMF are controlled by powers most able to lend capital to others. Although Russia and China benefit from membership in the World Bank and IMF, they have neither capital nor expertise to contribute. Nor was either country yet (by 1997) a member of the WTO because they were still unable to discharge the responsibilities of full membership.

The United Nations is vehemently criticized because it is inefficient and wasteful. Any political process has great difficulty in funding
and administering public programmes, all the more so when these
functions are conducted together by many nations. The charge of
inefficiency and waste is valid also because the 'political masters'
of the UN comprise 184 sovereign states, each theoretically equal
in General Assembly voting, no matter what the size of their respective populations or contributions to the UN's budget may be.

In the UN Security Council, the situation is different but also
unfair. Fifty years after World War II, the five victors of that war
still virtually make the decisions for everyone else – if they can
agree among themselves. One of these five is Russia, one China;
their 'veto power' can produce stalemate at any critical moment,
because they do not share the same degree of likemindedness (see
Chapter 6) as Britain, France and the United States, the three other
Security Council members with veto power.[14] The five Great Power
vetoes hamstring the Security Council, but under the circumstances
are irremediable defects which tragically remain essential if the
democracies wish to safeguard their common interests against countries whose governments are unrepresentative or unstable.

It has been proposed that the Security Council's permanent
membership be expanded, to include Germany, Japan, India, Brazil
or others, but such changes so far have been resisted.

During the Cold War, the Security Council was often paralysed.
Since 1990, it has sponsored many peacekeeping projects, occasionally with success. But the UN's unhappy experience, for example,
in the former Yugoslavia before NATO stepped in, and its inability
to stem the bloodletting in Somalia and Rwanda suggest its limits.
These stem directly from the political limits of the UN. The problem of getting concerted action for peace is grounded in the nature of the growth of mutual trust, not the goodwill or sagacity of
nations. A world-embracing group of disparate nation-states, each
jealously guarding its sovereignty, is inherently an undemocratic,
unstable and ineffective arrangement at this stage in history, no
matter how much we need it.

Somewhat contradictorily, the UN is also castigated because it
supposedly is the entering wedge of a 'world government'. This
criticism could be dismissed as outrageously laughable were it not
so widespread, especially in the United States. The UN's problem
is that it is too weak, not too strong. While the UN can surely be
improved over time, a working 'world government' – whether one

is for it or against it – is a pipedream. Those who fear the UN because they think it is a world government already, don't understand the world as it is.

RECAPITULATION: THE FIRST THREE PHASES

Most of human history was the age of empire (First Phase), now almost past.[15] The second millennium AD saw the rise of the nation-state (Second Phase) but led to system breakdown. As we approach the third millennium, it is likely but not certain that institutionalized international cooperation (Third Phase) will strengthen, but that will not be enough.

The most recent (Fourth Phase) trend, towards building *viable international communities*, is problematic and depends mainly on what the peoples of the democracies and their governments can understand and do. Based on common interests, shared values, cultural interpenetration and institutions capable of joint decision and action, i.e. of a supranational or *extra*national nature, Fourth Phase communities represent the wave of the democratic future, the best hope for world order. Perhaps sometime in the coming millennium, when democracy as a way of life will have spread solidly to an overwhelming majority of states and peoples, some kind of universal worldwide political institution – a much better kind of UN – based on law and democracy will be possible. This must, however, remain a very long range goal, a hope; for the time being it doesn't pay even to think about it. 'World government' is a chimera. The best we can do in the next few years is to study Fourth Phase institutions, try to improve those that exist and put together new ones as the opportunities arise, among countries that are ready, willing and able to undertake the common tasks. The rule should be: strengthen the core, expand the peripheries and depend on guided evolution.

Westphalia had signalled the waning of imperial and religious authority, in the form then of the Holy Roman Empire and the Papacy. The regime of sovereign nation-states replaced those authorities but soon, as the 19th century grew into the 20th, showed *its* appalling weaknesses. In the 20th century, Third Phase and Fourth Phase systems were potential replacement candidates. The supranational idea, very much the weaker, remained distinctly in the background until Europe grasped it after World War II. The attempt to build intergovernmental institutions and integrated, supranational communities – the latter only now beginning to mature – signals the rebuilding of central authority and world order, but this time on a *voluntary, proto-federal* and *democratic* basis.

This is something entirely new under the sun.

THE BASIS FOR FOURTH PHASE ORDER: NO MORE NATIONAL INTERESTS, ONLY DEMOCRATIC INTERESTS

National interest is whatever those in power say it is to get the public to agree with what they want to do.

James Moceri (1995)

Lord Carrington, of the United Kingdom, saw that much progress had already been achieved. He said, 'in the organizations for western cooperation which we have evolved among us, countries are generally disposed to relinquish particular interests from time to time without necessarily having a prospect of immediate return, in the expectation that others will be co-operative when their turn comes. It is a habit of give and take which western countries are beginning to acquire. . .'.

Reported in *NATO Letter*, February 1964

Some underbrush must be cleared away. 'National interest' is the prime candidate. This term, invoked often by politicians and journalists when they can't be more precise, is rhetoric meant to be all things to all co-nationalists, and usually to justify either unilateral action or isolationist inaction. Members of the military and diplomatic establishments take 'national interests' more seriously than the general public. But if you were to ask US officials, for example, why intervention in the Bosnian situation was *not* in America's 'national interest' from 1991 to 1994, but then *became* a matter of vital interest in 1995, they might be hard-pressed.

What made the Yugoslav case in 1991 different from the Iraqi invasion of Kuwait in 1990, which precipitated massive US and Allied intervention? Why was one in the national interest, but not the other? By 1995, what had changed in Bosnia?

According to James Rosenau, one approach to 'national interest', by those he terms 'subjectivists', is this definition:

[T]he national interest . . . is a pluralistic set of subjective pref-
erences that change whenever the requirements and aspirations
of the nation's members change.[16]

A classic example is the case of England's interests in the Low
Countries. Georg Schwarzenberger traces these back to 1101 and
the Treaty of Subsidy between King Henry I and the Count of
Flanders. The principle – valid until our century and especially
invoked in 1914 and 1940 – held that British security was threatened if the Low Countries were controlled by a potentially hostile
great power. After 1945, with the elimination of the German threat,
a new British security border was established on the Elbe. But
Britain's security interest in Europe by this time was no longer just
her own; she and the other NATO democracies *together* defined a
new interest – a common interest – encompassing Germany and
abutting the redefined Soviet empire.[17]

In the same way, any real substance in the concept of 'national
interest', with respect to any truly critical area of the world, has
over the past 50 years faded and been supplanted by a new *common
interest*, especially of the de facto community of experienced democracies. The shared political and economic values of these countries
dictates that it can hardly be otherwise. But even if this is so ob-
jectively, only likeminded countries whose peoples and leaders
understand this congruence of interests can adjust their foreign
policies to conform, and act in common accordingly. In other words,
democracies are beginning to serve common, not national, interests.
For such a new idea to become fully operative, the community of
nations involved must have Fourth Phase institutions.

Residual historical and geographical ties still impel some leading democracies on occasion to act unilaterally to pursue 'national
interests'. France and Britain still have special relations with former
colonies. Sweden feels a special responsibility for the security of
Finland and the Baltic states. Japan cares more about Korea's future than does Europe. The United States still asserts the Monroe
Doctrine on occasion. One cannot repeal the Laws of Geography.
But these Laws and those of History are increasingly irrelevant in
an age of jet travel, the Internet, and borderless currency and stock
exchanges. The Laws of Geography and History in fact have been
substantially amended by the growing reality of the common interests
of the democracies, largely replacing among them the old idea of
national interest.

Another reason 'national interest' is now a counterproductive concept lies in the decreasing importance of military power. Even the United States, the most powerful nation, has trouble imposing solutions on world problems. The awful potential of nuclear warfare has since 1945 dictated more reliance on diplomacy, persuasion, deterrence and a search for *humankind's* best interests. The visions and international structures evolved by the Western democracies and Japan after 1945 have provided a durable framework, so far, for the beginnings of a new kind of international politics, embracing the common interests of a large number of likeminded peoples. This is the essence of *Pax Democratica*.

Thus it no longer makes sense for individual democracies, even the United States, to base their foreign policies – and to continue to deceive their voters into relying – on an outdated set of nation-bound ideas about foreign policy.

Evidence that this evolution in thinking can take place is attested by Paul Nitze, whose extraordinary public career in international affairs spanned five decades. In one of his brief periods out of government, Nitze reflected on the character of American leadership in its most creative, community-building period, 1947–54:

> To my mind, the most serious modification in our national strategy in the period beginning in 1953 was the decision to emphasize that our first aim was to pursue United States national interests and to play down our interest in the construction of a working international order. The moment we began to emphasize that our policy was directed primarily to the pursuit of United States aims and interests, other nations were forced to look more closely to their own narrow interests. . . .[18]

Nation-states are still important, if increasingly less so, because only they for the time being have the power to create new multinational structures and processes that will better serve the common interest. And even when a durable Fourth Phase system has been put in place, the constituent democracies will still have to employ Third Phase institutions and – sometimes – Second Phase *Realpolitik* in their relations with states not members of the community. This may seem a paradox, but that is the nature of politics.

THE FOURTH PHASE: THE SEARCH FOR PEACE AND DEMOCRACY THROUGH POLITICAL COMMUNITY

The new Fourth Phase institutions are as different from empires, nation-states and intergovernmental bodies as modern *Homo sapiens* was from the Neanderthals. This Fourth Phase invention is the *supranational political community*, in its most advanced state the multi-nation federation. Here is its story.

After the breakdown of the Roman Empire, Church fathers, philosophers and occasionally secular rulers put forth schemes for ensuring peace. The idea of a unified Europe was espoused in 1305 by Pierre Dubois, a lawyer and adviser to the King of France. Dante, Erasmus, Henri IV of France, Grotius, Leibniz, William Penn, the Abbé Saint-Pierre and Rousseau are among those whose tracts on peace through federation have survived.

Immanuel Kant was the first to show that peace was morally and rationally imperative as well as empirically feasible. By the time Kant wrote his most famous essay on the subject, 'Perpetual Peace' (1795), the American and French Revolutions had taken place and, more importantly, the federal Constitution of the new United States was in effect. This inaugurated what Kant called 'the representative-republican' form of government, based on consent of the governed, on freedom and equality for all citizens. Kant was first to recognize that such states do not make war on one another.[19] Kant foresaw 'the time when the irrationality of war would . . . become generally apparent; and peace . . . a way of civilized life'.[20] Also, reasoned Kant, why could not the US example of federalism be applied to relations between the states of Europe?

Jeremy Bentham and Victor Hugo were among those during the 19th century who championed the idea of a united Europe. Following the terrors of World War I, a popular movement for European unification, led by Count Richard Coudenhove-Kalergi, was capped with a formal proposal by French Premier Aristide Briand (1928). Submerged by the rise of the dictators and the sleep of the democracies, the European federal idea came to the fore again after World War II. Intellectuals and political leaders, encouraged by the general will of the publics to banish devastating wars, moved forward with a patchwork design for a federal Europe. They also had powerful US support.

The European Coal and Steel Community (1952) was the forerunner of *political communities with federal elements* which now characterize the European scene. The European Economic Community and Euratom (1958) followed; all three Communities were merged (1962); the whole was woven into a European Union and a plan for a common currency and central bank (Treaty of Maastricht, 1992); by 1995, the EU had 15 nation-members and more were clamouring to enter. Appendix B contains a detailed account of this and other elements in the evolution of inter-democracy Third and Fourth Phase systems since 1947. NATO, OECD and the Council of Europe also represent important aspects of the Fourth Phase transformation.

While the EU bears distinct federal hallmarks – a supranational court, a European Parliament whose members are directly elected, an EU budget voted by Parliament and a single market with rules enforced by an independent commission – its powers remain short of the federalist ideal. However, it is clear, after more than 40 years of experimentation and evolution, that the quasi-supranational EU has accomplished overwhelmingly more than any other international body. How can this progress be measured?

First, there have been no wars in western Europe, the area covered by the EU, since 1945. In particular, France and Germany are now friendly partners. Second, there has been economic peace and indeed unprecedented prosperity under the EU economic union. Third, democratic government and respect for human rights have become the norm for Europe.

Consider what a revolution in human – not just European – affairs these three interlocked developments represent. Under Rome, imperial wars were the norm. After the barbarian invasions, both internal and external war became the general pattern – locally, between power centres, monarchies, and in and around the loose remnants of the Empire. Emperor Charlemagne managed for a few scant decades to bring peace within an area that now comprises France, Germany, the Low Countries and most of Italy. Otherwise, from around AD 450 to 1945 European armed conflict never ceased. In other continents, war and much democide had also been the norm for centuries, but from the 16th century, modern Europe began to colonize other parts of the globe and made war a truly worldwide institution. It seems therefore only fitting that in Europe the only true political revolution in international order in centuries should have begun. This revolution, the birth of Fourth Phase communities of peoples and nations, is based on the most fundamental ideas – including Kant's – of the transatlantic Enlightenment.

GERMANY, FRANCE AND THE FOURTH PHASE UNION OF EUROPE

After 1945, to bring about the broader transformation it was first essential that Germany be tamed and that France and Germany should be reconciled, under one human and political scheme. This was done because the Germans and the French wanted it and because the Americans insisted. The rest of Europe concurred; Britain put its moral and practical effort into the first goal – taming Germany – but waited too long to become part of the political scheme for unifying Europe and thereby eliminating war between ancient enemies. The other powers proceeded without the UK.

In contrast to 1919, when the victorious powers sought to pull Germany's military and economic teeth and hem her in in every way, in 1945 the victors helped the Germans simultaneously to recover morally and economically, build solid democratic institutions and enter on an equal basis the new European and Atlantic communities. This required a decade of diplomatic effort, tutelage and economic aid through the Marshall Plan. The result can be seen today: a peaceful, prosperous, democratic and self-confident German people, who have astonished the world by accomplishing the reunification of their country without violence, albeit with great sacrifice on all sides. The 40-year Cold War ended; the Germans had played a major role in the development of the Fourth Phase quest for world order.

The drive to unite Europe could not have been successfully undertaken without the wholehearted cooperation of the German people and their leaders. Nor could Germany have been rehabilitated unless she had been welcomed as a full participant in a uniting Europe and the wider, looser web of cooperating democratic nations.

Postwar French and German leaders deserve great credit for bringing about the reconciliation of their two nations and for supporting wider European unity. Little noticed today, for example, are the results of the Franco–German Treaty of 1963, which initiated an amazing programme of cultural interchanges . . . involving *350,000* citizens of the two countries *each year*. Without the steady, long-term dedication and willingness to pay for such programmes, as well as for the common defence, on the part of both electorates, and without the general support of the United States and the other European peoples for the idea and the institutions of European unity, this revolution in the attitudes of ancient enemies could never have taken place.

Europe and also the world benefited enormously from the economic unification of the Old Continent. The 1950s and the 1960s, when the European community process was launched, were golden years for Europe. Without the goals and political-economic institutions of a uniting Europe, that Continent would have been in a dismal state and the prospects for world peace diminished. Timely application of federal principles to the reorganization of inter-state relations in Europe was the crux of the matter. But by 1991, when the EU faltered in trying to deal with the breakup of Yugoslavia, it was clear that the process of unifying Europe was less than complete. Fresh leadership and ideas, after 50 years of progress, are needed.

Europe's post-1945 rejuvenation is generally applauded. But less attention has been paid to the march of democratic ideas and institutions, from the Atlantic to eastern Europe, from the North Cape to the Mediterranean, in Latin America, and to the promising modernization of domestic political institutions and economies on the eastern extremities of the Eurasian continent. History may show, however, that we have been too optimistic in believing that democracy will take root as deeply and firmly in fledgling free nations as it has in the Atlantic West. Democracy is a tender crop, difficult to plant and hard to nurture. But even if in the next two or three decades some nations find it impossible to ride the democratic wave, it seems fairly clear that the overall trend will continue and not only in Europe.

The extraordinary spread of democratic ideals and practices, coupled with the growth of market-based economies, was largely made possible by several unprecedented and momentous developments over the last half century:

- The United States, the world's oldest modern democracy,[21] resolved in 1941 to engage itself in the world, spread its principles, promote free trade, help others economically and fight anti-democratic forces.
- The west European peoples felt more secure, more able to communicate and cooperate with their neighbours, more protected in the exercise of their civil rights and more committed to Europe and to their nations because they had a say – no matter if the institutions worked imperfectly – in their own governments and in their fledgling supranational institutions. Democracy reinforced itself at all levels.

- Having reconstituted itself on Fourth Phase lines, Europe became a political and economic model for others, and a magnet for the peoples of eastern Europe.

- The North Atlantic Treaty Organization (1949) proved to be an extraordinary insurance policy, a joint force on which all members could call for external protection and to which all contributed, and a shield which ensured the long-term engagement of the United States in Europe and behind which the political and economic construction of the European community and the extension of the Euro-Atlantic community could take place. The OECD helped to ensure necessary economic discipline among the industrialized democracies.

- The global economic institutions, Western-led, contributed to the development of stability and predictability for entrepreneurs and ordinary citizens who wanted to reach out abroad in a shrinking world. Without the rules established by the GATT, the economic aid and monetary management of the World Bank and IMF and the international regulation of, e.g., air traffic and communications, the tender seed of democracy might have had less of a chance.

- Decolonization, while it demanded much – sometimes too much – of the newly-independent peoples, provided a spur to economic and political development.

- Within a cocoon of US security, as well as political and economic aid, plus opening world markets, Japan's rehabilitation and democratization provided new stability, commercial opportunities and development assistance for her east Asian neighbours, as well as a strong new partner for the United States and Europe. This development cannot be separated from that which took place in western Europe, and must be seen as a part of a general global advance towards freedom. Nor could this have happened unless the Japanese people had wished it, in particular wished for the hope and choices that democracy gives and the assurance that they were welcome in contributing to the community of free nations.

- The general spread of free market, liberal economies not only was promoted by the rise of democracy, but the freeing of enterprise in turn fostered the development of pluralistic political institutions, the rule of law and protection for human rights. Multinational corporations made their own important contributions to modern ways of life, including the habits of democracy.

- The burgeoning of communication, the lower costs of travel and the willingness of governments, foundations and non-governmental bodies to support vast interchanges, especially of students and of intellectuals and leaders, spread the modern ideas of democracy and of Third and Fourth Phase concepts rapidly.

FATHERS OF THE FOURTH PHASE

Technology and historical forces may have been midwives to this great transformation, but human thought, conviction and forceful leadership – at the right times and places – made the difference. A few notable individuals can be singled out as 'makers of the democratic community' – the Fourth Phase in inter-state relations – of the late 20th century.

Jean Monnet, the true 'first Citizen of Europe', who learned in World Wars I and II that peace and democracy were indivisible, worked untiringly in a long life to establish institutions that would enfold the member-nations into one-for-all-and-all-for-one behaviour patterns. The establishment of the first truly supranational body – the European Coal and Steel Community – was above all due to Monnet, who saw clearly the need to submerge the old nation-based competition for basic resources into a single market in which borders would be irrelevant. He championed the idea of further 'integrated' European Communities, which culminated in today's impressive, if still unfinished, European Union. Monnet, although French, was no nationalist; in fact his ideas went far beyond Europe. He saw early (1942) and more clearly than the great majority of statesmen, European or North American, that a 'Federation of the West'[22] (i.e. a strong community of democracies) should be formed. But Monnet was a supreme pragmatist, so he began with the six European countries most ready for community. He was the century's truest and most effective prophet of supranational integration, viz. of federal principles applied to relations between democratic states and peoples. To be realized, Monnet's ideas required the backing of top European statesmen. Paul Henri Spaak, Robert Schuman, Alcide de Gasperi and Konrad Adenauer were the most prominent; the early Communities are monuments to their vision, persistence, and political hard work.

Winston Churchill's public advocacy of Fourth Phase ideas predated those of the statesmen of post-1945 Europe. Churchill had written about a 'United States of Europe' as early as 1930.[23] In June 1940 he accepted the advice of Monnet – then a French diplomat working in London – to offer to the beleaguered French government an Anglo–French federal union, with common citizenship, a common parliament and full economic amalgamation. It was too late; much of France had already been overrun by the German armies. So the offer was rejected. In 1946, recalling these ideas in Zurich, Churchill urged the European nations to unite. On one notable occasion (27 June 1950) when the House of Commons was debating the plan for a coal and steel community, Churchill spoke strongly for British inclusion, stating that the Conservative Party:

> declares that national sovereignty is not inviolable, and that it may be resolutely diminished for the sake of all men in all the lands finding their way home together.

Probably no more eloquent defence for the merging of national sovereignty has ever been spoken, yet Churchill, when he became Prime Minister, and most subsequent leaders of his Party (with the notable exceptions of Harold Macmillan and Edward Heath) and of the Labour Party, failed to see the necessity for Britain to plunge decisively into creation of a Fourth Phase European system.

Despite Churchill's vacillation and his lingering nostalgia for the Empire, his unwavering belief in democracy and his intuitive conviction that the democracies must stand together lent powerful support to the forces of change. He and other British statesmen, beginning with Gladstone, spoke out over the years in support of proposals for Atlantic union, embracing the United States and at various times western Europe, the UK, the Commonwealth and others. In 1943, he told a group of US senators in London that he foresaw a day when Americans and Englishmen would share a common citizenship.[24]

Clarence K. Streit, soldier in World War I and *New York Times* journalist in Geneva during the dramatic days of the League of Nations, by the mid-1930s believed he saw with clarity what the democratic nations had to do to save democracy: just as the 13 American states had united in 1787, the Western democracies should form a federal union. In his book *Union Now*,[25] Streit concluded that the world's 15 democracies were in great peril with the rise of the dictators, that they were so obsessed by national thinking that they could not make common cause and that only a merger of sovereignties for limited but fundamental purposes – foreign affairs, military security, trade and money – would save them. Streit was *Time*'s Man of the Year in 1950. For more than four decades, he advocated calling a transatlantic constitutional convention of the democratic nations, incessantly pressing Members of the House and Senate to make the first move. Once, in 1962, an Act of Congress inviting representatives of other democratic nations to meet in an 'Atlantic Convention' was passed; distinguished people (but no members of Congress) attended; in the end nothing much happened. Against the inertia of elite and popular opinion, advocacy of Streit's sweeping formula for peace – a modern echo of Kant's – had little chance.

However, the basic concept left a powerful mark on American and other leaders. The idea of an Atlantic union underlay every major US political initiative taken with Europe from 1947 to 1970 – Marshall Plan, NATO, the Organization for Economic Cooperation and Development and the various forms of European union – considered by many a 'first instalment' on Streit's and Monnet's wider visions.

In 1940, Churchill, Monnet and Streit were tied together intellectually when the Prime Minister made his appeal for a Franco–British union. Jacques Freymond, the Swiss historian, recounts how Emmanuel Monick, France's financial attaché in London, 'struck by the ideas advanced by Clarence Streit and the proposals for Atlantic union, had seen in a union of France and England the first step toward Atlantic union'. Monick discussed these ideas with Monnet, who went to Sir Robert Vansittart, chief adviser to the Foreign Secretary, who took the project to Churchill.[26] Comparing the growth of Monnet's own ideas, from the time he was deputy secretary general of the League of Nations, with Churchill's intellectual development (always on several 'tracks', of which one was his own 1930 plea for a United States of Europe) and with Streit's federal convictions – gestating in Geneva when Monnet was there – one has the makings of a fascinating historical puzzle. Monnet and Streit met later in 1940, in Washington, if not before.

Churchill's offer of Franco–British union was highly – if fleetingly – publicized at the time; Sir John Colville, Churchill's private secretary, later said of it: 'There would have been great difficulties to surmount, but we had before us the bridge to a new world, the first elements of European or even World Federation.'[27] It cannot have escaped the notice of many of Europe's democratic politicians and intellectuals. When the nations and peoples were *in extremis*, even ideas this bold could be taken seriously.

British governments had steered Canada (1867) and Australia (1901) to federal institutions. India was also given federal form, which carried on after independence in 1947. Lionel Curtis in 1937 published the third volume of his vast work, *Civitas Dei*,[28] in which he called for an 'international commonwealth' composed of the British Commonwealth, the European democracies and the United States. His work, along with that of the economist Lionel Robbins and the statesman-diplomat Philip Kerr (Lord Lothian), inspired British intellectuals to form a 'Federal Union' in 1938, to press for international federalism.[29] These ideas were to have extraordinary impact on Continental thinkers who, in exiled governments, concentration camps and underground during World War II, began to form concepts that later would animate the drive for a United States of Europe.

It is ironic, given this powerful intellectual lead from inside the UK (1938–50), that postwar British governments and publics, encased in nation-bound tradition, were to lag far behind their most advanced thinkers.

FOURTH PHASE COMMUNITY IN THE NEW MILLENNIUM

What is 'international federalism'? How can it be applied to a complex but ineluctably interdependent world?

The basis of federalism is the simple idea that government functions should be devolved downward or evolved upward, depending on the political requirements of the entities involved. As a general rule, federalism says that every function should be concentrated at the lowest possible level. For example, fire protection is obviously a task of local government but protection of a country's seacoasts a national matter. Until recent decades, it was assumed that the regulation of trade, the defence of a nation, crime, pollution controls and foreign affairs were all adequately managed on a national basis. Only occasionally were military alliances or treaties to regulate commerce necessary. However, in the latter half of the 20th century some political leaders and thinkers began to see that evolution of certain governmental powers upwards can stop at the nation-state level only at great peril. And – the crux of Fourth Phase order – the power of decision must also be lodged at a level corresponding to each function. The modern proving ground for these principles has been western Europe.

The creation of the European Communities – now Union – not only signified the conviction of the contracting powers that wars among them must cease, but also recognized the crippling effect that continued reliance solely on national governments to oversee commerce and industry would have. Since 1950, the bulk of western Europe's national barriers to economic intercourse have been swept away. Although individual nations still control fiscal and other elements of economic policy, this is now seen as an inconsistency which should also be resolved in favour of a Europe-wide capacity to act. In the 1990s, efforts to create a common central bank and common currency moved forward, but public misgivings began to surface. However, the need for effective economic union remains, and increasingly on an intercontinental scale.

With the astonishing advent of the third industrial revolution – based on electronics, computers and the Internet, instant global communication, rapid travel, interlocking stock exchanges, open markets and a premium on knowledge as the main factor of production in the future – the capability of individual nations to control their own economic affairs is virtually at an end. European economic union is simply the forerunner, perhaps a good model,[30] of what will eventually have to be done everywhere. More – a good deal more – than simple cooperation will be required; this postulate is the essence of Fourth Phase inter-state relations.

But here is a true dilemma: to make the global economy, the international security system and space-ship Earth's ecology function adequately will require entangling supranational institutions. Yet these are currently beyond the capability of most countries to comprehend, let alone build and operate. Even in Europe, the barriers posed by ignorance and outdated but still powerful national feelings is great.

For the United States, the stakes in fashioning a workable, durable supranational system are greater than for any other single nation. This is simply because the US has more to lose if things go badly wrong, and because it will be impossible for it to exercise leadership in the future except within a truly collective, rather than hegemonial, system. However, many American leaders still believe that the United States can in the future continue to sit back and decide important matters solely on the basis of 'national interest'. And much of the American public, fearful of the gathering uncertainties attendant on the third industrial revolution – the Knowledge Age – are led by false prophets to believe that their salvation, once again, lies in insulating themselves from developments beyond the seas.

Japan – another indispensable component in any supranational effort to revitalize the world system – is an even more difficult case. While her democratic and economic metamorphoses since 1945 have astounded the world, and while she has played a responsible role internationally, Japan still is an essentially closed society, centred almost exclusively on economics. Centuries of Japanese cultural isolation produced a potentially dangerous case – for the rest of the world as well as for Japan – of emotional insularity. Nonetheless, many Japanese political, business and diplomatic leaders are enlightened internationalists. The broad instincts of the Japanese people are inclined towards peace and cooperation. Japan's capabilities could be more fully employed to make and keep the international peace, and to open up her markets still more. Because Japan's economy is likely to remain No. 2 in world ranking for some time to come, it simply cannot be left out of the movement towards Fourth Phase world order. But could Japan pull its weight in a full-blown supranational system?

Led by the rich and powerful democracies into the 21st century, a better world order – *Pax Democratica* – grounded in joint planning and action that goes beyond cooperation, and based on the bedrock of democracy itself will be necessary. The foundations of such a system have already been laid, but only the foundations; further courageous steps are essential. Essential or not, however, we cannot expect to move completely and at once from the accumulation of three great eras in world order (with even the oldest – empire – still existing vestigially) straight into an entirely new supranational system. One has to deal with historical and sociological realities. During the 21st century and perhaps beyond, old forms will continue to coexist with new. Some of the older tools will often have to be employed, even by those who prefer the newest.

For example, the Third Phase UN system demonstrates the limitations of intergovernmental organization, yet to try to discard the UN at this stage would be folly. Because it is the only universal political forum and because its specialized agencies perform essential global tasks, it will be needed for many decades. The UN might eventually be reorganized on democratic, representative and federal principles, but that will require a very long time-scale. Meanwhile, the UN is an important piece of the world puzzle, but not the critical one.

Many world regions can benefit from fostering intergovernmental cooperation, promoting freer trade and mutual help. Third Phase cooperation in east and south Asia, as well as in Latin America and parts of Africa is feasible and potentially helpful, even if most of these nations are not yet ready for Fourth Phase institutions.

Similarly, the world is not done with Second Phase balance-of-power systems. The realities of world politics and the imperfections of international institutions dictate that for a long time to come, the democracies and their allies will sometimes have to rely on *Realpolitik*. Even when a solid Intercontinental Community of Democracies has come about, ICD will often have to conduct its common policies towards less-than-friendly nations on Second Phase principles, moving to Third Phase wherever possible, with the hope that it can eventually assimilate rivals and adversaries to ICD's (by then) sturdy Fourth Phase system.

In the last half century, *Pax Americana* has defined our pivotal age and established guidelines for a nascent democratic community. This loose hegemonial system, however benevolent, will no longer do – for Americans or others. Now we are turning a corner to a new century, a new millennium. This can be the Era of Democracy, if we muster the new, *collective* leadership that the challenges ahead will demand. If the democratic peoples wish to use their combined capabilities, they can create the Intercontinental Community of Democracies . . . which will bring with it *Pax Democratica.*

But what should impel us to do this? Why not wait? Why do it at all? The burden of the next chapter is that the inevitable chaos and crises ahead will require joint foresight, planning and action by the democracies. *They* must lead; no others can.

4 The Challenge Ahead

Chaos and instability may prove a greater and more insidious threat to American interests than communism ever was.

Paul Kennedy, Robert Chase, Emily Hill[1]

The only thing necessary for the triumph of evil is for good men to do nothing.

Edmund Burke

The democracies will be called upon to cope with a future world of increasing complexity and danger, for which their present largely Second-plus-Third Phase systems are not equipped to deal. Leaders and publics today are complacent, drifting. The danger potential of the years to come – the challenge ahead – is set forth below. In Chapter 5, the inadequacy of the present system to meet that challenge will be examined.

ON CHAOS AND CRISIS

A crisis is 'an unstable state of affairs in which a decisive change is impending'.[2] It is inevitable, and perhaps sooner rather than later, that we shall be faced with the sort of overriding international crisis that will threaten the vital common interests of the democracies. It might be on the order of a major war, a great depression, full-scale disorder in a vital region, or a terrorist attack, on a scale heretofore not seen, by powers inimical to democracy and modernization. By definition, such a crisis would threaten the free order and the shared economic and ecological interests not only of the democracies but of the entire world. The nature and scope would be plain for all to see. Especially could such a Major Crisis challenge the underpinnings of a world community based on the Rule of Law and democracy itself.

This has to do with a *Big* Crisis, not your everyday garden variety. Press, TV and politicians thrive on minor 'crises' but these are usually ephemeral. For example, in a given week in the mid-1990s, if the crisis of the day were not another desperate juncture in PLO–Israeli or Israeli–Syrian peace talks, it might have been a little war on the Ecuadoran–Peruvian border, or the impending collapse of Japanese–American trade negotiations, or a vote by Québec which could break up the Canadian Confederation, or a breakdown in the fledgling Haitian electoral system, or the mass movement of Serbian refugees into Serbia-proper, or the failure of Japan to reflate or of the Bundesbank to lower interest rates, or Chinese naval manoeuvres off Taiwan ... or a hundred other serious or occasionally alarming disruptions. Now and then situations such as these can and do lead, through a chain of events, to true, major world crises, but for the most part they will not count for much in the general history of our times. We should consider only the larger crises that could be truly disruptive to international order and threaten the long-term interests of the democracies.

A number of smaller crises can merge into chaos, 'a state of utter confusion completely wanting in order, sequence, organization, or predictable operation'.[3] A heightened state of anarchy or disorder in one small state (e.g. Liberia in the 1980s–90s) can pose serious problems for near neighbours and inconvenience and bad consciences elsewhere, but it hardly threatens world order. But chaos in huge Zaire or in a strategic country such as Iraq or North Korea is another matter and could spread widely, suddenly presenting a major threat – a Big Crisis – to a developing *Pax Democratica.*

Some might prefer to believe that the state of world affairs currently is more or less manageable, that truly major crises and/or unmanageable chaos on a large scale are highly unlikely, and that this benign condition is likely to continue for some time to come. This is hardly a prudent assumption, given past history. The following pages propose a number of candidates for the kinds of major crises – most coming out of chaos or producing it – that could demand the joint and immediate attention of the democracies.

THE COMING CHALLENGES

This list is meant to be illustrative, not exhaustive. The examples are not presented as probability-scenarios, in the now time-honoured fashion of 'future studies', but are simply some of the fairly obvious crises-waiting-to-happen with which present mechanisms would be unlikely to cope. One could add others of comparable plausibility.

1. Potential Crisis of the Global Monetary System

Since 1970, when the United States, beginning to suffer a chronic balance of payments deficit, precipitated a switch from the gold exchange standard to 'floating exchange rates', the principal trading nations have been trying to adjust. Free floating exchange rates (explaining, for example, why your money can suddenly become worth more – or less – in terms of your vacation country's currency) haven't worked well enough. Turbulence in money markets has increased substantially, causing observers to wonder if governments are still in charge. Currency traders have tended to replace governments in the foreign exchange area. 'The $1 trillion a day being traded around the world is simply too much for any central bank to control. Only when there is concerted effort by many central banks have governments been able to thwart traders.'[4] Speculators have made big killings, sometimes with major political consequences, as when in 1992 they overran the pound sterling. Also, the expense of doing international business on a continuing basis mounts as companies and banks must incur currency exchange costs, extra paperwork and risks of rate-changes. Finally, the world trading system continues to rely inordinately on the US dollar as its chief reserve currency, although its value fluctuates; this situation is inherently unstable and, among other things, results in a continuing increase in the dollar supply *outside* the United States, and necessarily outside the control of the Federal Reserve.

Within Europe, pressures to change these money facts of life became great once the single market and economic union had evolved significantly. 'For a single market to prosper it needs to avoid the disruption of currency fluctuations and competitive devaluations.'[5] Monetary union was always on the long-term agenda of the European Community/Union; there is now supposed to be a European central bank and a common currency – the 'Euro' – by 1999. This kind of change, if indeed it can be brought about, would simplify matters (for the EU members) in many ways but also complicate them. There is as yet, for example, no 'European' political authority strong enough to oversee and support such a sensitive revolution in international finance. And moves to build yet another economic wall (this time financial) around Europe inevitably will bring problems in relations with great trading nations on the outside – mainly the highly-developed democratic economies of North America, Japan, South Korea and Australasia, which will be put at a disadvantage.

The advent of a 'Euro' would very likely bring pressures from top trading nations outside to get inside the Euro-zone, or to turn it into a much larger dollar (or yen? or DM? or 'Demo'?) zone, or otherwise spread the common currency's use intercontinentally, and in the process dilute the control over it still further. If Europe or some larger grouping does not adopt a common currency, even though a rational examination of the system argues strongly for it, exchanging currency and settling trading balances will pose a mounting problem as the new century begins. By the year 2010, given the increasing globalization of markets and banking, predicted Richard N. Cooper in 1984, 'real movements in exchange rates will be highly disruptive of profits, production, and employment in any particular location'.[6] Events since Cooper wrote have borne him out, but his timescale may not have been as generous as he thought. The US debates about NAFTA in particular and free trade in general beginning in 1993, the subsequent Mexican financial crisis as well as the French strikes in 1995, the lingering Japanese recession, the German recession of 1996–97 and the East Asian financial debacle of 1997, show how such dislocations can have serious political effects. One or two such events can be dealt with simultaneously by existing machinery; several, snowballing, might be overwhelming. But even if the rich democracies were to create a new monetary system, that probably would not be enough.

Four elements need to be addressed jointly by the industrial democracies before the global economy can be considered effectively structured: national economic policies; national taxation policies; national monetary policies; national social policies. To make a new system work, substitute for the adjective 'national' before each of these policy areas, the word 'multinational'. The longer the main nations wait to set up a broad common political institution for economic purposes, relying instead on flimsy and occasional bouts of 'consultation' in one area or another (by the G-5 or the G-7 or the OECD or some existing intergovernmental – but not supranational – body), the more risk there is of global economic chaos which could lead to a major crisis somewhere down the road, along the lines of 1929. A full-blown economic downturn, triggered by banking and other collapse, could cause deflation and disorder on a vast scale.

A common structure of economic rules and means of enforcement (i.e. an economic union), for a minimum number of advanced countries – not confined to Europe – will become a virtual necessity, and sooner than most people think. And others will want to join and should, as they can qualify.

2. Potential Crisis in Relations with China

Deng's death in 1997 opened the way for a struggle for power that will continue for some time to come. China under almost any likely scenario will pose major problems for the international community. The world's most ancient civilization and last working empire has undergone enormous upheavals throughout its nearly four millennia of autocratic, highly-structured and bureaucratic existence. After periods, sometimes very long, of chaos and conflict, China has always rediscovered order; the order has always been one of iron control.

Modern external influences on China, beginning in the late 18th century, have accelerated. As the 20th century has worn on, and especially now with extraordinary means of communication which do not acknowledge boundaries, it has become more and more difficult for the Chinese emperor (both Mao and Deng *have* been 'emperors' very much on the old pattern; Chiang tried in the brief brutal days of the Republic) and the emperor's efficient bureaucracy to control the impact of outside forces on his multi-millions. Well into the next century, one can foresee plenty of disorder and attempts to restore control. But in the process, despite the extraordinary pace of economic modernization and social change in southeastern China, outsiders would be foolish to count on a peaceful resolution of the pressures and the turmoil. Nor can the world outside be assured that as a result of such inner instability and the innate expansionism of a ruling clique China will not turn aggressively outward.

Mutual accommodation with China will be a major problem for the rest of the world for years to come. This is true above all for the advanced democracies (very much including Japan), who will bear the main responsibility because only they have the combined power and skills to manage these relations with any chance of success. To date, Chinese leaders from Mao through Deng's successors have shown themselves adept at playing the great democracies off against one another. Because China remains a permanent member of the UN Security Council, she will continue to hold veto power over vital decisions of that body. In the past few years, China's army and navy have been extensively modernized; their leadership is reportedly an increasingly powerful voice in the nation's policy councils and the economy; 'showing the flag' with naval manoeuvres, intimidating Taiwan with 'rocket tests' and live firing exercises and occupying islets in the South China Sea whose ownership is contested by several (decidedly) smaller powers had become routine by the mid-1990s. China possesses a formidable arsenal of nuclear, biological and chemical weapons – which she is beginning to share, profitably, with other authoritarian regimes disruptive of world order. China's entry into the world economy, but not yet party to all its rules, has come with a Big Bang; this economy is not free market/ private enterprise/rule of law capitalism, but state/bureaucratic capitalism, difficult to integrate into the modern global system. Projecting present growth, some predict that around 2030 China's will be the biggest economy of all, with the Chinese military controlling a good deal of it. Through a policy of 'engagement', the United States has attempted to handle China on behalf of virtually everyone else, but recent events show how weak are the outside levers – even those of the United States – that can be brought to bear to affect the behaviour of the Chinese state. Outside levers are especially feeble because there are many, not one; Western commercial interests have tended to outweigh the combined, long-term strategic interest of the democracies.

These imponderable but obviously weighty factors (and others we shall explore later) taken together suggest that managing the 'China problem' will be one of the greatest challenges – perhaps *the* greatest – facing the international community in the coming century. China's neighbours, unfortunately, are wholly incapable, on their own, of dealing with a Chinese policy of hegemony. A China sliding into chaos could readily bring about a major crisis demanding the overriding attention of the democracies; a China pulled together under iron leadership and projecting outward could pose *the* Crisis of the next 100 years, demanding truly desperate measures and not excluding nuclear war.

A *Pax Sinensis* – or at least a serious attempt at it – is probably the most likely single alternative to a *Pax Democratica* or the continuation of *Pax Americana* that one could envisage. On the other hand, if China could eventually subscribe to a general *Pax Democratica*, what a salutary unfolding that would be; if she resists it and attempts her own *Pax*, what a disaster *that* could be! For her own people, as well as for everybody else. Japan, Europe and America can no longer afford separate China policies. The stakes are simply too great. However, the mindset and institutional mechanisms for bringing about a joint policy are simply not there at present.

3. Middle Eastern Chaos and Crisis

This is yet another potential challenge of global dimensions: violent, disruptive, anti-democratic, Islamic fundamentalism or its still-living cousin, radical pan-Arabism. Consider:

- the disruptive lethal power of a tinpot but relentlessly determined and brutal dictator such as Saddam Hussein to covertly amass the beginnings of nuclear, bacteriological and chemical arsenals, from whose shadow his neighbours, the West and the world are still struggling to free themselves permanently;
- the possibility of foolish Israeli or Palestinian moves – or both – that rupture the Oslo process;
- the size, oil reserves, Shiite fanatacism and theocratic mobilization of an Iran aimed also at Mideast domination and the extermination of Israel;
- the social, political and economic flimsiness of the Kingdom of Saudi Arabia, built figuratively as well as literally on sand but strategically vital to the global economy;
- Egypt, with a benevolent autocrat attempting to keep his economically fragile nation and his demographically lemming-like countrymen from bursting the feeble bonds of their ancient community and turning to fundamentalism;
- the Sudanese Islamic dictatorship, seeking to obliterate the non-Muslim one-quarter of its population in the attempt to impose its fundamentalist regime, importing arms and fighting men from Iran, and exporting terrorism on a substantial scale throughout the Middle East;
- Libya, recently quiescent but still inherently unstable and potentially dangerous;
- a seething, populous Algeria, ruled by a military clique who fear democracy because it would very likely bring to power an Islamic dictatorship of a more brutal and uncompromising nature than their own, with – because of Algeria's relative weight in the Arab world – a potentially shattering effect on other Arab regimes;
- a few more modern and secularly-inclined Arab societies (Tunisia, Morocco, Jordan) struggling to resist Islamic radicalism, homegrown or imported;

- a still harsh and implacable Assad governing Syria in a less (for him) favourable post-Cold War climate, with his oligarchy holding down a nation which could erupt under future pressures and which continues to sponsor major terrorism abroad; and finally
- a half-modern, half-democratic, half-industrialized, half-secularized Turkey, desperately keen to join the modern West and Europe, yet held down by its autocratic Ottoman traditions, its lingering sense of ethnic superiority, the increasing attractions of Islamic fundamentalism, the 1000-year-old European fears and hatreds that continue to shut Turkey out of Europe's union, an apparently insoluble Kurdish problem, and its peoples' unbridled fecundity. Will Turkey be a leader in the Middle East or slip back into misrule and Islamic dictatorship? Turkey is by far the greatest hope, along with Israel, for a bright future in North Africa and western Asia, yet all could very badly go wrong there, in short order and with untold consequences for even distant nations.

There is reason to hope that an eventual if uneasy peace will settle over the Israeli–Arab conflicts; that the baleful influences in the Islamic and Arab worlds will not be able to coalesce; that positive Western and Israeli influences will grow ever stronger; that gradual economic and social improvement – modernization – and the containment of rogue states such as Libya, Iraq, Syria, Iran and Sudan will be able to overcome the instabilities of North Africa and the Middle East; and that the rest of the world will be generally vigilant and helpful. But do not count on it. The entire arc from Gibraltar to Pakistan (or even east as far as Muslim Indonesia) is a potential sink of anarchy and a powder keg. Widespread chaos is probably its most likely scenario in the next century, with the corollary of virtually unstoppable migration (already begun) from North Africa into Europe.

There can be little doubt that a series of important crises in North Africa and west and central Asia will continue to face the democracies. Europe, North America, Japan and the rest of the democratic world, even if they were to work fully in harness, hardly possess the means to put everything right in the Middle East, but they could make a significant difference with concerted measures of help, or of joint containment of trouble when necessary. As we enter the 21st century, not only do the advanced democracies badly lack a common set of policies, they lack even the institutions for fashioning such policies.

4. Chaos on the Eastern Margins of Europe

This could rather easily eventuate. While the liberation of former parts of the crumbled Soviet empire brought joy to the bulk of the former inmates and sighs of relief to the Cold War-bound Free World, five years later the situation in central and eastern Europe, the Balkans, and the entire middle Asian south, which rims Russia all the way to Mongolia, was crammed with fateful uncertainties. Poland, the Czech Republic, Hungary and probably Slovenia can hope for entry into the European Union and NATO – i.e. incorporation into the present community of democracies – early in the next century. The three Baltic nations, worried still about their huge bear of a former protector, may be able to find a fairly secure future within a Nordic sphere, buttressed by close ties to the European Union. Romania, Bulgaria, the chaotic lands of the former Yugoslavia (except Slovenia) and the rest of the Balkans will have – and will pose for others – more difficulties. These have no Western civic traditions. Indeed in all the former Soviet empire, only the Czechs possess proven, substantial democratic credentials. The others still struggle with difficult economic and political overhangs from their former colonial/autocratic regimes, and – especially in the Yugoslav case – face long periods of adjustment to modern norms for the treatment of ethnic and religious minorities and for democratic government. Most will probably continue to be subject to eruptions of irredentism and violence.

To these fringe lands of the former Soviet empire, add its once-integral parts, such as Ukraine, Moldova, Belorus, Georgia, Armenia, Azerbaijan, Uzbekistan, Turkestan, Tajikstan, Kazakhstan and Kirghizstan, and one has a second potentially ungovernable arc of instability running across the central Eurasian heartland that can cause great trouble for the rest of Eurasia and for the world balance in the coming years. And what happens in the former USSR could in many cases spill over into the next-lower tier of instability; from Armenia/Azerbaijan into Turkey and Iran; from Kazakhstan, Tajikstan, and the Khyrgyz Republic into Afghanistan or Pakistan; or from Ukraine or Belarus into central Europe or the Balkans. (And of course, some of these pressures could flow in the opposite direction.)

Still more: whether or not the Bosnian story finally unfolds with diminished bloodshed, the potential for Serb-inspired trouble in the fledgling Macedonia or the province of Kosovo, not to mention irredentist pressures on Serbia's northern borders with Hungary, could again foment another major Balkan conflict, involving Albania, Greece, Turkey, Bulgaria and challenging Russia and the Western powers in major ways . . . challenges with which the hastily-devised UN, OSCE and NATO machinery for Bosnia is hardly equipped to deal.

5. A Wrong Turn in Russia

Finally, the biggest question mark of all is Russia itself, still a great power by definition (if not a superpower in the lonely US class). Experts, consultants and freebooters from the West still clamber over Russia, trying to help or to secure supposedly lucrative business for the future. There are many encouraging signs of Russian metamorphosis towards modern Western models, but also signs of economic imbalances and of social discontent and backwardness, plus political volatilities. Perhaps Russia's worst problem is to replace the old Communist *nomenklatura* with a new and modern governing class. It is possible to find many reasons for optimism and to laud the alacrity with which Russians have taken to free markets, a free (if somewhat chaotic) political system, free speech and to general intercourse with the modern Atlantic world. But as we near the end of this tumultuous century, it is exceedingly difficult to forecast the Russian future with accuracy.

There was, beginning in 1991, a major opportunity for the West to bring Russia within its democratic/free market fold, thereby enlarging, potentially, the community of democracies. Some – but insufficient – efforts have been made. But no serious statesman outside Russia, hoping to help guide this positive process of re-education and reorientation of a large and proud people, can proceed yet with assurance. The golden moment – and one never knows if the democracies could have succeeded with a much more ambitious project – may have been lost.

Because of the size of Russia itself and the region around it, there is a distinct limit to what outside forces can expect constructively to accomplish. For Russia, how the future unfolds will depend more on its own social forces and its own creative leadership than on any external influences. Given this great uncertainty, chaos in Russia and in at least some of the lands around it is closer to a likelihood than one would like. As with China, Russia's historical burden is great and its future clouded.

The great democracies need to expect crises in the Eurasian heartland, some small and some very probably of major proportions, in the next two or three decades. Eurasia, termed the 'world island' by the father of geopolitics, Halford Mackinder, is still the strategic heart of the Earth; what unfolds there (and China is a huge part of its periphery) in the next century could have untold consequences for the democracies. The problem for them in this case is not so much that they lack a common policy, but that they simply have not done enough, together or separately; their estimate of the problem and of the dangers falls short.

6. Terrorism's Tremendous, Still Largely Untapped Potential for Chaos and Crisis

In the summer of 1995, US Senator Richard Lugar of Indiana lectured Ross Perot's 'United We Stand America' cohorts in Dallas. Sandwiched in a series of the usual windy talks by politicians from both major parties, Lugar's message stood out as serious, important and extremely sobering. It was, however, largely unnoticed by the press. He sounded a distinct note of alarm at the likelihood of nuclear terrorism, based on the known propensities and capabilities of international terrorist groups, the inadequate accounting for fissile materials in the former Soviet Union and the disappearance of bomb-grade nuclear matter from Russian stockpiles. Senator Lugar subsequently held Senate hearings on these dangers. But neither his Dallas speech nor the hearings were given media attention; the joys of hearing politicians damn one another in Dallas, for press and public, took precedence over the complicated details of potentially disastrous and all too likely acts of nuclear terrorism forecast by the Senator.

The potential danger is very great. The German government alone has reported more than 700 cases of attempted illicit nuclear sales between 1991 and 1994. The democracies and other governments are patently not moving in a sufficiently coordinated fashion, or on a large enough scale, to survey and control what is happening, to monitor and contain terrorist movements which could do this sort of thing, or to plan for the most horrible eventualities. Nuclear terrorism represents a true Achilles heel for any world order based on law. Terrorists have proven themselves quite capable of perpetrating grave atrocities almost anywhere. The work of such agencies as Interpol and the new Europol can be valuable, but a better understanding of the roots of terrorism and efforts to treat causes, plus more effective intelligence as to imminent dangers are necessary. The great danger is that one or more dictators in the Middle East could become a good deal more powerful and concert their efforts in a massive blow at the democracies, with or without nuclear weapons. The nuclear danger of course greatly increases the stakes.

7. Consequences of the Unrestricted Arms Trade

Closely allied to the dangers inherent in the access of international terrorists to weapons of mass destruction is the virtually indiscriminate, headlong sale of arms by those manufacturing or possessing them. Great amounts of surplus Soviet arms have found their way to renegade regimes in Africa and the Middle East; German, American, British, French, South African, Chinese, Czech and other armaments manufacturers have rushed to fill the insatiable maws of the military establishments of dictators and poor countries which can scarcely afford such useless expenditures.

The indiscriminate arms-dealing of one American citizen, Sam Cummings, was detailed in a recent Associated Press despatch;[7] he bought surplus arms anywhere he could find them, then sold them to any group or regime which would pay, from the 1950s to the present decade. A writer quotes Cummings as saying the gun-running business will never die, '[b]ecause it's based on human folly . . . and the depths of human folly will never be plumbed'.

During the Cold War, a 17-nation pact called 'COCOM' controlled fairly well Free World arms transfers to third nations, helping mostly those who were opposing Soviet inroads. The COCOM era, which saw the arming of many unscrupulous dictators on the right – as the USSR supplied bloodthirsty client regimes on the left – leaves a far from noble record, even if these arms transfers were at the time deemed necessary. Today, however, with the bipolar world regime splintered, there is little excuse for the democracies through unbridled competition to help arm those who would disturb international order or the domestic peace of nations. One day, major crises arising out of such folly can be expected, suddenly demanding high risks and great costs from the very democracies which seek in so many other sincere and effective ways to improve international commerce, damp down violent conflict, establish the rule of law internationally and promote democracy. We may come to see that in this particularly vulnerable area of purposeful inattention by governments (to characterize this in the most generous way) and powerful, ingeniously-conducted, vicious trade, lies another chain of potential crises for world order and another major challenge for democracy in particular.

8. Computer Chaos

A single act of terrorism could melt down the heart of the entire national/international information/communication system on which the world now depends. Such sabotage is a distinct possibility, given the extreme vulnerability to computer and communication systems that has been demonstrated in recent years by (more or less) innocent hackers. Antiquated government-by-government capacities for detecting and thwarting such vandalism on a vast scale, and the barely nascent systems of international cooperation in this field, are today incapable of coping with computer chaos of substantial magnitudes.

9. General Chaos in the Least-Developed Societies

In an eye-popping article for *The Atlantic Monthly,* 'The Coming Anarchy',[8] journalist Robert Kaplan traced the frightening outlines, as he saw them, of actual or impending chaos in the underdeveloped world, with special attention to West Africa. Here, the vicissitudes of one-crop or one-resource economies and of general mismanagement, the clash of tribal habits and loyalties with new urban conditions and artificially-imposed state boundaries, the existence of endemic poor health for large numbers side-by-side with birthrates out of control, the lack of experience in self-government, the enormous risks of general and rapid environmental degradation, and the prevalence of corruption and brutal rule by leaders no better than thugs, led the author to suggest that 'Africa may be as relevant to the future character of world politics as the Balkans were a hundred years ago, prior to the two Balkan wars and the First World War'. He predicted a 'coming upheaval, in which foreign embassies are shut down, states collapse, and contact with the outside world takes place through dangerous, disease-ridden coastal trading posts'.[9]

Perhaps things will not get quite that bad, but anyone who is optimistic about Africa need only look at the Rwandan tragedy, which erupted lethally soon after Kaplan wrote. By mid-1995, it had taken upwards of 1.5 million lives in an orgy of democide and 'ethnic cleansing'. Burundi, next door and composed of an ethnically similar mix, exploded soon after; the violence spread into Zaire in 1996. The UN effort to predict or control these events was scattered and ineffective.

What the ultimate outcome will be in Rwanda, Burundi or Zaire or what regional effects the breakdowns will have could not be predicted. But more sub-Saharan collapse on similar lines can be anticipated. Kaplan called the coming African chaos '*the* national-security issue of the early twenty-first century'. Perhaps, but there are a number of other troubled world-corners and systemic global problems (some suggested above), the dimensions and implications of which rival those of the impending African chaos.

It will be extremely difficult to nurture stable government and orderly, productive free market systems in states as fragile and underdeveloped as most of contemporary Africa, much of central and western Asia, parts of the Balkans and eastern Europe and perhaps some of Latin America. Impact these already problematical places with the jet travel and instant communications of our age – including computers and the Internet, fax machines, CNN, telephones, radio, movies and videos, 'virtual reality' and cassette tapes, bringing perhaps a degree of enlightenment but also waves of the worst cultural refuse of the West – and one has a recipe for general unrest, chaos and roiling crises on an unprecedented scale . . . McLuhan's 'global village' but on worse – much worse – terms than he envisaged in the 1960s.[10]

One can hope for the orderly development of the capacity for self-government in underdeveloped societies, but wholesale breakdown will often eventuate in more dictatorships; these usually result in upheaval and more chaos; then order is re-imposed; the cycle continues if unattended. Perhaps the Nigerian or Burmese militarists or the neo-Communists of Kazakhstan or a future dictator of, say, Haiti (when the US and UN have withdrawn) will not be as efficient at wholesale killing as were the totalitarian Nazis or Japanese, but surely there is a good case to be made that Professor Rummel's 'democide'[11] – 170 million victims worldwide in the 20th century – could easily be repeated or the numbers even exceeded, in the 21st. Bear in mind also that the technology of 'terminating' human beings has evolved rapidly since the 1930s to 1950s.

Ethnic cleansing, democide and chaos breed wars, and vice versa.

How much more of this disorder – and on what scale – can the responsible peoples of the world endure? International law draws a line (sometimes ignored by the world community) at genocide but the broader question of 'democide', so carefully defined and chronicled by Rummel,[12] is something that the democratic nations – supposedly the keepers of the flame of human rights – must also face squarely in the next century. The experience so far with the UN-sponsored war crimes tribunals for Bosnia and Rwanda does not give solid grounds for confidence.

It is unlikely that all these potentially convulsive emergencies described above will take place, or eventuate from just the chains of events suggested. The timing of each and all is unknowable. Some, however, and others just as serious, *will* eventuate. A few minor crises could roll into One Big One. History teaches us that this is so. And in today's fast-moving world, the democracies may not have time to prepare once the Crisis is upon us; this in turn could result in Chaos, which could become general and take decades if not centuries to deal with.

LEARNING FROM CRISES

With few exceptions, it is virtually axiomatic that the political classes seem unable to learn major lessons from the past and apply these to our situation. Still less are they able to assess contemporary trends and discern effectively what troubles the future is likely to bring. And if a single politician or pundit does see clearly and sounds the alarm, for the most part nobody listens, or they do not listen until it is too late.

In the 20th century, Winston Churchill and Franklin Roosevelt stand out as leaders who saw the portents of major crises far in advance. From 1911 until World War I broke out,[13] Churchill warned British politicians and public of the looming German danger. He did so again in the 1930s. So did Roosevelt, who understood the probable consequences of the rise of the dictatorships but could not rouse the American political class or the ordinary citizens. The Allies almost lost both World Wars.[14] Some of the lack of foresight of the political classes can be attributed to their chronic concentration on domestic matters, their short-term views of the national interest and their chronic inability to see crises until they become visibly imminent. Most political leaders are more willing to be led by public opinion than to lead it. The terrible risks run before and during both World Wars can also be laid at the door of poor – or nonexistent – coordination among the governments of the three great democracies in the first third of the present century, when the crises should have been seen and averted through joint, resolute action.

By 1945, some lessons had been learned. Economic crisis management was improved through the new United Nations affiliates. But UN security machinery could not handle the Cold War as it emerged in 1946–47; the NATO Treaty (1949) put an adequate scheme on paper, but it took the wholly unexpected outbreak of the Korean War in 1950 to alarm the West sufficiently to rearm and to put in place a system of concerted Allied planning and force preparedness in advance of crises. It was then that modern international crisis management was born; the system worked fairly well, at least as applied to Europe, for 40 years. It was an interallied effort, led by the United States.

A BRIEF *PAX AMERICANA*

Today, nearing the turn of another century, we bask in the declining light of '*Pax Americana*', which underwrote crisis management for 50 years. It was only with the 20th century defeat of the authoritarian challengers to Western democracy, in two world wars and a Cold War, that world order, for the first time since the end of *Pax Romana* 1500 years ago, has not depended on a balance of power. In the 1990s, no major power on the horizon is capable of challenging successfully the pre-eminence of the single superpower. This is a new but unstable hybrid system; *Pax Americana* is not like previous hegemonial orders, and shows tendencies of evolving towards *Pax Democratica*.

Over the last 50 years, major crises had positive outcomes on several occasions as the Allies acted together under American leadership. Here are five examples:

- the rapid deterioration of economic and political stability in Europe that led to the Marshall Plan (1947) and virtually all subsequent

efforts to build strong European and Atlantic institutions;
- the outbreak of the Korean War (1950), which led to the transformation of NATO from a paper alliance to combined forces-in-being and the institutionalization of transatlantic political cooperation on a continuing multinational basis;
- the Cuban Missile Crisis (1963), which signalled the high-water mark for Soviet attempts at an 'end run' around the alliance;
- the Arab Oil Boycotts (1973 and 1979), which led to creation of the G-7, the common adoption of energy conservation measures and the general reinforcement of interallied economic cooperation; and
- the overwhelming Allied response to a powerful but foolish challenge by Saddam Hussein (1990) to international law and world oil supplies, inaugurating President Bush's putative 'New World Order'.

An *overbalance* of power, with America and its democratic allies in charge and creating Third and Fourth Phase systems, was increasingly the basis of world order from 1945, and has been essentially unchallenged after 1989. However, this and *Pax Americana* with it may turn out to have been only a brief footnote to history.

The United States will probably retain its leadership position and capability as the new century opens. But alone, or sometimes as the leader on whom everyone else depends and whom they tend to follow, this supremacy is not likely to last. Equivocal signs of disintegration in the world, plus intensified commercial rivalry among the advanced powers, already are causing doubts about Allied cohesiveness and American hegemony, not just about the virtues of the latter (which doubts there always were) but also about US staying power. The responsibility for foreseeing and dealing with truly disruptive crises can no longer be solely, or even mainly, that of the United States, because *Pax Americana*, if it still exists, is a *waning Pax*. Unique in history, it always depended to a fair extent on at least the assent, and usually on the active cooperation, of key Allies – from a small group of the biggest to an across-the-board assemblage of all of them. But global hegemony by the United States, no matter how benevolent or convenient, is no longer a good prescription for world order. Most importantly, it is doubtful that the American people will much longer have the stomach for the kind of sustained leadership and burden-bearing that *Pax Americana* required of them over the past half-century. Unstable as it is, *Pax Americana* cannot last.[15]

TO CONFRONT LOOMING CHAOS, THE DEMOCRACIES MUST REGROUP

Peace has become divisible. After briefly glimpsing a new world order, the victors of the cold war have resigned themselves to tolerating anarchy in large areas of the globe, so long as their own material interests are not directly threatened.

Financial Times, Christmas Eve, 1994

Decline begins when people no longer ask 'What shall we do?' but 'What is going to happen?'

Denis de Rougemont

Chance favors only the mind that is prepared.

Louis Pasteur

The responsible powers – the great democracies – of this world are drifting. Citizens have lulled themselves into a false sense of security. They do not see, or do not want to see, our actual situation, which might be distilled as follows:

- although the world economy, on the whole, seems to be progressing, and particularly in the rich welfare states and several newly-industrializing nations, there is continuing complacency and a reluctance to look at the globe as a whole, at the fragility of the present framework for doing global business and at the potential long-term impact of socioeconomic inequality and political chaos on our economic house of cards;
- the wars, civil and otherwise, of the post-Cold War era, while lethal and disruptive enough, have not yet approached a scale which most people regard as intolerable, i.e. pregnant with danger for the international community. It's easy to dismiss each Somalia or Timor or Rwanda or Nagorno-Karabakh – individually – by alleging absence in each case of a 'real threat' to 'vital interests'. The extent of the cumulative, composite danger is not seen;
- there is not now an immediate, ongoing, and obvious global threat that signals citizens: 'it is imperative that we act'. The kind of overwhelming menace that formed the glue of the Cold War, holding the democratic coalition together and causing numerous people of goodwill and judgement in non-democratic countries to resist (often clandestinely) and to urge on the effort of the democracies, simply does not exist. The need to make sacrifices

to ward off future dangers that seem unclear and multifarious, even non-existent, is difficult to inspire.

Today's system is inadequate to deal with this kind of world, especially in the medium or long term.

The world could be dividing into three classes: the modern, rich democratic countries; the nations aspiring to join the democratic/ free market club; and the great number of peoples with little hope or chance for the foreseeable future. Depending on the degree of interaction, and the direction and volume of movement, among these groupings, the next century *could* be even more bloody than this one . . . or it could be better and more hopeful. The outcome depends in large part on the choices that the first group – the solid democracies – and the second group of nations, who share the first group's political values and with whom they wish to make common cause – will make and how these two will help, or (if that becomes necessary in a few cases) contain, members of the third group. A coalition of first and second group democracies is essential if the transition from *Pax Americana* to *Pax Democratica* is to be smooth and effective.

To create a truly *collective* leadership which can form timely crisis policy will be no easy task. Such a 'crisis policy' means a joint approach by the key democratic nations. We first need an early warning system – as we now have with weather satellites and globally institutionalized meteorology – to alert us to impending political and economic upheavals and other grave threats to the fragile new world system that has begun to evolve. Much better and more timely intelligence for the democracies *as a community*, and – in particular – the full sharing of that intelligence by each with all, and the joint evaluation of that intelligence, should receive top priority. Only with a common understanding of the major elements of global chaos, incipient or otherwise, and of prospective crises; a reconciliation of national interests into common interests; a joint ordering of priorities with respect to major problem-areas in the world; and a supranational mechanism by means of which the crises can be addressed *in concert, without delay, and on a continuing basis* by the great democracies, can we be sure that democracy itself will survive the coming turbulence. In brief: the most urgent task of the leading statesmen of the democratic world is to identify and understand the significant world problems which, if unattended, could evolve into major crises – deadly threats – and then wherever possible to work out strategies for dealing with such problems before they touch off crises, and to contain the crises or chaos if they eventuate.

PRESENT MACHINERY IS INADEQUATE

The democratic peoples must quickly develop a collective sense of overwhelming responsibility that goes with wealth and power. If the great democracies cannot arrange, *together*, to foresee, to plan, to prepare for action and – when the time comes – to act, there is even less chance that the UN or other 'universal' bodies, or even the existing hodgepodge of European, Atlantic and Pacific regional organizations, as we constituted them during the Cold War, will do the job. None of these is equipped to look at the entire global scene and make coordinated economic and political forecasts. None of these has substantial powers of its own. None is directly accountable to voters. Most are not equipped to make urgent decisions except by unanimity.

In five exceptional cases – the European Union's Commission, the European Council (of Ministers), the European Court and Parliament, plus the Council of Europe's Court of Human Rights – there are the beginnings of such supranational authority, but the scope of membership (Europeans only) is geographically incomplete to discharge the farflung tasks implied above, most of which have become intercontinental. The full involvement in the new Fourth Phase structures of not just Europe, but of North America, Japan, Australia, New Zealand and probably South Korea – as a minimum – is required. And the powers of European institutions still do not extend adequately into key fields – such as common defence, foreign policy, monetary and economic policy integration – where no single nation can any longer venture successfully on its own; these must now, in any event, be seen as intercontinental in scope.

In Chapter 5, we will examine how cooperation and crisis management among the democratic Allies has worked so far, what 'building blocks' from the present system can be salvaged for the future and what 'unfinished business' remains for the democracies.

5 The Democracies' Unfinished Business

> We'll deprive you of your enemy and then you won't know what you're doing.
>
> Grigory Arbatov, US–Canadian Affairs Institute, Moscow[1]

For the mature democracies at a minimum, the Fourth Phase of international relations – *community building* – should now become the norm. The changes in the international system since 1990 and the challenges in the century ahead demand a fresh approach, a new Intercontinental Community of Democracies (ICD).

The ICD must offer a sound replacement for the vestiges of the old Second Phase balance of power system and – incrementally – for Third Phase intergovernmentalism, which stops short of integration. This cannot all be done at one stroke, nor would that be desirable. Gradualism and careful planning, all within the scope of a new vision for the world to come, are necessary. Even when the experienced democracies have revised their structures and habits for working together accordingly, they will still collectively need to make frequent use of Second Phase methods and Third Phase institutions in their relations with the rest of the world.

How to fit some countries into an evolving Third-to-Fourth Phase world system poses many problems. China is a prime example. Because it is huge, the last empire and still ruled despotically, the Chinese leaders will often have to be dealt with in conventional *Realpolitik* terms. US and Western policy since 1972 has been to try to build China into a web of Third Phase intergovernmental relationships, such as the World Bank, WTO and APEC, where multilateral interaction is the norm. For China to fit comfortably, for itself and for others, into such Third Phase bodies will take time and luck. Fourth Phase integrative institutions are quite beyond China's present or foreseeable capacities. This, incidentally, is why it is currently impossible for the G-7 members to extend membership to China, or even – in a full sense – to Russia, as some are now urging. G-7 is a kind of halfway house – part Third Phase, part Fourth; its metamorphosis to the Fourth Phase should not be hindered by accepting partners not yet capable of engaging fully in Third Phase cooperation.

SUPRANATIONAL COMMUNITIES

Communities have existed since the beginning of time, but the concept of a *supranational* community – embodying the principles of the Fourth and most modern phase in inter-state relations – is revolutionary. Supranational communities, however limited in their functions, are based on the principles of democracy – the rule of law, non-negotiable civil rights, accountability of authority, living constitutions respected in practice and the ultimate sovereignty of the citizens. While it is possible and indeed essential for all kinds of governments, totalitarian as well as democratic, to participate in Third Phase institutions such as the United Nations, it is impossible for states not themselves grounded in democratic principles and behaviour to find enough in common with their new partners to integrate themselves into Fourth Phase structures. Whether they were to make a serious effort to participate, or simply 'join up' with the intent of subverting the enterprise, they would prove indigestible to an Intercontinental Community of Democracies.

In the following pages, we examine the fundamental bases for democratic thought and practice; the encouragement of the growth of democracy; and the unfinished building blocks at hand for building ICD. All of this is a work in progress, the 'unfinished business' of the democracies.

POWER, LAW AND LOVE

These three propensities are reflected in virtually all human institutions and behaviour. Other impulses drive people's lives, but these elements, combined in proper balance, distinguish modern democratic societies from all others. These are the foundation stones for ICD, the crux of the democratizing trend in modern civilization.

The rule of tooth and claw preceded democracy. Most humans have an innate drive for *Power* over others. Fortunately, this has been moderated historically by two civilizing impulses, that of making and respecting generally acceptable rules, or *Laws*, and that of regarding one's fellow humans with humanitarian compassion and benevolence, known in its highest sense as brotherly *Love*, by the Greeks as *agape*.

The *Power* to get things done, to control situations and to control others, is common to humans and essential to human affairs. In its primitive unbridled state, however, power spells danger. Through much of history, the uncontrolled exercise of power has skewed social evolution badly. To mention only the most egregious recent abusers: the unchecked power of the Nazis and the Chinese and Soviet Communists, reinforced by a military organization of society, institutions of repression, and modern technology, made this century a hell for millions. Power, the central principle of empires and authoritarian states, has risen uncurbed through most of history, only to be checked by *Law* in roughly the last third of recorded history. Greek and Roman thinkers recognized the necessity for law sanctioned by the community, as did the Jewish patriarchs. Their ability to think through, adopt and judicially compel compliance with laws stood in sharp contrast to the regimes of Asiatic despots. Today, the work of ancient Jewish, Greek and Roman lawgivers (despite flaws in their rudimentary democracies) form the basis for whatever freedom-within-order modern societies are able to enjoy, and whatever generally agreed rules make life together reasonably predictable.[2] The *Rule of Law* is the foundation of all modern democratic societies: no ruler is above the law.[3]

However, without including the impulse of *Love* – or whatever one chooses to call the fellow-feeling for one's co-earthlings – the story of democratic civilization would be incomplete. *Love*, a word overworked, misunderstood and susceptible of many different meanings, can confuse people, but it is still the best word for the purposes of this book, defined in this way: *Love* is sometimes called Brotherly Love, in the sense that William Penn hoped the Philadelphia he founded could be 'The City of Brotherly Love'. This love is what the author of Leviticus meant (19: 18) when he wrote, 'Thou shalt love thy neighbour as thyself'. Early Christians, writing in Greek, called this love *agape*: 'spontaneous, self-giving expressed freely without calculation of cost or gain to the giver or merit on the part of the receiver'.[4]

This is not about *eros* – sexual love – or platonic love, or the courtly love of the Middle Ages, or family love, or the love of warm affection we all feel now and then for those around us, or even the precise love of God, although that is a related idea from which, for many people in several religions, the love of others *in general* – as in *agape* – stems philosophically. Other words – philanthropy, altruism, benevolence, goodness, charity, humanitarianism, to name a few – describe aspects of this *agape* sense of Love, but none of them are so broad, expressive or all-encompassing as *Love* itself.

Love may focus on a particular person or a large group, but without regard to that person as a kindred class or a known acquaintance, and only because he or she is another human being. The parable of the Good Samaritan (Luke 10: 30–7) is a powerful Biblical inspiration for this idea of *neighbourly* love. The essence of 'neighbourliness' is that the Good Samaritan and the victim he helped *did not know each other*, and probably never had a chance to become acquainted. The Good Samaritan does good – what he can see is simply right to do – without seeking recompense or advantage for himself, and then goes on his way. This kind of love is an essential component of a modern community; the larger the community, the more impersonal and abstract – yet still tangible – the love that holds it together.[5]

In Old English, *love* is contrasted with *lagu*, law. The latter involves litigation, the former an amicable settlement. The phrase 'under law and love' in ancient Anglo-Saxon usage was used to denote the position of being a member of a 'frankpledge', which in turn was a system of 'free engagement of neighbor for neighbor'.[6]

So it would seem that the ancient Franks, reaching back into their pre-Roman, pre-Christian history, had some idea of mutual responsibility and of the interdependence of members of the community. This in turn gave rise to the word 'love' as a concept expressing 'amicable settlement' and covenant of neighbourliness, out of both goodwill and commonsense. The Oxford English Dictionary is quite clear that this behaviour is the *reverse* of an initial resort to law . . . the Frankish law which in ancient days rested on iron custom and the authority of the tribal chief. The Angles and Saxons brought these ideas with them when they overran Britain and pledged themselves, as situations called for it, 'under law and love' to aid their neighbours. Then, the OED tells us, this idea of 'love' as something freely given (not compelled, as by law) found its way, through translation into Latin, into the Roman concept of treaties (*foedus*) between equal partners. (Hence, the modern *federation*.) The fellow-feeling, plus the regard for superior law, inherent in these old ideas comprise the essence of *likemindedness*, a term to which we shall refer frequently, among democratic peoples.

Now we are getting closer to the underlying concept of the Fourth Phase of international relations, viz. a true supranational community – a voluntary compact between likeminded individuals, groups and today even nations – which is the main theme of this book: 'community' is directly derived from *Love* in the New Testament sense – *agape*, covering all mankind as a community, not just one's geographically near-neighbours, who would have necessarily the same skin-colour, same language, same fairy tales, same customs, and so on.[7] But for community to work in a political sense, at any level, more than *Love* or fellow-feeling is required.

Power is essential to enable a community to act, but is dangerous unless bound by agreed rules – *Law*. *Love* – mutual aid, the protection of human rights and the extension of humanitarian help to others – is essential to a truly humane society; but *Love* cannot be embodied in a community unless energized by *Power* and protected and encouraged by *Law*. These are the characteristics of an advanced community, small or large.

We may rightly deplore continued expressions of unbuttoned power at any level, but we should also realize that this same century which has seen appalling abuses of power has also welcomed the broadening of the Rule of Law within and among nations, as well as the expression of the Love of humankind which today typifies the highest modern values and has begun to permeate the interaction of peoples and governments. More and more, this has been happening throughout the world, as help is given to peoples less fortunate, as private charity and philanthropy grow in importance, as the world becomes smaller in every sense and more connected. The Red Cross, UNICEF, Amnesty International, Médecins sans Frontières, CARE and the work of the UN and NATO in Bosnia are all expressions of this surge in fellow-feeling and brotherhood.

In short, there is great hope for a better century to come. And the chief statesmen of the experienced democracies, who have made the greatest progress in curbing Power by means of Law, who try to use Power to rectify wrongs rather than perpetrate them, and whose citizens are reminded daily of their obligations to one another and their Love for those less fortunate, have a duty to design a new Intercontinental Community of Democracies based on these three principles. They have, in fact, already begun, even if the work remains unfinished.

Today there is little chance of civil war or widespread insurrections in western Europe, Canada, Japan, Australia, New Zealand or the United States. There is also virtually no chance today of war *among* them. This is because modern democracies have a framework of law which well circumscribes the power of the state, curbs violent expressions of 'popular' (or unpopular) will, and channels discontent and injustice to the ballot box and to courts of law. Humane principles permeate the political regimes of the experienced democracies; this is the essence of the likemindedness which enables these nations to work well together in world affairs, promoting a world in which Power, Law and Love are in humane, just and democratic balance.

The realist knows that mankind's social, economic and political arrangements can never attain perfection, even in the most just and well-ordered societies. But the modern democracies of Europe, North America and the western Pacific, with all their flaws and their strivings to improve in a turbulent world, remain the best hope and the best models, overall, for other peoples hoping to improve *their* lot.

Some say it is impossible to extend what has been essentially a Western vision of democracy to other parts of the world. But the modern liberal West's political values are universal. This is made clear by recent progress in Asia. The transformation in South Korea in the past decade is strong and heartening proof. Japan's stable democracy is further evidence. Turkey, which grew out of Eastern despotic tradition, has moved far into the Western democratic pattern. In 1995, Deputy Prime Minister Anwar Ibrahim of Malaysia confuted Asians who deplore an alleged attempt to 'impose alien political values on their countries':

> If we in Asia want to speak credibly of Asian values, we too must be prepared to champion those ideals which are universal and which belong to humanity as a whole. It is altogether shameful, if ingenious, to cite Asian values as an excuse for autocratic practices and denial of basic rights and civil liberties. To say that freedom is western or unAsian is to offend our own traditions as well as our forefathers who gave their lives in the struggle against tyranny and injustices. It is true that Asians lay great emphasis on order and societal stability. But it is certainly wrong to regard society as a kind of false god upon whose altar the individual must contantly be sacrificed. No Asian tradition can be cited

to support the proposition that in Asia the individual must melt into the faceless community.[8]

This is the real challenge for the 21st century: whereas the 20th embodied the struggle to 'make the world safe for democracy' (Wilson's gift of purpose, despite recurring cynicism) by defeating the bids of well-organized tyrannies for world domination, it will be the task of the 21st century to consolidate democracy's gains and to extend them – first, to individual societies striving for good self-government and second, to the plane of international governance. Democracy itself will be *the* fundamental building block of *Pax Democratica*.

By 2099, world affairs, like domestic affairs in advanced nation-states, should reflect the subservience internationally of *Power* to *Law*, the organization of democratically-controlled *Power* on a larger-than-state basis where essential, and the generous infusion into all government of the exercise of *Power*, circumscribed by the Rule of *Law*, and all tending to enable the ascendance of *Love . . . fraternité*, altruism, the good and caring society.

ICD'S FIRST BUILDING BLOCK: PROMOTING DEMOCRACY

> Your Declaration of Independence and Constitution inspire us . . .
> to be citizens. . . . [W]e must learn how to educate our children,
> run our elections, and organize our economy from you.
> Czech President Vaclav Havel, addressing the US Congress,
> 21 February 1990

Between 1960 and 1990, there was a considerable growth in the number of democratic regimes, based on comparative analysis of political liberties and civil rights.[9] In the past decade there has been some 'backsliding', but the net cause of democracy has still been advanced. If one takes a longer view, there is great progress, within countries and in the overall numbers now adhering to some kind of democratic regime. Looking back to 1900 or to 1945, as the end of our century approaches we see many more democracies now than then.[10] And their overall quality has been upgraded remarkably; what served as a set of standards for the few 1900 democracies would barely do for the weaker of today's aspiring free societies. In 1995, for the first time in history, more people lived under democratic than under non-democratic regimes. But past performance is not necessarily any guide to the future. Will this still delicate plant – democracy – continue to flourish as it has recently?

When the practice and institutions of democracy are fragile, it is often difficult to withstand pressures to resort to autocratic rule; then, often what begins as a temporary expedient becomes entrenched. But modern pressures and older traditions can also combine eventually to force the restoration of democracy. Theory or the experience of others are not always adequate guides; political cultures differ greatly.

To build an ICD, two questions should interest us deeply: 'What can mature democracies do to help aspiring democracies strengthen their regimes?' and, 'How can one best help from outside when regimes are not at all democratic, but their peoples are obviously keen to move to democracy?' There are no simple answers. Much of what the Western powers – often, to be sure, with conflicting motives – have tried to do by way of 'democracy-building' in the past half-century has not worked, or has even been counterproductive. In a period which featured de-colonization and a bitter Cold War, on top of all the normal difficulties experienced by new states or by old ones locked in ancient and basically anti-democratic traditions, the promotion of democracy could have been expected to be extremely difficult. Some of the methods used before, and which might be improved for future use, are set out here.

1. The Imposition of Democracy by Force

This was undertaken in Germany and Japan at the conclusion of World War II. It worked, especially as democracy-by-fiat changed to democracy-by-consent and then to general enthusiasm on the part of the 'new democrats'. Allied war aims had made it clear that autocratic governments in these powerful countries would not again be countenanced. Allied determination to 'democratize' led to major programmes of 're-education and reorientation', lasting several years and reaching deep into every corner of the two societies. The process continues today under its own power.

In Germany of 1945, the occupying nations – Britain, France and the United States on the one hand and the USSR on the other – had different ideas about democratization; these, along with strategic and economic aims, began to conflict soon after the occupation regime began. The three Western powers went their own way (1947) with an essentially tripartite policy and, in cooperation with thousands of excellent German leaders in all walks of life, transformed a broken society. Residues of Soviet and east German puppet rule in the USSR's former 'zone' of Germany remain, but today essentially the same process of incorporation into the Western democratic world is going on there, in a reunified and democratic Germany.

In Japan, the United States assumed sole responsibility for the switch to modern democracy in a programme lasting nearly a decade. Japan received a modern constitution; countless directives and educational efforts transformed the character of that idiosyncratic society. Although for various reasons the Japanese challenge was a greater one and 'success' still not entirely easy to assess, one can say fairly that neither Germany nor Japan – once such great threats to world peace and to the cause of democracy itself – today can be considered anything but an established, experienced democracy, and a firm partner in the evolving community of modern democracies. To analyse how these amazing changes could have been wrought, including the enormous receptivity of both the German and Japanese peoples, is beyond the scope of this book. But it is important to note that in both cases, the Allies had vanquished – and thereby discredited – the previous autocratic regimes, and furthermore had occupied both countries militarily. Holding the public power for several years, it was possible for the occupying powers to dictate what would be done and how it would be done. These were unusual historical cases.

Although Italy and Austria were not treated as defeated nations by the World War II victors, both were militarily occupied by the Allies and both were assisted (powerfully, it may be said) to install democratic governments and to develop the institutions and practices of modern democracy.

Nearly a century ago, the United States freed the Philippines from Spanish rule, put down a native insurrection (which might have begun its own democratic development), and proceeded – in the fashion of the time – to colonize. To its credit, however, US democracy-building efforts over the years were considerable, especially in the educational sphere. The United States also planned, then carried out, the independence of the Philippines. Now, nearly a hundred years after American tutelage in the Philippines began, many positive aspects of the uneasy association have finally begun to bear fruit as stable, democratic, modern government grows.

British colonial rule in many cases furthered the eventual establishment of democratic government. India is the prime example:
there was virtually no native democratic tradition. With Britain came
the Rule of Law and eventually the preparation for self-government. Most notable was the education in England of hundreds of
India's future leaders, including Gandhi and Nehru. Nor could the
emergence of responsible self-government and the end of apart-
heid in South Africa have taken place without the British civic
heritage, contradictory as that may seem. The English language
itself, in much of the Commonwealth and in American possessions,
has been an important vehicle for education in democracy.

The idea of 'imposing democracy' may be thought an oxymoron.
Only in rare cases – primarily those in which there is already some
basis in history and tradition (as in some aspects of pre-Hitler
Germany or early 20th century Japan) for democracy – can an
occupying power, governing autocratically, be expected to successfully impose the very ideals and institutions of liberty which the
instruments of its imposition deny in practice. It has been done,
but it is very, very tricky. In all societies, however, there is some
democratic potential.

2. Economic Sanctions to Force Democracy

This too is a tricky business. Sanctions were tried in the case of
Haiti (1992) to force the return of the democratically-elected Aristide,
but the military oligarchy was not brought to heel until it was clear
that the United States was ready to invade. Economic sanctions on
Iraq following the 1990–91 war were severe, but hurt the Iraqi people
more than Saddam's clique, which in 1997 still remained in power.
Fidel Castro's regime has resisted any change in its Communist
dictatorship despite more than 30 years of US economic blockade,
although this may change now that Russian support is gone.

In 1996 the Paraguayan military threatened a coup to oust the
legally-elected President. Paraguay, with Argentina, Brazil, Bolivia,
Chile and Uruguay, is a member of Mercosur, a fledgling common
market. The other members could not afford a collapse of Paraguayan democracy (and with it the efforts to establish economic
probity) behind Mercosur's common tariff. They threatened to expel
Paraguay from the 'club'. The military backed down.

Economic sanctions for other purposes have also had a sketchy
record, successful sometimes but often not. Under both the League

of Nations and the United Nations, economic sanctions in cases of war and peace were sometimes contemplated, occasionally adopted, seldom enforced, and rarely achieved the desired effect. Most recently, in the wars accompanying the breakup of Yugoslavia, economic sanctions were voted by the UN Security Council, apparently had some effect on Serbian policy in particular, were spottily enforced, but were hardly the main instruments in bringing the warring parties to the conference table (1995). NATO airpower, the resupply of the Croatian army and the exhaustion of the combatants did that. In the Yugoslav case, democratic government and protection of human rights were two of the ultimate aims, but not the main object, of the efforts to stop the conflict.

The recurring resort to military rule in Nigeria has been one of the most disturbing chapters in recent African history, especially important because of the great size and wealth of Nigeria, its potential as a model for Africa and the fair prospects it was thought to have had on gaining independence. Moral suasion, especially on the part of Britain and other Commonwealth members, had apparently no effect on General Sani Abacha, who annulled the results of democratic elections in 1993 to install the most recent of several military dictatorships. Britain and the United States restricted foreign aid to Nigeria; the US termed Abacha's actions an 'outrage'. Commonwealth and UN discussions have turned on the possibility of economic sanctions to try to compel the restoration of Nigerian democracy, but this has not been done – probably for fear that sanctions could not be fully implemented or, if they were, would not produce the desired result, especially in view of the conflicted interests of Western oil companies.

As an instrument to induce or compel democracy, economic sanctions are thus blunt, hard to enforce and largely untried, although they remain in the armoury of possibilities. Again, sanctions constitute the use of force and thus an undemocratic weapon to employ in a democratic cause. However, they may still be worth future consideration in certain cases.

3. Attempts to Promote Democracy by Political Intervention

It is tempting – yet sobering – to consider numerous efforts by established democracies to induce better government in countries within their spheres of influence. The history of the Cold War is replete with such instances, often flawed. In most cases, the

intervening power's motives have been decidedly mixed; promot
ing democracy was only one, and sometimes not as high on th
priority-list as others.

For the United States, the most effective such interventions oc
curred in Europe during the early stages of the Cold War, whe
the governments of some countries – notably (but not exclusively
France and Italy – might well have been overthrown by non
democratic forces supported by the Soviets, and were at the ver
least highly unstable. Several important countries, such as Spair
Portugal and Greece, had never enjoyed stable democratic goverr
ment and laboured under dictatorships of various hues. Germany'
new democracy was distinctly fragile and tentative. The worldwid
'agitprop' efforts of the Soviet Union – perhaps the most costly
longstanding and far-reaching propaganda campaign ever under
taken – concentrated for decades on western Europe and the weakly
governed countries in particular. It was natural, indeed necessary
for the United States to assist and promote democratic goverr
ment and counteract anti-democratic forces wherever possible, an
this was done.

The effort involved radio broadcasts, education coupled wit
economic rehabilitation under the Marshall Plan, grants to volur
teer groups for civic education at many levels, large-scale educa
tional interchanges, valuable work on the ground by the staff c
the US Information Service, political encouragement and suasio
by US embassy officers and a variety of activities, some open an
some clandestine, carried out by the Central Intelligence Agenc
to support democratic forces. These latter, for the most part, ar
not a part of the official public record as yet, but numerous ac
counts – many quite plausible and substantiated by often credibl
sources – have been published over the years. One example, tha
of the Congress for Cultural Freedom, reportedly one of the mor
successful CIA 'fronts', has been extensively reported.[11]

In the 1940s and 1950s, the CIA supported European nor
Communist trade unions in a decidedly non-academic 'war' wit
labour movements sponsored by the Soviets and indigenous Com
munist parties, notably in France and Italy. In the 1970s, the Com
munist parties in western Europe began to wither and transfor
themselves into 'Eurocommunists' and groupings along social demo
cratic lines who asserted that they now eschewed revolution.

The entire US overseas representation in Latin America was deepl
engaged in anti-Communist activities in the early days of the Col

War, on into the Reagan Administration and after. There were fewer democratic traditions and democratic thinkers and political leaders than in Europe with whom to work; thus efforts to introduce or support democracy in Latin America were handicapped. The CIA and its various front organizations fell into an old trap in the history of US foreign relations: in order to fight a left-wing revolutionary movement, backed since the 1920s by the USSR, the US relied more and more on the only organized alternatives available. Often, these were to be found among unsavoury reactionaries, militarists and opportunists. The genuine conservatives and liberal democrats were usually too few and too partisan to work effectively together as a counterweight to dictatorships of left or right. In recent years, this situation has begun to change, partly because of overt US aid, both private and governmental, in training leaders.

The history of British efforts to shore up democratic elements in the process of Latin American decolonization is a different one. In the 1950s, for example, the British put Guyana (formerly British Guiana) on a course for independence. They coaxed the few experienced Guyanan politicians of all stripes into a constitutional but shaky regime. Cheddi Jagan, a bright but also erratic local leader, whose wife was a Communist, was cultivated by the British, who hoped that the popular Jagan could learn from experience and lead Guyana to independence under democracy. The exigencies of the Cold War again intervened. The Americans pressured for Jagan's removal from political leadership; for years, he led the Opposition in a corrupt parliamentary system, dominated by Forbes Burnham and the 'Peoples National Congress' party. In 1990, with substantial technical help and encouragement from the Carter Administration, constitutional reforms were undertaken. Jagan's party, in coalition with others, won a fair election in 1992 and an ageing Jagan became a democratic President.[12] Transitions to democratic independence were easier in such British colonies as Trinidad and Barbados, more rocky in Jamaica.

The end of the Cold War changed the Latin American battlefield for democracy in major ways. With only one clearly anti-democratic regime, that of Cuba, left in the Western Hemisphere, US policies were bound to change. The thrust of the aid effort now couples the problem of 'political development' closely with economic modernization. The European Union and bodies such as the World Bank are also paying more attention to the nature, effectiveness and stability of political regimes everywhere as a precondition for economic growth, and thus for outside assistance.

In the summer of 1995, France intervened militarily in Comoros, a tiny island country in the Indian Ocean, to abort a coup perpetrated by mercenaries on behalf of a local clique, and to restore the lawful government. Comoros has had unstable, corrupt and only sporadically-democratic rule since independence from France in 1975. France has intervened in other former colonies; the result has sometimes been at least short-term stability but often not much democracy-building; this is a difficult task, especially for a former imperial power. Nevertheless, French colonial rule left a heritage, as did that of the British, of good administration and judicial systems. Also *liberté*, *égalité* and *fraternité*, taught in French colonial schools, became the birthright of the colonials as they fought for independence.

Although the Cold War skewed political intervention and possibly political evolution, too, in some developing countries in unfortunate ways, in the end the collapse of the Soviet imperial system gave the new generation of younger political leaders – especially in South America and the Caribbean – a much-improved opportunity to see what could be done with open societies and free market economies.

Since the 1970s, the effort to promote human rights by publicizing substandard conditions in various countries has also become a feature of political intervention. The US and its allies have worked hard through the United Nations to achieve agreement on international norms, and then to spotlight countries which do not meet these. Tussles with China have been especially notable; the US attempted after the Tianmen massacre to use trade sanctions to bludgeon the Chinese government, but this proved ineffective. For other countries, bilateral suasion and discussions in UN and other international fora sometimes appear to make a difference. Every year the Department of State publishes a roster of all countries in the world to try to nudge those with poor human rights records to respect international standards. The private efforts of such groups as Freedom House, Amnesty International and *Médecins sans Frontières* to publicize substandard cases sometimes result in efforts by spotlighted states to try to defend their cases or in occasional instances to make actual changes for the better.

4. Educational Efforts to Bolster Democracy Abroad

One cannot distinguish precisely where 'political' measures, described above, and 'educational' efforts actually begin and leave off. They often overlap and will no doubt continue to do so. While governments engage in considerable expenditures, through such programmes as educational exchanges and official grants, to encourage democratic development, today much is accomplished by private philanthropic bodies based in the wealthy democracies.

After the involuntary exposure of CIA activities (many of which were educational and constructive in their content and effect, yet kept secret so as not to compromise recipients) in the early Cold War days, the US government, both in the administrations of several Presidents from Lyndon Johnson through Ronald Reagan and in the efforts of many Members of Congress, sought in the 1970s to disengage the CIA and other official organs from any sort of clandestine activities to support democracy or otherwise intervene politically abroad. One important result was the creation (1982) of the National Endowment for Democracy (NED), a private grant-making foundation supported entirely by Congressionally-appropriated funds. Its Board of Directors consists of public figures drawn equally from both political parties and from business and labour. Its activities are entirely public. Its budget has hovered in the neighbourhood of $40 million per year. NED is seen as a creature of the US government, but also quasi-independent and politically even-handed in its grant-making. Its grants, given through US political party institutes and private American groups with special expertise in democratic questions, go to a wide variety of citizens' organizations and independent media around the world. Occasionally gaffes are made (a notoriously right-wing French students' group once received a small grant) but on the whole the NED's record seems unexceptionable and constructive. An important by-product of its activity is a substantial world network of people active in civic affairs and promoting democracy who, so to speak, constitute the 'alumni' of the Endowment.

NED was patterned in some ways after an older set of German quasi-governmental, grant-making institutions, the four political party foundations which receive Federal Republic funds from the Bundestag each year. These bodies have tended to work with their counterpart political (and always democratic) parties in other countries, i.e. the Konrad Adenauer (CDU) and Hans Seidl (CSU) Foundations with more conservative and Christian-oriented groups; the Friedric Ebert (SPD) Foundation with social democratic groups; the Lib eral Party's Friederich Naumann Foundation with foreign partie devoted to traditional liberal causes. Their activities range widely sometimes covering fields only indirectly related to politics.

In the United Kingdom, Parliament established the Westminste Foundation in 1992, in part at the urging of the United States an Germany, to make grants in support of democratic development The Canadian Parliament in 1990 created its own counterpart, th International Center for Human Rights and Democratic Develop ment. In the Development Assistance Committee of the OECI (Organization for Economic Cooperation and Development), th 20 or so rich democracies have recently set standards for linkin political with economic aid-giving. The US Agency for Internationa Development operates extensive democracy-support programmes i developing countries.

Official overseas information and cultural programmes of th established democratic governments, by their very nature, promot democratic values when they undertake to explain their own so cieties to others. The British Council, the Alliance Française, th German Goethe Houses, the United States Information Service an similar bodies all support educational exchanges, conferences, li braries, language instruction and other activities which in consid erable measure serve to promote democracy.

Private initiatives for public purposes which emphasize democ racy and human rights – mainly foundations, citizens' association and thinktanks – also conduct activities which on the whole ar highly beneficial. Without their work, the principle of citizen ac tion entirely separate from government, which is a distinct hall mark of a mature democracy, could hardly be sustained.

5. Organizations Composed of Democracies and International Courts of Human Rights

One of the most interesting and yet unnoticed forces in the post 1945 world was the tendency of Western, and especially Europear nations to promote democracy through: (1) international bodie whose membership was limited to democracies; and (2) internationa courts that mandate protection of human rights.

The Nuremberg Tribunal at the conclusion of World War II, se up to try Nazi war criminals, and its counterpart in Japan tried t cope with violent and unlawful, but state-sanctioned behaviour which took place on a vast scale in Asia and Europe. While some legal experts and others have argued that neither tribunal, relying on international civilized norms, was legally within its rights to judge crimes whose illegality was established *ex post facto*, it is generally thought that the measures and judgements were just. In any event, these trials established a precedent for the International Court recently set up by the United Nations in The Hague to try Yugoslavs who have allegedly committed genocide in the recent wars of secession, and a similar court for Rwanda.

A relatively unnoticed, and yet more far-reaching, development has been the institution of the Council of Europe's Commission and Court of Human Rights. In now hundreds of cases, individual citizens of member-countries which have signed the Council of Europe's Human Rights Convention have taken their complaints to this international body as a last court of appeal. Its decisions are respected as over and above the courts of the member-countries. Remarkably, nations whose own courts' judgements have been over-ridden by the European Court have accepted the verdicts and made necessary adjustments to their legal codes. The British government, for example, accepted the European Court's verdict that jailed IRA members were political prisoners, not ordinary criminals, and thus could not be compelled to wear prison uniforms.

Even less-known than the human rights activities of the Council of Europe are that body's indirect democracy-building efforts. No country can be a Member of the Council unless it is a recognized democracy. Belonging to the Council does not confer as many benefits as membership in, for example, the European Union or NATO, which vitally affect life and limb and pocketbook. But the Council of Europe is nevertheless a body which aspiring nations believe confers a badge of democratic respectability. In 1967, Greece came under the military rule of a colonels' junta; the Council was set to expel Greece; the junta withdrew before it could be forced out. Only when democratic rule was re-established was Greece re-admitted to the Council. In the late 1950s and early 1960s, powerful popular forces in the swiftly-changing Spanish society wanted to replace the Franco regime with democracy; membership in the Council of Europe (and later the European Union) was an avidly sought-after certification of modernity. These democratic pressures eventually resulted in Spain's full entry into modern Europe. Portugal's experience was similar.

Turkey, after many years in the Council of Europe, sometimes wavers on the edge of expulsion because its democratic and civil rights norms are not yet unequivocally established. Turkey was the first Associate Member of the European Communities (now Union) and in 1995 joined a customs union with the EU, but has not yet become a full Member, in large part because many leaders of the current 15 Members of EU believe Turkey is not yet a full democracy. The preamble to the 1957 European Economic Community treaty states that the signatories are '[r]esolved by . . . thus pooling their resources to preserve and strengthen peace and liberty, and calling upon the other peoples of Europe who share their ideal to join in their efforts'. In 1961, anticipating the addition of Members to the original six, the Community's European Parliament laid down as a further condition of EU entry that an applicant 'must accept the rule of law, agree to respect human rights and fundamental freedoms and have a parliamentary democratic system of government'.[13]

The preamble to the North Atlantic (NATO) Treaty is also specific: 'The Parties to this Treaty . . . are determined to safeguard the freedom, common heritage and civilization of their peoples, founded on the principles of democracy, individual liberty and the rule of law.' In Article II of the Treaty, the signatories pledge to '[strengthen] their free institutions, by bringing about a better understanding of the principles upon which these institutions are founded, and by promoting conditions of stability and well-being'.

As the former Communist states of central and eastern Europe apply for membership in NATO, the EU and other Western bodies, the question of their democratic credentials must arise. Many of them have already been accepted as at least nominal democracies by the inclusive Council of Europe; Russia, in a controversial move, was welcomed in 1995. But the EU's hurdles are higher; the EU will demand of new aspirants from the East that they prove the depth and stability of their democratic institutions. NATO will also be more demanding, insisting – in addition to meeting democratic criteria – that new Members be peace-loving, i.e. resolve in advance all territorial disputes with neighbours.

These are clear indications that something new has appeared on the international scene: acceptance of the principles of democracy, and their implementation in practice, has become the touchstone for membership in the various organs of the 'club' of Western democracies. By banding together in the name of democracy, by refusing admittance to non-democracies, by the willingness to expel members which backslide, and by effectively protecting individual civil rights through common judicial institutions, a new form of suasion has been developed by the advanced democracies. As time goes on, this new set of methods might well be applied intercontinentally or in regions other than Europe.

DEMOCRACY-BUILDING REVIEWED

We have explored several ways in which experienced democracies have helped countries less well established in the modern civic culture.[14] Some of these methods, especially those depending on the use of force or on clandestinity, cannot be recommended for the future. But if the experienced democracies were to undertake *jointly* to help aspiring democracies, making use of appropriate educational and other tools, in a broad permanent programme designed to enlarge gradually the community of democracies in the world, much could conceivably be accomplished. Chapter 6 attempts to define 'likemindedness' as a touchstone for determining which nations should be members of the ICD. How such a coalition for democracy-building and other purposes might be put together is discussed in Chapter 8.

This chapter has paid somewhat detailed attention to the process of democracy-building, not only because it is little understood and under-valued in discussions of world affairs, but also because the spotlight should be trained on *democracy-building itself*, as one the four overriding tasks of the democracies' future community, a key element in *Pax Democratica*. The other three tasks are well understood as continuing challenges: security and defence, economic well-being and the important catch-all, 'survivability of the planet'. All these and democracy-building are interrelated:

What point is a common security system unless one knows what one is defending?
How can prosperity and an open world economically be separated from how participant-countries are governed?
Is not responsible government one of the first requirements for less-developed nations struggling to advance economically, or to attain world environmental norms?

One cannot overemphasize the high priority which should be given – and which has not been given in the past – to democracy-building.

If, for example, the experienced democracies had in 1990 or a bit earlier begun a joint large-scale educational programme of helping Russia to rebuild its society on democratic principles, a record of more solid achievement in all spheres might well have been established by the end of this century.[15]

USING THE OLD BUILDING BLOCKS IN A NEW ICD

The 'unfinished business' of the West is the construction of an Intercontinental Community of Democracies, a process well started in the Cold War years but now largely stalled. Some of the 1947–70 structures are now unnecessary or even a block to progress. Some remain vital. Most need remodelling. Let's examine each important foundation-stone which could be suitable to ICD's new architecture.

1. The North Atlantic Treaty Organization (NATO)

Until NATO was furnished (1951) with substantial forces in being, under an international command and general staff, and supplied with a secretariat and Council consisting of representatives of the 16 member-countries in continuous session to review the foreign policies and defence arrangements of the members and to give political sanction to the plans for mutual defence, NATO was literally a paper tiger. But structures and a well-defined mission gave it credibility and the organizational capacity to do what it was meant to do: deter general war in Europe, especially one threatened by the USSR. NATO also bound the Germans into an interdependent military system, and kept the United States in Europe; these remain key factors in that continent's stability.

Since the end of the Soviet threat, there has been much cogitation as to what new purposes NATO should serve. Quite apart from the necessary discussion as to whether and how to involve Russia (and other former parts of the USSR) in a broader, NATO-led European security system, one should recognize that NATO is the best existing – indeed virtually the only – model for a collective security and mutual defence organization based on democracy and the needs of democracies.

Bodies with similar democratic memberships and purposes, such as the Western European Union (perhaps an EU defence ministry of the future), the US–Japan alliance, ANZUS (Australia–New

Zealand–US) and the various close US–Canada defence arrangements, are all weaker and less-inclusive than NATO. NATO, in one way or another, should gradually become the defence and security arm of the Intercontinental Community of Democracies.

With time, solid democracies which are presently outside NATO's geographic limits should become members and NATO's defence perimeters extended correspondingly. Any democracies, stable and meeting advanced criteria for self-government and the protection of human rights, fully capable of bearing their share of the burdens of Alliance-membership, and sharing the vision of the experienced democracies which started NATO, should eventually be welcomed into membership. The Alliance should be capable of intervening anywhere in the world for peacekeeping or peacemaking, if circumstances – as in Bosnia (1995) – require it.

In the late 1990s, it was evident that Russia was not yet ready or able to meet the criteria for NATO membership suggested above. The burning question of Russian membership in NATO must eventually be decided by unfolding conditions on the Eurasian continent and – above all – by the direction of political-economic Russian evolution. At this stage in Russia's history, the NATO powers can and should make all kinds of special arrangements for a broad (and at this stage, necessarily loose) collective security system, covering as much of the Eurasian north continent as possible. Korea and Japan need to be involved, and perhaps eventually the Indian democracy. But all of this will take time and great wisdom. The essential thing is not to lose sight of NATO's original purpose: to protect and expand the realm of freedom.

In passing, it should be noted that the 1997 discussions of expanding NATO made no mention of including Finland, Sweden, Ireland or Austria. Given their outstanding democratic credentials and their obvious interests, how could this be?

The mutual defence clause (Article 5) of the NATO treaty is a nearly-automatic commitment of all to go to the aid of any member attacked. But in the present state of affairs, this is really a standby provision. Much more important in a Europe (and a world) in which the breakup of a peripheral country such as Yugoslavia could conceivably lead to a nasty regional war and worse, are the twin questions of how NATO sifts and analyses world intelligence with respect to 'hot spots', and how decisions to act – when there is an obvious need to act – on the basis of these analyses can be taken and implemented expeditiously. A major structural problem with NATO is its unanimity requirement. A situation in which, say, Luxembourg or Greece or Portugal can block NATO action with a veto is intolerable. Practically, a decision to send NATO troops to Yugoslavia, for example, can usually be taken even if Greece opts out; but if one of the four great powers – US, UK, France or Germany – disagrees, or if several of the middle powers – Italy,[16] Spain or the Low Countries – demurs, then NATO could be immobilized.

The only answer, in principle, is to devise some new voting methods. Former Secretary of State James Baker calls these 'supermajorities'; others, drawing on provisions in the partly-supranational EU treaties, refer to them as 'qualified majorities'. No matter. Any arrangements by which a healthy majority of NATO member-nations could override the hesitations of a minority (even if substantial) would constitute a portentous constitutional step for members. But the management of dangerous international conflicts with which the UN proves unable to deal, which call for quick action, and which clearly affect the security of the democracies (and therefore world security) may well require such measures. We shall come back to this question, because other organizations – some in being, others to be imagined – could be affected.

All things considered, NATO is an indispensable building block (perhaps *the* indispensable one) for the new ICD.

2. The European Union (EU)

This began as an essentially economic set of arrangements with a broad political purpose, i.e. to marry France and Germany in such a way that war between them would become impossible. Now the EU is a well-established single market, with executive, parliamentary and judicial institutions involved in broad aspects of European life. Its 15 members hope to consummate a monetary union by 1999 and aspire to a joint defence and foreign policy. Within a decade or two, there could be as many as 27 EU members; most of east and central Europe wants to join.

Although the process of unification went well in the beginning, the EU has in recent years bumped up against psychological limits. Countries are reluctant to give up more sovereignty, for understandable reasons grounded mostly in hard-to-shuck-off traditions and worries about the economic future. The Germans so far have felt they had least to lose in a strong federal union with their neighbours; their past was one they have preferred to forget; they have believed the fears of their neighbours could only be allayed permanently if they – the Germans – were indissolubly bound to Europe. As pressures to expand EU membership to the east accelerate, this German requirement to be saved from the need to exercise the normal (and perhaps ultimately abnormal) behaviour patterns of a Second Phase rather than a Fourth Phase nation becomes more and more apparent. The desire, at least among some supposedly realistic Germans constrained now to distance themselves from their neighbours and go it alone, can be expected to increase as uncertainty about the EU's future grows.

The uniting of Europe, concretely by means of the EU, is one of the great projects of history. The EU is the first instance of a group of nations voluntarily entering a political union grounded in democracy.[17] A successful EU will help extend modernization in the world, keeping the way open for the continued expansion of democracy. If the EU falters, Europe and the world could slip back into unhealthy patterns of the past. As a model for integration in other regions, such as Latin America and southeast Asia, the EU has already provided inspiration. The North American Free Trade Area (NAFTA) is another harbinger. As a model for further integration among the larger group of established democracies – moving to Fourth Phase ties within an intercontinental community – the EU's general approach seems made to order.

The future of the world economic scene is cloudy. Such bodies as the World Trade Organization (formerly GATT) are pillars of the world effort to promote free trade, yet the WTO is like the proverbial convoy which can proceed only as fast as its slowest ship. The EU has shown how a full customs and economic union can be formed, fairly quickly in the eye of history, if the members are sufficiently likeminded... i.e. if they share clear and important interests which they understand in a common way, and if they share political habits and institutional capabilities which permit them to conduct extremely complex and difficult business jointly on a regular basis. Because NATO and the EU have been grounded in this kind of likemindedness, they have worked; for a broader, deeper Fourth Phase effort at international integration to be effective, these characteristics are essential. Chapter 6 and Appendix A explore likemindedness in some detail.

Beyond Europe and the EU, Canada, the United States, Australia, New Zealand and Japan understand that they share basic interests with EU members. These countries are also used to conducting common business in the same way, i.e. democratically. Within Europe, a few seasoned democracies are not yet part of the EU but ought to be: Norway and Switzerland principally. For the very special reason that Turkey: is in an absolutely strategic position – geographically and as a 'swing country' between the West and Islam; belongs to or is formally associated with all the institutions of Western and European amalgamation which have risen to prominence since 1949; has striven mightily to become a modern democracy; and has been willing to defend freedom with the West (in Korea and as the most exposed part of NATO, for example), it must also be included in any larger political-economic grouping of democracies.

This discussion leads to some conclusions: (a) the EU is the most forward-looking model for a larger, integrated, Fourth Phase Intercontinental Community of Democracies (ICD); (b) the EU has come to a resting place in its amalgamation process; so (c) why not use the EU as the core of the new ICD – incorporating as accompanying building blocks NATO and the OECD (see below), whose members would all become charter subscribers to a wider political-economic union?

Chapter 7 explores the serious implications for such a major switch for the Europeans and the extra-European experienced democracies.

3. The Organization for Economic Cooperation and Development (OECD)

For those who do not follow intergovernmental economic cooperation day by day, the OECD is a 'sleeper', an important building block for the new ICD.

The members of the OECD[18] comprise the seasoned industrial democracies plus two or three others (notably a newer member, Mexico) which have been included for geopolitical reasons rather than for the character of their political regimes. The OECD's purpose is: 'to help member countries promote economic growth, employment, and improved standards of living through the coordination of policy [and] . . . to help promote the sound and harmonious development of the world economy and improve the lot of the developing countries, particularly the poorest'. The Organization collects and compares a wide range of social and economic statistics concerning its members; reviews annually the economic performance and prospects of each; thinks out possible solutions to common problems (such as unemployment); and oversees and encourages members' resource transfers to developing countries. Through its International Energy Agency, the OECD has been instrumental – vitally so in 1973–80 – in coordinating the response of the industrial democracies to the Oil Crises.

The OECD grew out of an earlier agency (the OEEC) which coordinated Marshall Plan aid. When the United States joined the OECD as a full member (1961), it was in part to press other countries (notably Japan) to carry more of the financial burden of aid to poor nations outside Europe. It is now the economic talk-shop of the industrial democracies. The OECD is not a supranational body like the EU, nor does its executive, the Secretary General, exercise an important public role. It is very much a behind-the-scenes, innovative, idea-sharing organization. But it could conceivably become more important and visible. The members of the OECD, plus a few others, might form a free trade area leading to an intercontinental customs and economic union based on democratic and free market principles. At the very least, the OECD needs to be kept and its scope and powers strengthened as a kind of economic policy planning council for ICD, as that new body develops.

Belonging to the economic 'club' of the most advanced democracies is a powerful carrot to dangle before some of the big struggling democracies, such as India or Brazil. OECD economic and social standards would be difficult for some to attain, and the implicit connection with democratic government a further problem. But it would be a carrot, and an important one, in moving societies-in-transition towards an Intercontinental Community of Democracies.

4. The Council of Europe and its Court of Human Rights

The Council is the largest, and the oldest, of several intergovernmental organizations founded after World War II to promote European unity. From the beginning its structures – in contrast to the supranational European Communities – were weak and its purposes general, so that it became a large but formless 'tent' under which all of western Europe could talk and try to address common tasks, such as inhibiting drug traffic or protecting historical monuments. The one criterion on which everyone could agree was that its members had to be democracies. And as it has turned out, the Council's principal and most important activities by far have come to be democracy-building and the protection of human rights.

In 1997, the Council comprised 40 members, some 'special guests'

– aspiring democracies considered not yet fully qualified – from eastern Europe, and three observers: Israel, the US and Canada.[19] The Council of Europe asks that its members meet minimum democratic standards, but has recently relaxed its terms to encourage untried democracies to move ahead. Members' governments sit on the Council's Committee of Ministers and are also participants in the Parliamentary Assembly. Past experience suggests that countries on the outside, or accepted only as 'guests', will work to improve the democratic character of their regimes to gain membership.

The Council of Europe convenes international conferences on democracy, bringing legislators from outside Europe to meet with its own parliamentarians. The Council also helped the Organization on Security and Cooperation in Europe (OSCE) to establish its own parliamentary body. In addition, the Council in 1989 sponsored the creation of an International Institute on Democracy, to train leaders in civic development. More important than these aspects of Council of Europe membership, however, is the activity of its European Court of Human Rights (1953), whose rulings – as a kind of supreme court for civil rights cases – the members have pledged to respect and carry out. There is nothing like this elsewhere. Gradually, by accession to its Convention on Human Rights, the Council gathers nations which acknowledge the Court's jurisdiction above their national judiciaries and in this way widens the scope and deepens the commitment to the protection of human rights in one continent.

Two aspects of the Council of Europe thus constitute attractive 'building blocks' for the future ICD: (a) the Court of Human Rights, which could be expanded by opening it to signatories from other continents; and (b) the process of inclusion, or exclusion, by means of which democratic countries are brought together in a body that is theirs alone . . . another device which could be enlarged to comprise democracies from all parts of the world.

5. Economic Summits (G-7)

This is not a formal organization, unlike the four bodies cited above. Yet it is probably more important – at least potentially – than any of them.

By 1975, the economic system which had run well for the Western democracies in the 1950s and 1960s was severely shaken. Recession, exchange rate disorders, the oil threat and poorly-working institutions (such as the IMF, GATT, and the changing European communities) were sapping the energies and sense of common purpose of the leading powers. Then-French President Giscard d'Estaing worried 'that we never have a serious conversation among the great capitalist leaders to say what we do now'. Such conversations, he said to James Reston of the *New York Times*, should be undertaken 'between a very few people and almost on a private level'.[20] German Chancellor Helmut Schmidt and President Gerald Ford agreed that such consultations would be helpful. Schmidt suggested that the heads of government be advised by an independent group of 'wise men' and this was done. After numerous consultations, Giscard invited President Ford, Prime Minister Harold Wilson, Chancellor Schmidt and representatives of the Japanese and Italian prime ministers to join him on 15–17 November 1975 at the Chateau of Rambouillet for 'small, select and personal' discussions.

The annual Summit has remained in this mode, 'limited to countries which carried weight and influence . . . bring[ing] together those directly responsible for policy . . . [and] able to talk freely and without inhibitions'. Herr Schmidt is reported to have said, 'We want a private, informal meeting of those who really matter in the world.'[21] At later Summits, the Canadian Prime Minister and the President of the Commission of the European Communities were added to the original six. The Summit grouping has come to be called the 'G-7', and – from 1997 – the 'G-7/G-8', with Russia now more 'in', but still partly 'out'.

The first convenors of the Economic Summits shared a strong conviction that international economic issues required treatment by heads of governments, not in the first instance by officials, who tend to get bogged down. And because heads of government had responsibility for both domestic and foreign policy, they were best placed to reconcile the needs of both. Also, if agreement among the leaders could be reached, they had the authority to see that decisions would be carried out.

As with all human institutions, formal or – as in the case of the Summits – informal but growing organically, change takes place and not necessarily always in ways the founders anticipated. The G-7 Summits became institutionalized, even though there was no treaty and no permanent international secretariat. Early on, governments recognized the need to prepare for the annual meetings. Accordingly, groups of 'sherpas' (the deep-winded Nepalese who carry baggage up the Himalayas for the high-climbers) were appointed within each G-7 government. These sherpas tend to be chosen from the treasury departments and economic councils of the members. As soon as a Summit has been held, the sherpas go to work again to get ready for the next year's meeting and to see what ought to be done about implementing the decisions of their masters. Every year the Summits are held in a different G-7 capital; the host government's sherpas take the lead in preparing for that meeting. And so on.

The summits became somewhat less ambitious, as the complexity of the constantly-changing world situation affected planning and implementation of decisions. The eruption of a second world Oil Crisis in 1979 inevitably brought more political considerations into the discussions. The Japanese were especially reticent to be involved in wide-ranging political exchanges,[22] but these became inevitable as Western–Soviet relations, for yet another time in 1985, deteriorated. Nuclear proliferation, human rights, the Middle East, terrorism, environmental concerns, the Soviet invasion of Afghanistan and other burning security and political issues found their way on to Summit agendas. The Iraqi invasion of Kuwait was an especially hot item in the 1990 G-7 meeting.

So, for practical purposes, the annual G-7 Summits plus the intensive interaction between foreign offices, treasuries and sometimes defence ministries have become a broad – if somewhat disjointed – process of continuing consultation (eventually at the highest levels) on political, economic and other topical questions that the seven members believe are important or urgent to treat. However the G-7 process, for several years, has become stuck on dead centre. It is useful, sometimes important, but in the welter of international and domestic activity that surrounds the complex governments of the members, it has not achieved the public visibility or the high priority that it should. It remains a fundamentally Third Phase institution. The complex reasons for this are not useful to argue here, but the fact remains that as a potential body of strategic importance to the conduct of inter-democracy affairs, the G-7 stands out in any survey of building blocks for the future. We will examine the possibilities of a restructured Fourth Phase group of the most experienced democratic powers in Chapter 8.

6. Other Relevant Intergovernmental Bodies

The five institutions sketched above are not the only 'organizational building blocks' from which a new Intercontinental Community of Democracies can be constructed. Other international bodies, developed over the past 50 years and involving the democracies to one extent or another, will be relevant to the architectural design of a new edifice ... one which can empower the full, new vision of a *Pax Democratica*.

One must at least look over one's shoulder at organizations such as the *Western European Union*, a companion to NATO and a possible defence ministry for the EU, the *US–Japan Alliance*, the *US–Korea Alliance* and the *ANZUS Defense Treaty*. All combine countries which should be incorporated into a mutual defence/security arm of an Intercontinental Community of Democracies. Important too is the *Nordic Council*, which has pioneered the integration of social and economic measures among the Scandinavian countries and shows what 'likemindedness' can do. The *European Economic Zone*, the *North American Free Trade Area*, the *Australia-New Zealand Economic Zone*, and *APEC* (*Asia-Pacific Economic Cooperation forum*) are all relevant, working at various levels for economic cooperation. As a forum for security and human affairs discussions among 53 nations (most of them democratic or at least proto-democratic) spreading across north Eurasia, the *Organization for Security and Cooperation in Europe* (formerly CSCE) has some importance in helping to stem the tide of destructive nationalisms in formerly totalitarian areas. Charts showing membership of most of these bodies will be found in Appendix B.

But for practical purposes, NATO, G-7, the OECD, the EU and the Council of Europe will constitute the principal building blocks for constructing the new edifice of an all-democracy community. This is because of the solidly democratic nature of most of the member-countries; because of the impressive practical accomplishments in cooperation and integration of these bodies from 1949 to 1990; because of the ingenious nature of their mechanisms – precursors of the Fourth Phase in building world order; because the more advanced of these countries understand their strong common interests and share important habits of working together; and because they represent collectively the financial and governmental power to get things done in keeping with their democratic norms.

Recent accessions to membership in the OECD and the Council of Europe require, however, that the foregoing statements be taken with some caution. Countries such as Moldava, Mexico or Azerbaijan can hardly be classified as important world political or economic players, yet half-finished democracies, aspiring to be part of the modern world, can certainly be absorbed conditionally into outer circles of democratic cooperation to prepare them for fuller involvement. It should be emphasized that the 'unfinished business' of the democracies will never be 'finished'. It is a long-term project whose next stage, the ICD, might require the first half of the 21st century. It is important that we define ICD's initial composition and goals, as well as its new structures and working methods, sharply and clearly; Chapter 8 attempts this.

The most important change from the 1940–90 patterns in establishing the goals of the new ICD is to place the protection and extension of democracy first. The most important change in working methods and character will be to adopt Fourth Phase ways of making decisions and assuring democratic accountability. The most important change in composition will be to provide a solid core which can undertake the hardest initial work, and around which aspiring democracies can gather and gradually accept the fullest responsibilities. How the pre-formed building blocks of community, transformed and re-shaped, should be combined to form the new ICD and extend *Pax Democratica* will be discussed in Chapter 8. In the next chapter, it is first necessary to consider which nations and peoples look as if they are sufficiently prepared and willing to enlist.

6 Likemindedness and the Democratic Peoples

Democracies are particularly capable of making constitutional commitments to each other. For self-regarding states to agree to pursue their interests within binding institutions, they must perceive in their partners a credible sense of commitment – an assurance that they will not exit at the least sign of disagreement. Because policymaking in democracies tends to be decentralized and open, the character of commitments can be more clearly determined and there are opportunities to lobby policymakers in the other democracies. Democracies do not just sign agreements; they create political processes that reduce uncertainty and build confidence in mutual commitments.

G. John Ikenberry[1]

DECIDING WHO CAN JOIN THE CLUB

Without a framework of goals, plans and structures, an ICD will not work. On the other hand, a mere constitutional scheme, no matter how conceptually or legally magnificent, does not guarantee success. The International Community of Democracies must be made up of 'likeminded' countries; an infrastructure of habits of mind is essential. Likemindedness is the state of mind, the mixture of attitudes, beliefs, social habits and capabilities that characterize countries apt for Fourth Phase integration. Some characteristics of likemindedness are suggested below.

There are *degrees* of likemindedness. There are no perfect democracies. But some countries fit the pattern more precisely than others. And stages of development – social, economic and political – are relevant. Countries do not remain static; some that today seem only marginally likeminded may develop their fitness for interdemocracy integration rapidly.

In assessing likemindedness, nations of the world might be divided into five groups: (a) a *core group* of experienced democracies which recognize a broad range of common interests and are

97

thoroughly used to working with one another; (b) a *second tier* of less-experienced democratic nations which share interests with the core group and which already know how to work with them; (c) *aspiring democracies* in a kind of half-way house of political and economic development but which strive to join the 'club' of modern democracies; (d) *tiny democracies* whose weight in the world is inconsequential, but whose voices should be heard as members of ICD; and (e) the remaining *despotisms and autocracies*, pre-modern regimes which show little interest in or aptitude for democracy or the protection of human rights, or for close collaboration with others.

States with high degrees of likemindedness might be characterized as follows:

1. *Stable, experienced, advanced, politically democratic regimes*, where political freedoms and representative government, protection for civil rights and the Rule of Law are essentially unchallenged and the habits of democracy pervade the conduct of civic business.[2]

2. *Advanced economies*, characterized by sophisticated free markets, close monetary cooperation with similar states, substantial overseas investment and aid programmes, open trading and other economic exchanges with likeminded nations, high levels of exporting and importing dependency, comparatively low degrees of business and governmental corruption, and deep involvement in the integration of the globalizing economy.

3. *Knowledge-based socio-economies*, integrating the most modern forms of science, education, communication and high-technology industries.

4. *Modern humane societies*, which accept a high degree of responsibility for the general welfare and quality of life of their citizens, enjoy high standards of living, and embrace and express the ideal of *agape* – the caring society. There is also a high incidence of private initiative working for the good of the community, the hallmark of a civil society.

5. *A deep and widespread understanding that the vital interests of their people are widely shared* with likeminded peoples. Vital common interests of the democracies include: mutual defence, security, and the diminution of war, terrorism, civil strife and democide; global economic growth and prosperity embracing free markets and widely accepted rules; the sustainability of Planet Earth – emphasizing development and growth, protection of the environment, mitigation of crime and the drug trade and other destabilizing

transnational phenomena; the growth of stable democracy and the indivisibility of human rights.

6. *Proven capability for engaging in joint efforts with likeminded countries* to serve the common interest, expressed through participation in a number of cooperative and integrative schemes – especially in building past foundations of multinational architecture (Chapter 5). This comprises not only adherence to sophisticated treaties pledging mutual aid, but a sustained commitment of political and diplomatic 'muscle' to the service of the common interest and a demonstrated willingness to share burdens fairly.

7. *A substantial body of diplomats, civil servants, military officers, political leaders, academic experts, business leaders and others who are trained, available and oriented towards international cooperative work.* This denotes a society so rich in human resources that it can – and does – afford to share them with likeminded partners in the ICD's own integrative venture, and – especially – with less fortunate countries needing help in modernizing.

There is an *eighth, very important criterion: the relative economic weight and political-military power* of the various countries. This is important to consider because it fits under the heading of 'what does the nation in question bring to the table?' when the Community is under construction. In a thoroughly advanced Fourth Phase community, which would constitute a limited federation of its members (probably some years off), this question would be less important; in the US federation, for example, the comparative weight of New York as against that of, say, Delaware or Idaho is much less important than is the relative importance in today's unfinished European Union of Germany's weight as against that of, say, Portugal or Belgium. Within half-built Fourth Phase communities, as well as with respect to those communities' relations with countries and groups outside, composite economic-political heft must still count for a great deal.[3]

The foregoing guidelines have been set forth with some trepidation; the problem of applying the standards, attempted in the paragraphs below, is even more touchy. Men and women from different cultural and educational backgrounds may define such loaded terms as 'democracy' or 'interests' differently. However, one has to start somewhere. It is to be hoped that others will take this as a signal to improve on the work in progress.

APPLYING THE LIKEMINDEDNESS CRITERIA

> We start from different poles. We start from a philosophical base that is based on the Greco-Roman traditions of democracy and the Chinese start from a Confucian base, so there is a problem.
>
> Hugh Davies, British negotiator
> in Hong Kong talks, 1995[4]

Now comes the difficult part: Which countries, of the 200 or so in today's world, fit the 'likemindedness' criteria, and how closely? This is obviously no simple matter.

It helps to use such economic templates as Gross Domestic Product, because a country with a very low GDP, and especially a low GDP per capita, is unlikely to be an important player in the global economy.[5] With respect to the sixth criterion (proven capability for joint undertakings), another rough template[6] will show the scale of a nation's involvement in cooperative and integrative enterprises with others. For example, there is no comparison in this respect between a highly-sophisticated democracy such as the Netherlands, whose neighbours are advanced democracies and which participates actively in a dozen or more Third and Fourth Phase bodies, and a country such as Costa Rica, whose democratic credentials are high but whose opportunities for international involvement are limited by its size, economic capabilities and the lack of nearby modern partners.

Also, in a world in which Second and Third Phase systems – and even, in China's case, First Phase systems – of conducting world affairs are very much alive, there will have to be political considerations which go beyond straightforward accounting calculations as to which nations are 'likeminded'. For example, even though Israel and Taiwan meet most of the criteria as well as do other second tier wealthy democracies, it would be political folly to invite either nation in the near future to join the core of a new organization which would shut out – at least initially – China and many Arab countries.

By the same token, for historical, geocultural and strategic reasons, Turkey must be part of the initial Community, even though it scores low on several criteria. For seven decades Turkey has been a testing ground, a 'swing' Islamic country which is trying – at times desperately – to join the West and to meet modern standards. As Turkey goes, it is likely, so will much of Islam go in the next few decades. To shut Turkey out of the full range of integration within the coming ICD, after having welcomed its participation in vital organizations such as NATO for more than four decades, would be a grave mistake.

For the most part, however, it is not impossible to categorize states into the likeminded, the partly-likeminded, and those who – at least at this point in history – lie outside the pale. In Appendix A, the reader will find a fairly systematic analysis of degrees of 'likemindedness' as a basis for composing the Intercontinental Community of Democracies.

On page 102 is a list of the 'Core Group' of democracies which meet substantially the highest levels of the first seven criteria. Each has also been assigned special weighting based on political and economic power in world affairs (the eighth criterion). These conclusions are based on basic works and standard sets of statistics the analysis of which enables one to screen countries for present purposes. The annual survey of political rights and civil liberties published since 1978 by Freedom House in New York,[7] makes it possible to drop out readily from the Core Group and the second tier certain nations which are attempting to establish democracy but which have not yet stabilized their institutions and practices. Similarly, using OECD and UN statistics,[8] it is possible to set aside still other countries on social and economic grounds; in many ways, they do not share an important 'common language' with the more advanced. Finally, an examination of countries deeply involved for years in community building among the likeminded (Appendix B) further screens out countries which have been weak to identify their common interests with others, or which currently lack the capacity to engage in sophisticated international community-building.

The following set of recommendations for determining initial membership in ICD is no static thing. Many countries which today are in one sort of political or economic 'half-way house' or another will nevertheless be able and presumably willing to take part in some, but not all, ICD activities; many can be expected gradually to become full participants. ICD in its early stages should be thought of as a series of concentric circles of integration and cooperation, with the deepest forms of commitment at the centre.

AT THE CENTRE: CORE GROUP AND SECOND TIER

There is a *Core Group* of twenty advanced democracies which clearly meet all the criteria for the initial inner circles of an Intercontinental Community of Democracies (ICD). Ranked more or less in order of their 'fit' with the criteria, these are:

United States of America	Belgium
Germany	Denmark
France	Sweden
United Kingdom	New Zealand
Canada	Austria
Australia	Finland
Italy	Luxembourg
Japan	Switzerland
Netherlands	Spain
Norway	Iceland

Some readers may want to quibble with rankings within this Core Group of twenty. For example, why is Japan at eighth place and not higher? Why rank Canada and Australia so high? Why is Switzerland – a 'loner' in many respects – still in this first twenty? Appendix A will suggest some answers.

The *Second Tier* of democracies – although each is somewhat less advanced in various ways – belong with the Core Group as founders of the ICD. These six belong there because they joined long ago to help construct NATO, the European Union or other cooperative enterprises in the north Atlantic and western Pacific areas and because they share most of the likemindedness criteria at fairly high levels. A few do not quite measure up in some important respects, yet on geopolitical and historic grounds these anomalous nations cannot be left out. Second tier countries are listed below more or less in order of how they fit the full set of criteria.

Second Tier for the ICD:

Czech Republic	Republic of Korea
Portugal	Greece
Ireland	Turkey

Of all the countries liberated in the disintegration of the Soviet empire after 1989, Czechoslovakia was alone in having strong democratic credentials antedating World War II. When Slovakia seceded in 1992, the Czech portion of the old union was no longer forced to carry along a more backward partner. Today, Czech democracy is rated a '1.5' by Freedom House (on a scale of 1 to 7), the same rating as advanced countries such as the UK, Germany, France and Italy. By most economic indices, the Czech Republic is in good shape – relationship of debt to GDP, foreign reserves, inflation, unemployment rates, etc. – and is advancing rapidly to parity with such western European countries as Spain and Portugal. Among users of the Internet, the Czechs ranked 18th in the world in 1994.[9] The Czechs have been foremost, among east-central Europeans, in joining world and European cooperative bodies. Czechs are, per capita, among the most talented and forward-looking people in Europe. Beyond all this, the West owes more to the Czech Republic than to any other east European or Balkan people, because of our pusillanimous acquiescence in 1939 to Czechoslovakia's dismemberment by Hitler, when the Czechs were ready to fight. In 1947, Czechoslovakia was the only country east of the Iron Curtain which opted to join the Marshall Plan, yet it was prevented from doing so by its Soviet 'protectors'; the West, again, acquiesced and in February 1948 Czechoslovakia slipped behind the Iron Curtain. When the USSR forcibly overturned the 'Prague Spring' reforms of 1968, the West once more stood by passively. More than any other country which lay for four decades bound in the Soviet grasp, the Czech Republic has the moral, political, economic, educational, human, industrial and humane qualifications to join any new community of democracies. It will need some years, however, to 'catch up' fully.

Portuguese democracy (rated 1.0 by Freedom House) puts it high on the list of the politically qualified, although a few more years could be needed to confirm the long-term stability of its institutions. Important strides in economic and social modernization have been made by Portugal since its leap from dictatorship to democracy in the 1970s, but it is not yet in the same economic league as its advanced European Union and Atlantic partners. Portugal plays its part internationally; it should be able increasingly to share fully in the common burdens and responsibilities of the most advanced countries. All things considered, an essentially constructive future for Portugal seems assured.

Ireland's democratic and civil character can be certified, even though in many ways it is still on the sociocultural fringes of Europe and lags behind economically. It has not seen fit to join NATO;

until its mutual security commitment becomes stronger, Ireland will be less than a full partner with the other democracies, despite its membership of the EU. Yet no one could countenance leaving Ireland out of an ICD, for cultural, historic, strategic and geographic reasons.

By all economic indices, including its rapid transition to a knowledge-based society, (South) Korea is in the forefront of newly-industrialized countries which have come from far behind in the modernization stakes. Its democracy is still young, plagued by continuing large-scale corruption and occasional abuses by the security forces. However, its political development is far ahead of all other Asian countries, with the exception of Japan. Strategically, the Republic of Korea is an essential partner in the defence of democratic interests in the Far East. It recently was accepted into the OECD; this brings it into the ambit of the two dozen or so world economic leaders.

Finally, neither Greece nor Turkey, although each fails in important ways to measure up to some of the criteria for 'membership', could possibly be left out of the coming ICD. Greece's democracy does not yet meet the most advanced European standards. Greece became a full member of the EU in 1981 but economically and socially is not fully modernized. Above all, Greece does not show the same degree of commitment to the common interest and to institutions such as NATO and the EU, as do the other members. However, because it belongs to these and other key Atlantic and European groupings, because of its strategic position in the Balkans, and not least because it was the birthplace of democracy, Greece belongs among the founders of the ICD.

Turkey is about on a par with Greece in meeting overall ICD criteria, but there are major differences. Turkey has made great strides in economic and social modernization, but in many ways it is still a developing country. Turks can change their governments democratically, but countenance widespread human rights abuses. Military coups have been frequent. Reforms are proceeding, spurred by Turkey's entry into a customs union with the EU (achieved in 1996), but most Europeans remain dissatisfied with Turkish progress. On the other hand, no other partly-developed country has shown the determination to modernize, or to do its fair share and more in the mutual defence of the West, or to take part in the full web of cooperation among the advanced countries. Turkey's military commitment in the Korean War, for example, was greater than that of all other Allied countries except the United States. Its sheer size alone – more than 60 million people, on a par with the largest European countries – makes its future a priority item on the West's agenda. Since the modernizer Kemal Atatürk wrenched his country-men from their ancient despotic, imperial and Islam-bound past after World War I, Turkey has occupied an absolutely strategic position between West and ancient East. If Turkey completes a successful transition to modern, secular, Atlantic-style democracy and to full participation in the advanced global economy, the im-pact on the entire Middle East will be profound. It is the second non-Western nation, after Japan, to have participated in the laying of the so-far essentially Western foundations for the democratic community. Given Turkey's deep involvement in Atlantic security and economic affairs, its strategic position and its unshaken com-mitment to the West, it would be unthinkable not to include it in an initial ICD.

ASPIRING DEMOCRACIES

We have now proposed 26 'founder-members' for an ICD, initial signers – presumably – of a broad framework treaty. Beyond these, there is a sizeable number of democracies with varying qualifica-tions which do not measure up well against our criteria in impor-tant respects. These could be considered *aspirants*, prospective full members sooner or later if things go well, for the 'club' of democ-racies, and candidates for forms of partial – or associate – member-ship now. None of these nations, because of their size, power or strategic position, and their demonstrated desire to 'belong with the modernizers', can be ignored. Indeed, if the founders of the ICD were to shut out from a larger community-oriented circle all democracies which were seriously deficient in one way or another – that is, not sufficiently likeminded or not yet equipped to bear full responsibilities with all the others – but which clearly are striv-ing mightily to modernize and therefore 'belong' in spirit, a major purpose of the ICD would be thwarted.

To create a Pax Democratica and make it last, freedom's realm must be continually extended. There must be no let-up. Creative ways therefore need to be found to involve around two dozen as-piring democracies as 'associates' alongside the inner group of 26. Aspirants are not yet able, for example, to share fully in the man-agement of a global economy the full responsibilities of which they are not yet ready to assume. Russia is the prime example, India yet another. But it would be unwise not to involve these two major struggling democracies as closely as possible and to open the doors to ever-deepening participation as their approximation to the standards of the Core Group and second tier members evolves.[10]

There are also ways in which aspirant democracies can deliberate general policy with the full members of the ICD without compromising the ability of the inner group-plus-second tier to act when necessary on significant and urgent questions. This will be discussed more fully in Chapter 8.

In rough order based on relative approximation to the likemindedness criteria, here is a suggested list of 26 *aspirants*, which would be launched on a sliding track towards full membership in ICD.

Israel	Philippines
Taiwan	Venezuela
Poland	Russia
Singapore	India
South Africa	Latvia
Hungary	Bulgaria
Thailand	Lithuania
Malaysia	Estonia
Argentina	Costa Rica
Slovenia	Mexico
Uruguay	Ukraine
Chile	Slovakia
Brazil	Romania

(Note: Taiwan should be considered for special status, especially with regard to economic cooperation. It is already, for example, an observer nation in APEC, but its unique position with regard to China rules out a full part, for now, in ICD. Until a secure peace reigns in the Middle East, Israel's inclusion in all aspects of ICD could be problematical, although by most 'likemindedness' indices it should participate.)

Aspirant nations will each have to be handled as a separate case and involved in ICD in as many ways as its perception of its interests and its capabilities for sharing ICD responsibilities fully will allow. Geographic, historic and strategic factors – and not only the systematic attempt to rank these countries according to how they measure up to the 'likemindedness' criteria – must also play a role. As an example: Russia is in the first rank of nations requiring special involvement in the ICD because of geopolitics, although it fits most of the criteria rather poorly. Since the collapse of Communism, the Atlantic nations and Japan have not worked out an adequate strategic partnership with Russia that will best ensure that that great country is given, to the fullest extent possible, the economic, educational and other forms of technical and financial assistance that Russia needs, and also to make sure that Russia will *feel* itself to be a partner, growing into what one hopes will eventually be full membership in the ICD. Nor has Russia yet been able to do its full part. A major impediment has been the poor Japan–Russia relationship, the product of unfortunate historic and nationalistic forces. Transition for Russia may require some years – even decades, but what counts is establishing clear markers on the way to the goal, and then making a start. Just as the two powerful despotisms of Germany and Japan were brought into the democratic fold after 1945, so the aim should be to bring Russia fully and safely into the modern post-Cold War *Pax Democratica.*

Some countries striving to modernize and making some progress, have been left off the list of aspirants. Marginal cases would include, for example, Pakistan, Jordan and Morocco, each of which could become a serious aspirant. The cut-off point for invitations to the ICD could admittedly be lower, or higher. In Appendix A, rough calculations are supplied on which these 'aspirant' rankings are based. These involve subjective judgement of a variety of factors bearing on the seven criteria and also on the eighth, or power, criterion. Opinions on this will differ greatly; these suggestions are offered to stimulate debate.

The list of 26 aspirants, beginning with Israel and cutting off at Romania, is offered mainly to suggest that the ICD, not long after its founding, would have to consider countries such as these for various forms of association in order to serve its broadest goal: the enlargement of the community of democracies, which process will always remain 'unfinished business'.

THE TINY DEMOCRACIES

Some very small countries have been judged in Freedom House surveys for several years as fully democratic, with high standards of political liberty and civil rights.[11] Individually and perhaps not even collectively, they do not figure in any important way in the global economy. Outside pressures which many of them may experience in years to come could force some to amalgamate with larger countries against their will, or slip into dire economic and political straits. Because they embrace democratic ideals and put them into practice consistently, they need the sense of solidarity with other democracies which membership in the ICD could give them. In some way, perhaps in a large representative assembly of all democracies (proposed in Chapter 8), the voices of these nations – many indeed minuscule – should be heard. Here are 21 small candidates:

Andorra	Tuvalu
Barbados	Bahamas
Belize	St Vincent/Grenadines
Cyprus[12]	Dominica
Kiribati	Grenada
Liechtenstein	Mauritius
Malta	Monaco
Marshall Islands	Palau
Micronesia	St Lucia
San Marino	Solomon Islands
Trinidad and Tobago	

If all the foregoing nations – the Core Group, the second tier, the aspirants and the tiny democracies – were included, a very substantial Intercontinental Community of Democracies (around 70 countries) would have been formed.

KEEPING THE DOOR OF COMMUNITY OPEN

Pax Democratica, the Fourth Phase of world order, rests on a central principle – democracy – that played only a peripheral role in the three earlier phases. More often than not, even during the Cold War when the European and Atlantic democracies were fighting to preserve their liberties and those of others, economic and power-political considerations obtruded into decisions that took scant account of such factors as human rights and their negation – democide, the Rule of Law, devotion of countries to representative government, and so on. *Pax Democratica*, in contrast, assumes that the most fundamental decisions of the coalition of democracies will be made by countries whose political regimes are stable and meet high standards, that the nature of their association together will be democratic in its essence, and that in the great majority of instances, the question of how a particular case bears on democracy itself will head their checklist of priorities when questions external to the Community – its 'foreign affairs' – have to be decided.

If this is the case (and we will discuss in later chapters how this kind of apparatus and decision-making might work), then it is important to reserve the most fundamental powers of decision to the most democratic and likeminded nations. But to be true to itself, the ICD will have also to bring aspirant democracies, in various ways, into the processes of cooperation, consultation, debate, decision-making and eventual integration of common functions to serve common interests.

An 'open door' policy and a series of graded forms of association will need to be devised. No democracy should be left out which meets certain minimum standards (based on the seven criteria) and which demonstrates a desire to be included in the *Pax Democratica* process. As the Community in its variegated aspects and membership grows, its value and its power will become more and more evident. Ultimately, the ICD should be able to do the things that the founders of the League of Nations and the United Nations wished for but could not do, plus a good deal more, because its members will be of like mind, and they will exclude from their 'family' deliberations and their web of close cooperation countries that have neither the desire nor the aptitude for democracy.

No exclusions should be considered permanent or final. It is important that the ICD establish clear and well-publicized criteria for membership, and that such important nations as China understand that the door is open to them as well as to others still 'outside'. Nor does the creation of ICD mean that all non-democratic nations will be shut out of world decision-making; it simply means that within the United Nations and other universal bodies, a 'caucus of the democracies' (see Chapter 8) will operate to define and advance the collective point of view of the free nations on major global issues.

Moreover, it should be made clear that the construction of *Pax Democratica* will be done in such a way that it strengthens the United Nations and its processes. Eventually the UN and the ICD should grow together; by that time democracy will have become the international norm, in two respects: (1) it will characterize the domestic regimes – and therefore the international interests and habits – of the great majority of nations and peoples; and (2) the trust of the ICD peoples in their own democratically-constituted international institutions will be so great, and their combined accomplishments so manifold and manifest, that all international/universal bodies will quite naturally and gradually become democratic in their governance.

This chapter has set forth some experimental and illustrative guidelines for determining which nations and peoples should be involved in any future ICD, and to what extent. If an ICD is to come about, a small group of nations will have to lead. When they have determined that there should be an even wider coalescence of democracies, they and others will then have to attack the question – among others – of 'Who is in? Who is out? Who is partially in?' in a much deeper way. And there will inevitably be important political considerations which elected leaders of great countries will be compelled to take into account. Such decisions will greatly tax the ingenuity of the founders; they will have to work out the devilish details when the time comes. The foregoing pages represent only a 'first cut' at the question, to suggest one way that the founders might proceed.

The next few decades will be an inevitably messy period internationally, but if ICD's goals and methods are clear and consistent, then the growth of the democratic community will eventually make the hermetically-sealed nation-state, the present undemocratic web of 'universal' bodies which purports to represent humankind, and – ultimately – the institutions of despotism, war and democide themselves, anachronistic and irrelevant.

The Intercontinental Community of Democracies should be *the* growth industry of the future . . . if we want it badly enough. However, there are many who will not want it badly, and some who will not want it at all. Their views are considered in the next chapter.

7 The Vision and its Critics

Now we have examined three sets of 'building blocks' for a transformed Intercontinental Community of Democracies: (1) the be-
havioural underpinnings of the caring society; (2) some key Third
and Fourth Phase structures from the past half-century which can
be reshaped and built upon for an ICD; and (3) a total of around
70 democratic nations which, in different ways, could be involved
as members of the future ICD.

In Chapter 8, we will look at the overall concept for an ICD and
how the building blocks might be incorporated in a new international
edifice, suitable for the needs of the next century . . . a new world
order, in the true meaning of such a phrase. But first, in this chapter,
we look at some possible pitfalls and serious objections to the concept
of *Pax Democratica* and an ICD.

Before we start making 'architectural plans' for an ICD, it must
be pointed out that other architects and engineers were here before us. Their structures, and the visions which animated them, in
some cases have been in use for a time, while in other cases the
designs are not yet off the drawing boards. Many experts and practitioners of international affairs will not want to abandon their chosen
schemes or at least will be extremely sceptical of *Pax Democratica*.
Some will say that to do nothing is better than to embrace some
new concept which might only make things worse. Some are
nationalists, in a time-tested but now – more than ever – inadequate tradition. Some espouse what they believe to be still better
ideas for changing the international system. Others believe in mud-
dling through. We should consider their cases carefully before laying out plans for implementing *Pax Democratica*.

Here are the main arguments which have been advanced for doing
nothing – or for doing something else – along with some responses.

THE ICD'S INNER GROUP OMITS SOME VERY IMPORTANT COUNTRIES

Argument: In the 26 proposed 'initiators' (Core Group and second tier) of the Intercontinental Community of Democracies (pages 102–5) there is no place for such large and important countries as Russia, Brazil, India, China and Indonesia. How could a group of other countries plan global schemes without these?

Answer: First, Russia, Brazil and India are in a different category from Indonesia and China, as the former are today practising – if struggling – democracies. China is still an empire; Indonesia once was, hangs on to some imperialistic but limited pretensions, still is ruled by a repressive military regime, but is fashioning a modern economy and is fairly cooperative with its neighbours. Neither dictatorship is ready for international Fourth Phase integration with democracies.

Second, in Chapter 6 the 'likemindedness' prerequisites for any form of association with the ICD are set out at length. Russia, Brazil and India should be involved to the fullest possible extent in the *business* of the ICD but they are handicapped in different but important ways for *full participation* – i.e. for undertaking the most demanding responsibilities of membership, including the taking of crucial decisions – any time soon.

Russia, Brazil and India represent societies in various half-way stages of political and/or economic development. More importantly, none of the three yet identifies closely with the common interests that the ICD Core Group and Second Tier have already come to embrace in their years of working together.[1] The founders of the ICD will be using the most durable and soundest 'building blocks' from the older architecture of the 1947–90 period as fundaments for future structures; the leaders of thought and action of the stable democracies understand – as fully as still nation-bound humans can be expected to at this stage in history – why and how they have done these things collectively, how to make the ties still stronger and, as new political Fourth Phase structures, democratic in nature.

India is the longest-practising democracy of these 'big three', enjoying the Rule of Law and a multi-party legislature. It has made great economic strides in recent years and begun significantly to free up its state-dominated economy. It is a peace-loving nation, but its neighbours, especially China and Pakistan, threaten it. Other unsteady neighbours, such as Bangladesh, Sri Lanka and Burma, add to the instability of South Asia, the old 'sub-continent'. Furthermore, the sheer size and great masses of India (projected to be more numerous in the next century than those of China) pose major problems in modernization that a smaller, better-integrated democracy might find easier to deal with. India's foreign policy is still more or less self-centred, although the passing of its early and socialistically-inclined independence leaders, plus the acceptance of the realities of today's calmer and economically competitive post-Cold War world, have made a difference. But to try to get Indian leaders, at this stage in their country's development, to think globally and to recognize – let alone undertake – global responsibilities, and to see their interests as congruent with those of the proposed Inner Core of the ICD would be asking too much at this stage. The ICD's broader tiers of cooperation – principally the Democracies' Caucus in the UN, an ICD interparliamentary assembly (see Chapter 8) and many forms of close economic collaboration and 'opening' by the democracies – should, however, find plenty of room for India. The future should widen these opportunities. If present modernizing trends continue, India could conceivably emerge to greatness in the 21st century.

Brazil has for decades been 'the land of the future' – and still is. Although its huge industrial cities and immense back-country resources are powering a great engine of economic development and laying the basis for a modern political system, its widespread poverty and poor level of social integration still pose great problems for Brazil and for those democracies who would propose to enfold her into sophisticated and demanding new Fourth Phase international systems. Brazil still looks inward, although her recent sponsorship of Mercosur with her neighbours is encouraging. It has been proposed that Brazil should be a permanent member of the UN Security Council, and also of the G-7. While the time is not far-distant when Brazil might be brought into the OECD – which now includes even less democratic nations such as Mexico – to put her now into G-7 or still more important counsels of the rich, powerful democracies would be premature. But the time will come.

Russia, discussed in other contexts, poses the most important and difficult set of dilemmas in regard to the democracies' inner circle. On the one hand, the liberation of the Russian people from seven decades of totalitarian Communist rule is a history-making event of the first rank, and poses great opportunities. If the Russian people could be brought fully into the core of the modern democratic community, as Germany and Japan have been brought since 1945, the advantages for Russia and for the world would be immense. If this were to happen, there would be little to stop the momentum of the modernizing and humanizing power of the democratic way of life in world history. With Russia firmly in the camp of the democracies, China and Islam would seem to form the only substantial resistance to a powerful long-term trend. But – on the other hand – if Russia, despite all efforts of its reformers plus whatever aid the West can give, slips back into old patterns of autocracy and imperialism – trying in a First Phase way to ensure its security by expanding its dominion over neighbours, which never ends – then all its neighbours and indeed the world as a whole, are in deep trouble again. This Bad Scenario may look rather unlikely at this juncture, but then neither is modernization yet a secure and powerful trend in Russia. By the late 1990s, Russia's future was clouded. In its half-way house towards stable democracy and a market economy, it unfortunately seems likely that Russia will continue for some time to prove unable: (1) to identify its main interests fully with those of the West, although it will try; (2) to take on the full responsibilities, mainly economic, financial and political, of a member of the Inner Core – today, the G-7, tomorrow the much tighter planning-steering group of great and powerful democracies proposed for the ICD in Chapter 8; and (3) to quiet its old fears of encirclement by powers, such as Germany, Islam or China, that impel it to play Second Phase power politics in the great international game and to try to restore the old First Phase empire of the Czars and the Soviets.

In short, Russia is not yet ready for Fourth Phase integration with democratic likeminded partners, but should be involved and encouraged nevertheless in every other way to play as constructive a part as it can in the web of Third Phase intergovernmental cooperation. Russia's participation in the EuroAmerican Contact Group and NATO force in Bosnia (1994–) and meeting ad hoc with the G-7 powers on common matters (from 1991) are positive, as is the NATO–Russia Permanent Joint Council (1997). As in the cases of India and Brazil, full involvement for Russia can and should eventually come, the sooner the better. While the West's policies and assistance are important for the process, the defining metamorphosis is largely the task of the Russian people.

As for China and Indonesia, large countries with rapidly expanding economies but backward forms of government and primitive regard for human rights, the door to the Democratic 'club' can only be slightly ajar for now. Their cases are obviously different. Inwardly repressive and anything but democratic, Indonesia – fifth most populous country in the world – nevertheless is no serious threat to its neighbours. While it has (in old imperial fashion) conquered the western half of the great Island of New Guinea, known now as 'West Irian' and is engaged in ethnic cleansing and 'Indonesianization' there and in East Timor on a major scale, Indonesia in the 1990s has become externally a positive, at least benign force in Southeast Asian Affairs, having taken the lead to form ASEAN (1967) with its neighbours. But if one considers the criteria for likemindedness (Chapter 6), it is evident that Indonesia can today be nowhere near the forefront of Fourth Phase world politics. In any case, it can hardly be considered a serious candidate for the ICD until a peaceful and democratically-inclined transition from Suharto to his successors has taken place.

The case of China, like that of Russia, deserves long and careful consideration. Unlike many troublemaking middle powers such as Iran, Iraq, North Korea, Syria, Libya or the Sudan, China cannot be ignored or isolated in resolving major global questions simply because of its tremendous demography, size and potential power. Economically, China is poised on the verge of entry into the modern world, although it is ambivalent about cooperation with its neighbours and trading partners. Its leaders, as in ages past, seem as yet in no mood to adjust China's imperial attitudes or political system to its changing economic requirements.[2] This represents overriding reality and a great source of potential inner conflict with important external consequencies.

The ways in which the advanced democracies move to involve China in global decision-making must be carefully conceived and developed. The buzz-word of the US foreign policy establishment for relations with China in the 1990s has been 'engagement', although there is also an implicit readiness, if absolutely necessary, to slip into a policy of containment if China proves more – not less – imperial in its future behaviour. Meanwhile, 'engagement' sounds like a fair word for characterizing a future ICD Second Phase policy towards China based on a clear common interest of the democracies and a proper recognition of China's interests. China should be given increased opportunities to enter the Third Phase 'club' provided it is moving towards likemindedness (the seven criteria) in important respects.

To recapitulate: The main answer to China and any others which choose for now to remain outside the modern democratic club must be: (1) You are already involved in the UN and other universal bodies, and we will work with you there to further universal interests that we agree we have in common; and (2) As you prove your peacefulness, your humane regard for your own people and others, and your capacity for sophisticated international cooperation by moving towards democracy and a free economy . . . you will find a place at the democracies' special table.

Finally, those who would advocate some new international condominium of all the great powers, irrespective of their likemindedness but based only on their power and the identification of a few important – but inevitably ephemeral – shared balance-of-power interests, should remember that the long-term overall priorities of an Intercontinental Community of Democracies are different, viz., to: (1) mitigate violent conflict worldwide; and (2) put a halt, insofar as it can be done, to democide and other gross violations of human rights. The best strategy for doing this is gradually to expand the community of democracies and free market economies on a generous but absolutely realistic basis . . . grounded in democracy itself.

These are the main guideposts for the founding group of democracies (the 26 Core and Second Tier members). Questions as to which other major powers, not now obviously part of an inner group (or in some cases, e.g. China or North Korea, not even in layers of an outer group), must be secondary to measures to create and make workable and durable a strong inner grouping of democracies. We must get our priorities straight, keep them that way, keep the doors open for new members, and work as closely as we can, using Third or even Second Phase old methods, with non-democratic nations whose goodwill we can hope for and whose cooperation in many areas we need, but on whom we cannot count without reservation – at this stage anyway. And in some cases, the democracies as a group may have to contest the designs of such peripheral or external nations if they persistently flout ours. That is an essential principle of *Pax Democratica*.

THE ICD SCHEME IS NEO-COLONIALIST

The Argument: The Intercontinental Community of Democracies would begin with mainly rich, powerful and mostly-white nations –

our 20 most likeminded from Chapter 6 – as its core, and six more in a next tier of founders. This will be seen by some as racist, neo-colonialist, capitalist-imperialist. These arguments will be especially strong in countries not grounded solidly in modern political (i.e. democratic) or economic (i.e. free market) systems, or by individuals anywhere who believe that Western guilt for past imperial transgressions necessarily invalidates what are essentially Western-inspired plans for a fresh start at world order. The peoples of developing countries which still need major help, some of which are democracies of sorts, may understandably ask: 'Why aren't *we* included in the founding inner counsels of the democracies? Are we but second class peoples and nations?'

The kindly but firm *Answer* must be: Inevitably there will be short-term dislocations involved in such a broad and far-reaching approach as ICD and *Pax Democratica*, but *in the long run* and on the whole, such an open-ended, free community will surely result in better and safer world conditions for *all* peoples. The recent record can help us.

Since the 1950s, when the Allies began in earnest to build the Euroatlantic community, the objection was often heard that the rich West was 'ganging up' on poor developing countries in order better to exploit them.[3] The fault in this argument is clear: There will always be powerful business interests seeking to profit in the developing world; in most – but not all – cases, these help the local economies as well as themselves. But if the most underdeveloped countries need capital transfers in the form of loans or grants or more open trade opportunities, they will have a much better chance of getting that aid if the countries capable of giving it are working closely together on all global economic problems, including those of development. And needy nations will get still more help if they can approach potential givers multilaterally rather than one-by-one. This is clearly borne out by the experience of the World Bank and the EU, whose development assistance programmes rely on collective, agreed aid from a group of givers. The OECD is also a good example of how the developing nations profit from collaboration among the wealthy democracies; each year OECD's Development Assistance Committee rates each of its rich members as to the percent of GDP represented by its development assistance, and analyses the overseas aid programmes of each. Over more than 30 years, this process has publicized both the outstanding and the dismal records of rich givers;[4] these annual reviews of each by all in turn have influenced public opinion and parliaments and have generally spurred increases in overall aid.

Unless the big players – a relatively few large, advanced democratic governments with an overwhelming stake in the global economy – are able to much better integrate their several economies, arriving at rational, growth-oriented, harmonized policies, they will not be able to accumulate the necessary wealth to transfer to the less-developed. And this is even more true with respect to prospects for increased trade than for development aid. The prospects of the developing world, for better or for worse, depend to a very great extent on the economic health, cooperation and continuing growth of the big rich countries. For example, the currently fastest-developing part of the world, east Asia, could not have progressed so rapidly without the markets and investment capital of the highly-developed countries.

One must yet again recall the central purpose of the ICD founders, viz., building a democratic framework for peace, prosperity and freedom in which there will be a place for the Egypts, Jordans, Bolivias, Moroccos, Papua New Guineas, and others in various halfway or 'quarter-way' stages on the road to modernization – some sooner, some later. Their leaders should see the obvious advantages of hastening their own evolution so that they can gradually increase their capabilities for outreach and their commitment to the purposes of the ICD, and join with it. This process should move even more quickly if the ICD's initial core proves as strong and dynamic as it should, and gives powerful leadership.

As aspiring democracies, many of the countries which formerly were colonies and in the 1950s and 1960s may have been part of such anachronistic blocs as the Bandung Non-Aligned Conference, would be included from the outset in the Caucus of Democracies at the UN and the ICD interparliamentary assembly, both described in Chapter 8. They would be welcomed, as and when ready, to take on greater responsibilities in the ICD overall. This has been the patttern over the past half-century for aspiring nations, such as Spain, Portugal and Greece in 'joining Europe'; it has worked well and should be a model for ICD's global evolution.

To understand the full scope and psychological nature of the 'neocolonialist plot' argument, however, one must break down the sources. First, one need hardly take account of the objections of governments such as Iran, Iraq, Burma, Nigeria, Cuba, North Korea, Libya or the Sudan. Without substantial changes in their respective internal order or their world-views, it is hard to see how they could take part in an ICD, as associate members or even as observers. (Even in the UN, their present roles are largely negative, often destructive.) However, given time, the yeast of internal change, the pressures to participate fully in the world economy and the attractions of a modern way of life for their peoples could be expected to bring most of them along, one way or another. But for the immediate future, we need not worry much about their views, or their propaganda . . . as we can do very little, beyond giving humanitarian aid when asked or offering educational opportunities to their students if they will let us, to help them to change their attitudes or social or political conditions. The onus for change and inclusion will be on them.

Other states not especially dangerous to their neighbours, but still poorly-governed and unstable, are trying hard to move rapidly into the global economy and are beginning to understand the idea of commonality among the likeminded. They are trying to work with their neighbours and with the West, and are strategically important to the democracies. Here, one should cite countries such as Egypt, Vietnam, Indonesia, Saudi Arabia, Cambodia or Angola, for whom places should be open at the democratic table when they and we feel ready. These countries aspire to modernization and international acceptance. We should continue to work with them in Phase Three international bodies, such as the UN and its subsidiaries, and encourage their modernization. But Phase Four involvement is beyond them at this stage.

If one attempts at the outset to include, in the most vital and decisive activities of the ICD, too many nations beyond the core group – whose commitment to democratic and free market values is strong and tested, and who are in all respects ready, willing and able to engage in political and economic integration across a wide spectrum of Phase Four activities – one risks failure of the entire enterprise. Likemindedness – in all its aspects – must be the basis for ICD; if early members of the critical 'inner circle' are not sufficiently likeminded the new Community will founder. The ICD must not be watered down, but – in the last analysis – must proceed at a pace and with the members that can be counted on, gradually gathering strength and expanding.

It must also be pointed out to critics crying 'racism' that with the initial close involvement of the Japanese, South Korean and Turkish peoples in *Pax Democratica*, the 26 founding democracies will demonstrate clearly that the ICD is not a 'white man's club', and that it bids fair to become less and less confined to democracies of Western origin as time goes on.

The founding democracies must above all tell the world and their own peoples how vital is *Pax Democratica*; the process by which we arrived at our formative conclusions; and our own conviction that what we are doing is for the good of *all* peoples, not just our own. We must explain that a democratic world order which – as its top goal – can eventually eliminate genocide and keep damaging wars to a minimum, and which will promote all forms of progress, holds far greater prospects for mankind than any other conceivable form of order.

There may still be Naysayers who maintain that this will simply usher in a new era of imperialism, that *Pax Democratica* is just a new and clever means of preserving the privileges and domination of the Western democracies. After having made clear our aims and pointing out the untruths in such arguments, the founding democracies of the ICD had better just get on with the job. 'The proof of the pudding is in the eating.' There need be no apologies. The main democratic powers must do what we have to do. In the long run, the world will benefit greatly, and most people will understand, eventually if not at the outset, that it does. There may be risks, but we have to take them because we will have set the deepening and widening of the community of democracies as our *first priority.* If we are timorous, everyone – not just the democracies – will suffer in the long run. Millions of lives are at stake, if the record of this passing century is any indicator.

ASIANS ARE DIFFERENT; WON'T AN ICD PIT ASIA AGAINST THE WEST?

Argument: To form an intercontinental community around the central principle of democracy assumes that 'democracy' comprises a universal set of values, good for all peoples; this (goes the argument) is patently not true. Asian critics in particular contend that this is not the case because the 'Asian way' is different, stemming from different cultural and historical roots. Some go so far as to say that an ICD or even such weak attempts at 'Pacific Rim' cooperation as APEC[5] constitute an imposition of Western values on people who just don't think or act as Westerners do. Lee Kuan

Yew, Singapore's venerable founding father, is a prime exponent of this view. He believes that because unbridled American democracy leads to the kind of social decay supposedly now prevalent in the United States, a more orderly and authoritarian form of society (like Singapore's) better serves the aspirations and needs of Asian peoples.

Answer: Not all Asian leaders agree with Lee; Malaysia's deputy prime minister Anwar Ibrahim, for example, believes that Asians 'must be prepared to champion those ideals which are universal and which belong to humanity as a whole'.[6] The outspoken advocate of democracy, Nobel Peace Laureate Aung San Suu Kyi of Burma, has inspired not only her own people, but thousands in every part of the world. Some of the proposed founders of the ICD – Japanese, South Koreans, Turks – are Asians, already practise democracy and work well with the established Western democracies.

The broad principles of human rights and democratic government are valid for people everywhere. There are, of course, many variations in the forms and practices by means of which democracy's principles are given effect. Such differences are not just understandable, they are positively healthy. Indeed they epitomize the very essence of the open society, which enshrines diversity, protects it, thrives on it. Democracy is never static; it is always a work in progress. We must acknowledge that not every society is ready to institute government based on the irreducible essentials of democracy. However all peoples, with time, can reasonably aspire to this indispensable aspect of living in the modern world.

It is instructive to look at Europe, where the ideals of democracy and human rights first took root (and took a long time to develop) and where their practice has evolved furthest. In that continent, the forms and habits of free government nevertheless vary greatly, depending on historical accident and cultural idiosyncracies. The 'constitution' of the United Kingdom, for example, is unwritten, depending on what precedent and the House of Commons say it is; the Swedish constitutional monarchy has different structures from those of modern Germany; the Swiss have evolved a federal cantonal system which encompasses a great deal of 'direct democracy' and a collective executive; while the French presidential constitution poses yet another substantial variation. But each of these systems rests ultimately on the will of the people.

Similarly, electoral procedures differ considerably between west

European states, but basic principles such as the secret ballot, universal suffrage and free choice between several parties and candidates are shared by all. Constitutional provisions and laws governing civil rights also differ within western Europe, but virtually all of its nations today observe the same general standards, and this observance is spreading to virtually all European countries which until 1990 lay east of the Iron Curtain. Thus, uniformity in the forms and conventions of democracy is not the rule in Europe, but adherence to common principles *is*, more and more.

Within Asia, one sees substantial advances in democratic government and the safeguarding of human rights. Japan, for example, today enjoys a stable and democratic system. South Korea, although its governmental evolution has taken longer, today bears comparison with Japan. India, with all its problems, is embedded in a democratic framework. Thailand, the Philippines, Malaysia and Taiwan are in different stages of political modernization and practise democracy in quite different ways, yet all three are tending to the same general way of political life, which is gradually becoming a universal standard in much of Asia.

There are regional and country-to-country differences in Asia and other continents. To help accommodate differences and develop cooperation among the culturally likeminded, regional groupings are a natural and desirable development, even a useful prelude to associations of wider scope. An ICD does not assume that all cooperation among democracies should take place within a single all-embracing, worldwide framework; the European Union, for example, will no doubt continue to develop on its own, with close ties to the larger ICD. ASEAN (the Association of South East Asian Nations) is a regional organization which aspires to be a counterpart of the EU. There are budding combinations – some successful, some less so – in Latin America, the Caribbean, Africa and South Asia. The new NAFTA (North American Free Trade Area) is another example. If these can gradually build in methods and approaches that are compatible with the ICD's goals, and eventually become linked more and more with that intercontinental body, the world as a whole will profit.

Some Asians who believe democratic values are Western and cannot be imported could derive backing from an important Western dissent from the assumption running through this book, viz., that democratic values are universal and that democracy can ultimately be the cement of a global community. Samuel Huntington published a eye-opening article in *Foreign Affairs* (Summer 1993), followed by a book and another article in 1996.[7] He contends that 'the fundamental source of conflict in the new [post-Cold War] world will not be primarily ideological or primarily economic. The great divisions among humankind and the dominating source of conflict will be cultural'. Huntington divides the world into six or seven great civilizations (the West, Islam and China are most easily recognized) which, he believes, will inevitably clash. He believes that democracy is a unique Western growth, transplanted to other 'civilizations' only with the greatest difficulty. The danger in his idea – taken seriously by many – is that it could lead to a 'circling of the Atlantic wagons' and make conflict with, for example, Islam or China or even Japan, inevitable. He ignores the progress already made towards a global community based on democracy, which already includes both established and aspiring democracies in all continents and provides the basis for *Pax Democratica*, a potentially durable world order based on universal values.

WON'T ICD BYPASS, AND WEAKEN, THE EUROPEAN UNION?

The people of North America share with us the same cultural background. In setting up their societies they have been guided by the same concepts of the leading thinkers of our world who have also determined our structures . . . The 'European House' is no home for us: We belong in the 'Atlantic House'.
                                   De Telegraaf, Amsterdam, January 1990

A larger union of democracies will thwart the great project of European union. This is one of the most serious arguments for not changing present arrangements. The ICD supposedly questions an amazing enterprise of community-building which has been undertaken over several decades, with tremendous effort and to great effect, in western Europe. The Europeans have made considerable progress in creating their own 'United States of Europe'. Let them complete this (goes the argument) and only when that has been done, form some durable 'partnership' with the United States. Together, this formidable transatlantic partnership would then gradually be able to sort out any major world problem. But if the other democracies of North America, east Asia and Australasia were to press ahead with the

ICD before Europe's union is complete (say the Europhile critics), would this not decrease the potential importance of Europe, weaken the EU and greatly discomfit at least some of its members?

Answer: Perhaps, but this case is a lot weaker than it was a couple of decades ago. The global economy and the world political stage have become much more complex and demanding of the now-inextricably interdependent democracies than in the 1950s and 1960s. Regionalism for North America, Japan, South Korea, Australia and New Zealand, as well as for Europe, is now outdated. The economic world of the coming century is seamless by comparison with anything that went before. The stakes of the various advanced democracies in a workable, peaceful world are therefore now virtually indistinguishable. This is not a question of what we might *like*; it is simply a fact. A suitable integrative framework for the world's most interdependent economies is a must.

Some psychological losses for Europe may be involved in moving rapidly to construction of an ICD which in key respects will supersede the EU. Europe will not itself become an independent superstate on a par with the USA or other potential superpowers, as many of its ardent advocates – Americans as well as Europeans – once hoped. But whether or not this was ever a good idea, is European superstatus now achievable? The considered answer must be: No, and less and less will this be so. Europeans are now bumping up against the political limits of their plan for Union. These limits are imposed by residual national feelings, fears of inevitable German dominance, the political and financial impossibility of creating a truly autonomous common defence force complete with nuclear arms, and the obvious inadequacy of regional economic steps in the face of the headlong pace of economic globalism. What good is it, for example, to carefully craft a European patent system or a vast set of product standards for Europe alone, if commerce and industry among the most advanced nations are now virtually global in scope? Even the huge American market is now so intertwined in the global system that it cannot return to continentalism – even if its people wished. NAFTA can be nothing but a way station to global free trade.

Some further examples of the limits of European supranationalism: The Germans persuaded the other Europeans, in the Maastricht Treaty which deepened EU ties (1992), that a common money and central bank were necessities for Europe.[8] By 1995 it had become evident that many European countries feared this would mean

German control of their economies. Also, opinion polls showed that a preponderance of Germans would probably not want to give up their stable, cherished Deutschmark for a more inflation-prone all-European currency under (they believed) looser supranational control. Monetary unification has been put off to the end of the century, and now seems likely to take place for most EU powers. However, monetary union with a larger group of the most stable, advanced economies might become a good deal easier – indeed essential – than if confined artificially to Europe. And if a common currency is truly necessary for Europe, then by definition it must also be good for a larger number of highly-developed economies.[9]

Not just in monetary affairs do the principal powers – Germany, France, Britain – show a measure of distrust of one another sufficient to stop European amalgamation. While additional mini-steps towards economic unification, well-begun over 40 years, still seem possible, the big *political* steps necessary to provide a central executive power to oversee a common monetary system, foreign policy and military establishment now seem much further away than ever . . . and receding beyond the political horizon. Because the union of Europe has been proceeding *voluntarily* and democratically, a development historically without precedent, no single power – not even today's more powerful Germany – could, or even would, *compel* union. Empires, one trusts, are finally out of style in Europe. But there is simply not yet the high degree of mutual trust that is required to proceed much further with voluntary union.

Another reason why Europe cannot complete its union is more fundamental. This lies in the inherent structural contradictions of European political, economic and security arrangements as they developed after the onset of the Cold War. The principal institutions which 'did the job' have been: European Union (initially, 'Communities'), the North Atlantic Treaty Organization, the Council of Europe, Western European Union (WEU) and the Organization for Economic Cooperation and Development (OECD). As the dimensions of the Cold War became apparent, initially it was thought that Europe could provide the military strength to balance off the USSR through the Brussels Pact (1948; transmuted into WEU in 1954). The North Atlantic Treaty (1949) was required to bring the power of the United States into the alliance to secure Europe. When the Korean War started (1950) European and American observers believed that more than a paper treaty was needed to make Allied resolve credible: major US forces would have to be stationed in Europe and the new Federal Republic of Germany would have to be rearmed, the latter truly a formidable undertaking politically. The US nuclear guarantee and permanent stationing of major US forces in Europe constituted the ultimate shield for these political-military developments, and for all aspects of community building, including the economic burgeoning of the Old Continent.

The first European Community – for Coal and Steel (1952) – was launched more or less simultaneously with the general political and military efforts to amalgamate Europe because the founder, Jean Monnet, believed that an international pooling of these once-vital industries into a single market was a good way to get the Germans and French to bury their ancient enmities for good. In the minds of the founders, the economic advantages were purely secondary.[10] Other communities, one for atomic energy and another embracing a full common market, were brought into being (1958) as a substitute for proposals which proved too bold for the French to accept, i.e. a European Defence Community and a European Political Community. These latter would have been truly momentous steps towards a full European federation. The US government of the day backed these ideas enthusiastically but, when political and military union proved impossible, settled for Europe's economic union. Successive US administrations accepted a certain amount of trade discrimination from the new integrated Europe for over-riding political reasons, i.e. Western security solidarity. When the defence community project failed, another way, through Western European Union (WEU), was found to rearm Germany and bring it into NATO.

Thus, by 1958 and the height of the Cold War, the management of Europe's common affairs – in which the United States had become inextricably entwined – were bifurcated: the three European Communities became the heart of Europe's economic management, with lots of US advice and cooperation but no direct participation; NATO, accompanied by WEU as a powerless but politically important bit of face-saving, provided for Europe's defence. In guaranteeing Europe's *security*, the Americans were by far the senior partners, and seldom silent ones. But no one took very seriously after the late 1950s the idea that the North Atlantic, not just Europe, was the proper scope for a large *economic* union. Nor – conversely – did anyone seriously propose that Europe should really undertake its own defence by itself.

Among other things, a full European defence system would have required a substantial all-European nuclear force, independent of the United States, directed by a European political authority, and capable of providing its own integrated, credible deterrent to Soviet power ... i.e. at least approaching the scale of the superpowers' arsenals. The Europeans have never been willing to pay for this, and no one wanted it anyway. More than any other single factor, this has ensured that a European union would never be a super-power on the order of the United States. And this is still the case.

In the 1990s, as – on the one hand – the European Communi-ties were dubbed a Union and further stages of economic unifica-tion were initiated fitfully, and – on the other hand – the Cold War wound down and NATO's future and the possibility of a Eu-ropean foreign and security policy and independent European force were more actively discussed but so far rejected, it has become increasingly clear that the limits to a true United States of Europe have been reached. (For a glaring example, one need only look at the inability of Europe, and specifically the EU, to resolve the Yugoslav crisis from 1991 to 1995.) As we approach the new cen-tury, it seems highly unlikely that this state of European affairs will change, even though there may be a 'euro' and some enlarge-ment of the single market eastward is no doubt on the cards. The widening of the EU is thus likely, but not any substantial deepen-ing, at least for a fairly long time to come.

The dangers of the EU process stalling are, however, very great. Seldom in history do major projects of political reform stay on dead centre once they have come to a standstill; a reversion to old patterns becomes inevitable. How can one move forward, regain momentum? Without foreign policy and military union, and even with monetary union, the EU may continue to enjoy the benefits of free trade for some time but the old particularisms are bound to grow. France will likely become more fearful of Germany and more keen to recapture the shadows of lost glory; Britain will try to insulate itself from the integration process as much as ever and look across the seas to an old American connection which is no longer there, or to comparably nebulous Commonwealth ties; the German people, who had hoped overwhelmingly to bury their past in an indissoluble federal future with their neighbours, will be forced once more to play out the role of the single greatest Euro-pean power in the centre of it all, facing unsurely both East and West. The support of the United States for a united Europe – loose and German-dominated, something different than earlier envisaged – must then inevitably fade. Even though nation-states are now truly an anachronism, everyone in such circumstances will no doubt have one more try at the billiard-ball system of 'vital national interests', ghostly 'sovereignties' and the balance of power. Back to the Europe of Bismarck or, worse yet, to that of Kaiser Wilhelm II, or perhaps to something now unimaginable but even worse.

Russia's future course must also be considered. The European powers could never welcome huge Russia into fullfledged EU membership, even if her democratic and free market evolution remained on track. However, with the United States, Japan and other stable democracies fully part of a larger ICD system based on EU principles and experience, there would be a logical place for a modern Russia at the table. But if an EU were shorn of its close links to the US and unwilling to bring Russia into its union, then troubles and dangers would become manifold, in the Far East as well as in Europe. And back again we would go, by still another route, to old-fashioned Phase Two balance-of-power politics.

There is a further, politico-philosophical question: Was a European superstate, a huge new nation, ever a good idea, or what the founders intended? Jean-Marie Guéhenno contends it was not: 'Europe defined itself by its ambition of universality [extension of democratic values], and it cannot abandon this ambition without betraying itself'.[11] By the same token, an ICD should not be thought of as simply a new nation-state, written even larger; it would be yet again something new under the sun, never-finished and always enlarging to realize its universal values.

Therefore, the response to the question, 'Won't the ICD stop the essential European process of unification?' has to be: *Only* an ICD can now preserve what EU has already gained, and make possible the further gains it has always hoped for. Europe's pioneering steps towards unity are *the* model upon which – indeed, *around* which – to now build the larger Intercontinental Community of Democracies, the 21st century's *Pax Democratica*. It is not necessary to dismantle European Union; one should go on improving the EU but make it part of something even greater. To go forward, Europe should become part – a truly indispensable part – of a great experiment that is even more breathtaking than its own successful effort to change the world from 1950 to 1990: the next stage in the history of democracy.

THE UNITED STATES WILL BE DIVERTED FROM URGENT DOMESTIC PRIORITIES

... if it attempts such a far-reaching international scheme, goes the next *Argument*. And so will other democracies which should be involved; every nation has many serious problems at home to attend to. Besides, the present crop of leaders and their publics demonstrate flagging willingness to undertake international tasks. In short, there is no 'political will' to bring about a truly durable and effective world order.

Answer, especially for Americans: Just as World War II ironically raised the United States from a ten-year slough of economic despond to heights of international achievement, and just as the Marshall Plan and the protection of US vital interests in Europe through NATO demanded an outpouring of US creativity and money ... and thereby invigorated the nation ... so a great new international challenge in the 21st century would call forth undoubted American reserves and moral purpose. To ask Americans and their rich democratic allies to begin laying the firm basis for a radically improved, more peaceful, more humane, more prosperous and enduring world order is something simultaneously to fire imaginations and allay many contemporary doubts and fears. The democratic peoples can all rise above petty squabbling over fanciful limited resources to resolve our own problems *in the process of* getting the world safely through a dangerous period ahead, in a great common effort. Furthermore, they will save money in a closer defence union; still more will be saved as the world becomes gradually more peaceful and predictable.

Ronald Steel, a strong partisan of the narrow approach to American interests, is one of those who argues that the United States must first give attention to its domestic social problems if it wishes to be a respected international citizen.[12] Steel and others fail to understand that not only will we lose our own freedoms in the long term if we fail to protect the freedoms of others – with the places to make a stand, to be sure, judiciously chosen – but that many of our most critical 'domestic' problems can no longer be addressed successfully unless we (and our likeminded partners) understand the need for doing so in concert. An excellent example is the problem of unemployment and related social and economic dislocations attendant on the near-total interpenetration of the world's economies in the Knowledge Revolution. Especially among the advanced nations, the distinction between 'domestic' and 'international' economies is now irretrievably dissolving.

Finally, one must point out that the United States is not a nation like any other. For the bulk of this century, we have been the strongest in all respects, if at times our strength was not fully mobilized because of domestic irresolution. As the new century approaches, the United States is the only superpower and, in the light of new knowledge about the true weaknesses of the old Soviet Union, has been so for the past 50 years. A superpower – especially one like the US which seeks to preserve its moral dignity as well as its power – is not entitled to the same range of egocentric behaviour as a middling nation, such as France under de Gaulle. If the President and Congress, for example, had decided in 1995, after four years of indecision, that after all Bosnia was not worth the bones of a single US infantryman (paraphrasing Bismarck and Pomeranian grenadiers), there would have been no power capable or willing to pick up the Balkan pieces afterwards. The Europeans might have again tried, as might the Russians . . . or the Serbians after another long and bitter war. But in the end, after the failure of European diplomacy and UN peacekeeping, it was the United States alone which could provide the manpower, technological, logistical, communications, and command and control systems, plus the overwhelming reality of its great political and economic power, necessary for decisive Allied intervention.[13]

The calculation to intervene in Bosnia was not a straightforward calibration, à la Ronald Steel, of America's vital national interest in the traditional sense, but an overall and complex conclusion that the historic American interest in Europe's peace was at stake, that the credibility of the 45-year American commitment to NATO and the community of which it is the shield and chief symbol was at stake, and that by extension US commitments to peace and security all over the world and to the UN system itself were *also* at stake. Intervention in Bosnia represented US recognition of the extent to which the *common interest* of the entire community of free countries were entirely congruent with *its own* interests – to an even greater extent than for any of the other vitally concerned participants. Regardless of the historical and quasi-legal conditions surrounding Bosnia and Yugoslavia (and they were dire matters), the United States in the end had to intervene.[14]

This Bosnian incident alone illustrates, as history will no doubt show, that the United States does not enjoy the comfortable op-

tion of standing aside when its closest allies, the future of the democratic community and its vital interests, the principles of respect
for human rights, and the European geopolity for which so much
American blood has been spilt in this century are all in serious
danger.

DOESN'T AN ICD IMPLY UNDERCUTTING THE UN?

Answer: The UN and its agencies suffer from inherent weaknesses
which goodwill and more effort can hardly repair. Like the EU,
the UN has begun to bump up against its political limits. Although
it is for the most part bloated, inefficient and cost-ineffective, trying to do too much and succeeding too seldom, the United Nations
as a world forum nevertheless is indispensable. It is the one universal body where every nation, no matter what the character of
its government, can have its say. In many peripheral fields, such as
world health, agricultural development, cultural and educational
interchanges, and the care of refugees, the UN family of Third
Phase organizations does work that no other body or individual
nation could or would do. And often the cooperation of inadequate
or even evil governments must be importuned in order to get humanitarian assistance to the wretched; who can or would do this if
there were no UN?

Also, some nations are delinquent in their dues for the UN budget,
cavalier and negligent in their responsibilities. Despite the need
for UN reform, it ill behooves such countries to criticize the poor
weak reed that serves as a surrogate for a strong world political
community that the nations are unwilling to endow with real powers.

These things said, the structural inadequacies and severe limits
of the UN system must still be acknowledged. Some things could
be changed for the better, but the UN cannot manage major security
issues regardless of how much reorganization or tinkering takes
place. It has shown over 50 years that it is unable to handle big
conflicts involving major powers, or indeed any of the challenges
of peacekeeping or peacemaking that might involve fighting. This
is not because the Secretary General or his staff have been pusillanimous or incompetent, but because with 184 members, each with
one vote, the resolution of the world's common political affairs – if
some of them could indeed be resolved – is inevitably reduced to a
lowest common denominator. It is true that in a few cases, after

long inaction and millions of democides, it became possible for the UN to intervene more or less successfully in Cambodia (1993–). Namibia and Mozambique may also be counted as UN successes. But these are exceptions; Haiti, Rwanda, Burundi, Zaire, Somalia and other troublespots bode ill for UN security operations. Yet, in the absence of a better mechanism, the UN and its Security Council remain indispensable; things may not be good but without the UN they would be worse.

Because the UN is not based on democratic principles, a good 40 percent of its members (all non-democracies) pay only lip-service, if that, to its Charter of Human Rights. The UN can hold conferences on the rights of man, but it has no powers of compulsion. It is a talk-shop, not a Phase Four organization with powers of its own. Thinking again of democracy and the UN 'constitution': if every country, no matter what its domestic standards or size, has an equal vote in the UN, not too much can be expected of that body. The lowest common denominator of decisions, plus the same weight in voting for Bhutan and the Seychelles as for France or Japan, makes for public indifference, if not disgust, with the UN process.

Can this situation be changed? Probably not much, by means currently employed or contemplated, such as management studies. But something might be done if the credible democracies were to organize a *Democratic Caucus* (see Chapter 8) within and alongside the UN. Chapter 6 lists more than 70 countries with a commitment to democracy that should be involved with the building of an Intercontinental Community of Democracies. All are members of the United Nations, with permanent delegations in New York. A caucus of these delegations could meet as often as necessary to consider major issues before the General Assembly and the Security Council. The caucus would provide a forum to develop and express a consensus of the democracies on important questions, to muster a comparable vote and strong influence, and to back up by all means available the UN actions of which it approved.

Over the next 30 years or so, reform of the UN and its agencies should be sought determinedly by the democracies. The UN should be strongly supported in the things that it can and must do. As ICD efforts would tend continuously to enlarge the number of functioning democracies in the world, so should the membership and influence of the ICD's Caucus in the UN increase proportionately. One could hope that the democratic way of life would more and more become the international norm, and that Third Phase inter-governmental organizations, such as the UN group, could eventually begin to take on Fourth Phase attributes, and thus democratic characteristics. But no responsible democracy, on the other hand, could countenance qualified or supermajority voting practices until it were sure that the overwhelming preponderance of participants were democracies – each governed by democracy's principles, protecting the civil rights of its own people and fully representative of its electorate.

In time, following such a strategy might well cause the ICD and the United Nations quite naturally to grow together, rationalizing their joint structures and serving the world in a system of democratic institutions and practices. I say 'in time'; this might take decades or centuries. Yet this long-range goal, which has a good chance of becoming reality if the democracies remain resolute and unified, should be better than simply trying to patch up the UN system the way it is. The Intercontinental Community of Democracies, growing like coral by accretion and able eventually to represent and mobilize for the common good the vast majority of the world's peoples – those who will have modernized sufficiently to accept democratic responsibilities as well as privileges – is surely the best hope to pursue.

Unfortunately, the peoples and governments of some key countries are quite fed up with the UN as the century draws to a close. These feelings may not be justified and the actions of some governments – such as the United States, which in the late 1990s had UN dues arrears reaching into the hundreds of millions – seem unfair and counterproductive. But if the UN appears increasingly unable to manage big world crises, then the major nations responsible must arrange other ways of dealing with them. In 1995, this was the conclusion to which the NATO countries came with respect to the burning fires of former Yugoslavia; the UN was asked to step aside for a force, under NATO, organized more on Phase Four lines and run by clearly likeminded countries. In future comparable cases, an ICD developing along lines explained in the next chapter, will probably be the main answer – if not always the only one.

ISN'T AN EVEN FREER GLOBAL ECONOMY LIKELY TO RUIN THE RICH WEST?

Argument: The dislocations of the Third Industrial Revolution – the Knowledge Economy – are forcing workers in the developed democracies, including Japan, out of well-paying jobs, wrecking the welfare state and spoiling hard-earned gains, as trade and investment barriers around the world are reduced. This causes enough disruption as freer trade progresses (with great difficulty, sometimes) just among the advanced economies, but opening up to less developed economies, such as Mexico under NAFTA, or North Africa or eastern Europe through accords with the EU, or half-developed Pacific nations through APEC – and to all nations under WTO accords – is making these changes even more disruptive for rich economies and for individual working families.

These critics will further argue that an ICD, necessarily embracing free trade, will increase these risks. Even within the highly-developed OECD group, differences in productivity, the social difficulties of rationalizing agriculture and computerized investment pools which slosh instantly across borders to maximize returns already conspire to lower standards of living and harm established ways of life. If an ICD means building a strong new – but even more open – global economy, we want no part of it, say these critics. Time to put up barriers, not lower them. In short, those who believe that such measures cost them or their neighbours jobs or profits are truly frightened.

The Answers to all such arguments point in the same direction, viz.: (1) the potential gains of freer trade – based on past experience – fully justify some risks; (2) the rich democracies will weather the storms of adjustment much better if they coordinate their approach; (3) trade and investment in developing countries play only a small role in labour market tensions in the developed democracies; (4) the global economy is coming whether we like it or not, so we'd better make it work to the advantage of all rather than just sit back and let the devil take the hindmost. Finally, (5) the failure to go forward together and fully exploit the tremendous new economic possibilities of a more open world will condemn both the rich *and* the poor to ruinous zero-sum games that could lead to world depression, or even in some cases to armed conflict.

Addressing the November 1993 conference of the Asia Pacific Economic Cooperation (APEC) forum, President Clinton said: 'If

American investment creates two new jobs in Indonesia, that will mean one more new job in America.' The opportunities for the mature economies to create more wealth lie not only at home, but even more in the rapidly developing corners of the world, where not only new industries are being created but great new markets as well. The markets take time, but the history of world trade expansion in the past half-century confirms that the two go together. In a recent book, Bill Gates incisively made the case for freeing trade:

> The economy is a vast interconnected system in which any resource that is freed up becomes available to another area of the economy that finds it most valuable. Each time a job is made unnecessary, the person who was filling that job is freed to do something else. The net result is that more gets done, raising the overall standard of living in the long run.[15]

The impediments to world-wide trade, especially tariff levels, have been steadily reduced through a 40-year series of GATT negotiations. GATT – now the World Trade Organization – has a new mandate to reduce non-tariff barriers to trade and investment, and new powers to adjudicate trade disputes. GATT's accomplishments have been a major spur to world-wide economic growth, better standards of living and higher incomes.

The experience within the European Union's single market – involving not only free trade but free flows of capital and labour – over its 40 years of development also tell us something. Around the EU's single geographic market a succession of arrangements to improve trade among neighbours has taken place; this has also impelled countries not yet full members of the EU to accept restrictions on their economies in return for full benefits. West European standards of living and economic growth have taken off in ways that could never have been imagined before 1950.

The North American Free Trade Area (NAFTA) has succeeded in reducing trade barriers impressively among Canada, Mexico and the United States, even though the collapse of the *peso* in early 1995 slowed the process. APEC countries around the Pacific Rim have accepted a general commitment to lower tariffs to zero in a few years, with dispensations for less-developed members. ASEAN and Mercosur make similar projections. Much remains to be done, but the general liberating trend is clear.

In recent years, however, putting these kinds of regional and global trade deals together has gotten increasingly sticky. Some side-effects of the new Knowledge/Communications Revolution have slowed growth (or at least our ability to measure it) and created unforeseen complications. Additionally, the effects of the powerful oil-supply-led and Vietnam War inflations of the 1970s took many years to squeeze out of the world economy. The economies of western Europe, in particular, are not as flexible as that of the United States or as single-mindedly directed and neo-mercantilist as that of Japan; therefore Europeans have felt the pulls of protectionism and the supposed 'export of jobs' even before the United States and Japan. But with the negotiation of the NAFTA treaty, the supposed loss of jobs to the Far East, to Mexico and the rest of Latin America became a major US political issue. There are parallel fears in Europe of freeing trade with former Communist states on the EU's eastern borders. European unemployment levels have risen – in some countries to a socially dangerously point – during the 1990s.

The downsizing of many companies in the Western world and Japan, plus worries about the growing burdens of the welfare state, have given workforces – now white-collar voters as well as blue – a strong sense of insecurity. Nor are domestic economies in the industrialized democracies producing the results that consumers and workers had gotten used to from 1950 to 1990. Furthermore, the public debt incurred in four decades of Cold War is still being carried in many countries, requiring high taxes to pay interest – money that could otherwise be invested in economic expansion.

Voters in the West, understandably, find much to complain about. Against this discontent, proposals to drop trade barriers still further – and especially to lower them for the goods of low-wage developing countries – encounter strong resistance. But the world is undergoing a major economic transformation, akin to the impact of the printing press, the steam engine, the telephone and telegraph, railways (these comprising the First Industrial Revolution); and the automobile, the assembly line, interchangeable parts, and the airplane (the Second) on people's lives and their interconnections. This time, led by the computer into the global knowledge revolution (the Third), the dislocations are much more rapid, more widespread and more highly publicized. However, there is no resisting these changes, just as the Luddites could not stop the first industrial revolution by smashing weaving machines. But it is easy to understand such feelings.

Some statistics that might help further to illustrate our situation: in 1994 the United States economy produced the equivalent, measured in (constant) dollar value, in manufactured goods that it did in 1965. But in 1994, it did this with only *15 percent* of the US workforce, as against *one-quarter* of the workforce in 1965. That demonstrates the tremendous gains in productivity and in living standards as well, in those 30 years. By 2005, the share of manufacturing jobs will drop to 12 percent, by 2015 to around 8 percent. In other words, many fewer people are needed to produce the same amount of manufactured goods; by comparison with the impact of technological change on manufacturing, the impact of foreign job competition is minor.[16]

Seen from another perspective, Harvard's Robert Z. Lawrence has pointed out that '[B]etween 1979 and 1989 . . . the 2.7 percent annual rise in output per work-hour in US manufacturing was exactly the same as the rate between 1955 and 1973', when average incomes in the United States were doubling, as they had every 35 years for a hundred years. Because of productivity improvements in manufacturing, it has required fewer and fewer workers to produce the same amount of goods; the percentage of the US GDP derived from manufacturing has not varied for decades, and the displaced workers have gone into the service industries. 'The primary reason for the declining share in manufacturing employment in the United States is relatively rapid productivity growth, not foreign trade.'[17]

Similar trends are taking place in other highly-industrialized economies. Another set of figures, this time from France and representative of most west European countries: in 1960, 25 percent of the French workforce lived and worked on farms; in the 1990s, the figure is around 8 percent and still dropping. What are all those 'displaced workers' now doing – those 'unemployed farmers' and factory workers? Answer: In most cases, working in service industries or in the new higher-tech industries that didn't even exist in 1960.

An anecdote: Around 1990, an 'American' firm named Hitachi brought suit before the US International Trade Commission against another American firm, Burroughs Inc. Hitachi said that office machines Burroughs was manufacturing in southeast Asia (with lower labour costs) were being 'dumped' unfairly on the US market, and competing with similar office machines that Hitachi (Japanese-owned but *incorporated, manufacturing, operating and marketing in the US*) was making in its US plants! Strange, but true. This case, no doubt replicated in its essentials in at least every highly-developed country many times over, is an accurate symbol of what is happening to everyday products (and services too) that consumers in the West are used to. What, one may ask, now are imports and what are exports?

The world's economies are thus hopelessly inextricable, more interdependent than the ordinary voter could imagine. This is difficult to understand. *However, free trade and investment is the essence of the coming, interlocked world, and its main economic hope for the future,* just as they have enriched earlier ages. Boiling the argument down to essentials: If Country A's industries produce *widgets* with high efficiency, but a re-tooled industry could add even more value by making *gadgets* instead, then if lower-wage Country B can make the widgets, and Country A instead sells its new gadgets to B and many others ... both countries' workers and consumers will be better off. Economists in abundance have made this case for 'comparative advantage'[18] over the years.

As the new century approaches, there are problems in freeing trade, however, that were not thought about a generation ago. Protecting the environment, which is managed by different rules country-to-country, with the less-well-off nations usually following poorer conservation practices, is one. Questions of differing labour standards and social practices are also increasingly important as markets are globalized. These and other not strictly economic matters were taken into account, for example, in the NAFTA Treaty of 1993; Mexico especially must improve its working conditions and environmental standards. All parties to freer trade agreements make adjustments, and transition arrangements are usually necessary, but in the long run all benefit. The European Union, over four decades of such adjustments, has shown that when countries once poor, such as Portugal or Greece, entered the common market, everyone gained.

There is a further consideration, broader than economics. It was best expressed by Henry R. Nau in the *Wall Street Journal* (26 August 1993):

> trade policies are not just about jobs. They are about creating an atmosphere of openness and freedom that enables reforming countries to find their own way peacefully toward greater prosperity and pluralism. If the old democracies fragment over trade issues, the new democracies will surely fall.

The nub of the problem of spreading the fruits of productivity growth seems to lie in the service industries – which today account for about 80 percent of America's total output. Services productivity has grown markedly slower than in manufacturing. Here, not in foreign competition, lies the primary challenge: 'The real problem has been the failure of producers in services to apply these [new] technologies in ways that raise productivity'.[19] In the US, these dislocations have led to declining real wages for middle- and lower-income workers; in Europe, the problem manifests itself in increasing unemployment. Slower economic growth, all over the developed world, has brought problems, but these will no doubt be resolved when economies and societies have adjusted to the new conditions of the Knowledge Revolution, and especially have found ways to restore high levels of productivity in the services sector.

But the advanced nations – Nau's 'old democracies' – will also have to ask themselves a more profound question: what happens in a society in which labour-saving devices have reduced drastically the requirements for what we used to think of as meaningful work, when demand can be satisfied with a small part of the workforce? Social service, further education and other constructive leisure activities for many, re-defined and compensated, might be a partial answer.[20] Meanwhile, freer trade is not our culprit and in fact should continue to expand because it helps consumers and opens new markets everywhere.

The message? Voters in the affluent democracies should not panic when they face the economic world of tomorrow, but instead support party platforms and individual political leaders who understand the inexorable globalization of everyone's economies, who see Nau's connection between trade and an open, free world, who wish to to re-fashion advanced societies, and who are prepared to work with neighbours, especially the likeminded, to create gradually a minimum but workable framework of commercial, industrial and investment rules to make the playing field not only as free, but also as fair, as possible.

It is vital for leaders of thought and action to explain to publics the tremendous (and more than offsetting) opportunities ahead, and to smooth the way towards taking advantage of them. As they undertake these tasks of public education, could leaders also think through – again – the doctrines which must underlie the changing free enterprise economy, including 'a more human face for capitalism',[21] i.e. an advanced society based on Love, as well as Law and Power?

QUESTION: WON'T AN ICD LEAD TO 'WORLD
GOVERNMENT', A BAD THING?

Critics in several countries say, of Fourth Phase arrangements when
proposed, 'Doesn't this imply "world government" and "loss of
sovereignty" for the nation?'
  'World government' – with powers approaching those of a typi-
cal nation-state – is a chimera. Theoretically, a universal government could solve a lot of problems that spill over borders. Practically,
it is an impossibility. If it ever comes about, it is centuries if not
millennia away; in our time this cannot be foreseen or hastened.
Handfuls of good people, some quite zealous, in many countries
believe that only a world federal constitution, along the lines of
that of the US, will 'save' us. If one only regards the 200 or so
extremely varied nation-states that not only would have to agree
to such a plan but be capable of carrying it out, the inherent
inachievability of a world government becomes immediately obvious. An ICD's goals are much more modest: to achieve a beginning unity of planning and execution of around two dozen likeminded
democratic peoples to attack together a limited but extremely important set of international problems that none of them – not even
the United States – can resolve on its own, and gradually to involve more and more younger democracies to work with them.
  Such an ICD, some will say, involves 'giving up sovereignty' to a
supranational body. This is a more serious argument, insofar as
'sovereignty' can be inherent in a *state*. But the concept of sovereignty itself must be defined. Political theorists and legal experts
do not agree on the meaning of the term.[22] In the 18th century the
theory of federalism was put forward to contradict that of sovereignty. In modern Western democracies, there seems to be a widespread conviction that all government rests on consent and that
the *people* are sovereign. Modern theories of democracy could hardly
countenance a contrary idea; if so, then what is at stake in the
formation of an ICD is not the 'sovereignty' for example, of the
states of France, the United States or Japan, but the sovereignty of
the French *people,* the American *people* and the Japanese *people*.
No democratic people can 'lose sovereignty' unless they choose
voluntarily to give all their rights and powers to a dictator. But
they can share their sovereignty with likeminded partners.
  Voters in the big countries – the USA, Germany, France, Japan,

the UK – tend most to fear the loss of independence. Some Americans labour additionally under the illusion that their country could and should 'go it alone'.

In Europe, the case for sacrificing independent powers of decision in building a continent-sized market where there was none, was generally accepted more than 40 years ago. But now, even in the big countries of western Europe, further steps towards economic integration, such as a common currency and central bank, find doubters. In security matters – such as the breakup of Yugoslavia in the 1990s – the European Union nations saw the need for an integrated foreign policy, tried it, but still couldn't manage because politicians and voters perceived differring 'national interests', in most cases illusory but grounded in history. It remains exceedingly difficult for Europeans, especially in the biggest countries, to make the leap to full Fourth Phase relations among states.

Japan is even further behind the Atlantic countries; some of its politicians understand political and economic interdependence, as do a good many of its public servants, especially diplomats and businessmen who live and work abroad. A few major industrialists such as Akio Morita, founder of Sony, appreciate the ineluctable requirements of interdependence acutely.[23] Japan's Prime Minister, Ryutaro Hashimoto, and President Bill Clinton upgraded the security ties between their countries somewhat in April 1996 and again in 1997. But in general, most Japanese still are mentally 'freeloaders' who cling to the idea that they can do the minimum and still take advantage of the international system that the West built and into which it welcomed them after World War II. This attitude is changing, probably not fast enough, but the Japanese people have shown that ultimately they know how to face facts, if sometimes with agonizing deliberation.

But it is in the United States that the political class and a fair percentage of the electorate, plus many of the talk show rabble-rousers, still cling to the idea that the US can go it alone if need be . . . that we should cooperate with our likeminded Allies only when it suits us. Critics of multilateralism aver that the US should basically make its own decisions and carry them out unilaterally when necessary. Such unilateralist attitudes are perhaps not those of a majority – yet – but they are held by enough people so that unscrupulous politicians can express them publicly with impunity and sometimes gain votes thereby. A variant of this attitude is a return to isolationism, which is patently impossible but that does not prevent many US minds from entertaining a withdrawal from – a denial of – the world.

An influential group of more sophisticated Americans look at the world and accept close and cooperative arrangements currently in place with America's allies, but maintain that in today's world there is still no substitute for the traditional balance-of-power/national interest system. So – by perhaps a more tortuous route and with more effort to 'bring along' the Allies – these 'realists' reach substantially the same conclusion as the unilateralists, i.e. that America must go it alone when it *has* to, when 'the chips are down', that pragmatism should be the first touchstone of our diplomacy, and so on. But in the view of these realist pundits and decision-makers, the chips seldom *are* down. They believe that unless American 'vital interests' – defined as countering a direct attack on the United States or an ally to which we are legally (and narrowly) bound by treaty or as protecting overseas resources, such as oil, on which we depend – are at stake, we should husband our power parsimoniously, and especially not get too bound up in entangling arrangements with other countries, even if they are – more or less – old friends. The views of the situation in the former Yugoslavia between 1991 and the summer of 1995 were preponderantly of this ilk among US foreign policy makers and the political class generally. Henry Kissinger's opinions have remained, for a generation, the most prominent example of the realist approach.[24] This path to policy leaves a great deal – in fact, too much – to be desired.

There is yet another – more extreme – strand of contemporary American thought that must also be taken seriously. This is the emotional and dangerously unthinking view of large numbers of American rank and file voters, gathering force with the uncertainty of the post-Cold War period, who believe that the UN is a dangerous conspiracy that threatens their nation. The radical populist form of this view is that of the so-called 'militias' and other right-wing, closed-minded paranoids. Such attitudes are usually part of a more complex bundle of general suspicions about government; in 1996 national polls showed about one-quarter of Americans as 'deeply distrustful' of government, including the relatively feeble institutions of international cooperation.

More and more, Americans seem to be turning their attention inward and assuming that 'outward' will take care of itself. We begrudge, more and more, the development aid given to less fortunate countries. We fail to pay our UN dues. We penny-pinch our diplomatic and information services overseas, dangerously. Congress, more and more, reflects these views and in some cases leads in their propagation.

Older Americans lived through history – the Cold War, Korea, and in some cases World War II; most of these people understand our situation from personal experience. In recent generations, something has gone wrong with our educational system, broadly defined to include the ubiquitous TV as well as schools. For example, a sizeable majority of US highschoolers recently professed not to know of the American Civil War (1861–65) but also hadn't even heard of the Cold War! In a world flooded by 'news' and information, it is easy to think that Americans are 'well-informed'. But if our citizens have no historical basis for filtering the information which washes over them daily or – even worse – if they simply don't bother about world affairs – it is easy to postulate an increasing number of American voters who are either apathetic, complacent or terribly frightened to the point of paranoia by gross misinterpretations of the world situation. This serious defect is one that only US political leaders with courage and integrity, media moguls and the purveyors who work for them, and – especially – educators can remedy.

Unfortunately, the creation of a better world order is so urgent and demanding that we cannot wait for the process of long-term reform in education to bring about the necessary change in public climate.

Over the years, I have discussed the concepts of this book with many political figures, academic experts and civic leaders in the great democracies. A goodly majority say they favour the creation of something like an ICD and a *Pax Democratica*, but some sceptically question whether or not 'our leaders have the political will to take such far-reaching steps'. This is a 'chicken or egg' riddle: How can leaders act in such a major case unless the electorates are prodding them to do so? But how can the preponderance of voters be expected to understand the perilous times ahead and the need to take far-reaching action when they are not in possession of the facts? The obvious answer is that leaders of thought and action in the affected democracies will have to analyse our common situation, reach a consensus that spans borders, and convince heads of governments and other top political leaders that action is required. If heads of governments themselves are far-seeing and take the long-range view, then they can use their powers to educate the electorates. If they are not sufficiently percipient or courageous, then their advisers and broad groups of leadership in their countries – civil society – will have to convince and energize prime ministers, presidents and cabinets by going directly to the public, convincing them that intergovernmental institutions are too *weak*, not too strong.

Enlightened private citizens have a crucial role. Citizens' groups helped powerfully in the 'making of Europe', influential private bodies lobbied for passage of the North Atlantic Treaty, and – before the United States entered World War II – the prestigious Committee to Aid the Allies demonstrated how involved private and public partnerships of concerned citizens can help elected leaders change the public climate at crucial times.

THE CRITICS AND THE CONCEPT

Since the end of the Cold War, the chief democracies – electorates and leaders – have been floundering around, trying to understand the new outlines of the world challenge and what to do about it. It is the chief argument of this book that a truly Great Debate should begin soon. This book tries to set forth a concept with which to start: *Pax Democratica* and the purposeful evolution of Fourth Phase world order.

One might summarize the riposte to the critical views presented in this chapter thus: most of the arguments have at least some merit, but none are unanswerable. Instituting *Pax Democratica* will certainly require major adjustments – in important international institutions, in foreign policies of important countries and in public thinking everywhere. Leaders of international business for the most part understand the need for such adjustments, as they will clearly benefit. In particular, however, it will be the political classes of the participating countries – the elected officials and high civil servants, diplomats and military officers – who will be most affected by the creation of an ICD. The military of the NATO countries, in the process of building a credible Cold War deterrent, have already made most of the necessary mental and emotional adjustments; they work together smoothly in multinational harness. But it is particularly difficult for, say, national legislators to think about transferring some of their prerogatives to a multinational plane and to educate their electorates accordingly. And civil servants and diplomats simply fear they may lose their jobs, if some tasks are translated internationally.

There are always risks in any great enterprise such as *Pax Democratica*. But if one looks at what is at stake, and then at all the alternatives for action, including doing nothing and drifting, or pursuing a futile effort to transform the UN hastily, or tinkering at the edges of traditional diplomacy . . . one must conclude that the democracies have not only the opportunity, but the duty, to begin bringing a decent and workable degree of order to the world by engaging their peoples in a wide-ranging, gradual effort to integrate their most crucial and sensitive international undertakings . . . in other words, to gear up for a truly joint, Fourth Phase, approach to the world, on behalf of all its peoples.

How can this be done? That is the subject of the next chapter.

8 The Architecture of *Pax Democratica*

I consider our principal foreign policy challenge to be the main-
tenance and strengthening of the core of democracies which won
the Cold War.... It is going to be harder to keep this core
together when the inherent forces of multipolarity will conspire
to drive us apart. If, however, we want to avoid a return to the
dangerous balance of power politics which characterized the world
prior to the Cold War, we will have to strengthen the economic,
political, and military ties which link the Western democracies,
as well as the mutilateral institutions we have established over
the past half century. If we do not succeed in strengthening those
collective links and institutions, we will never be able to confront the instabilities now arising beyond the Western fold.

Secretary of State Lawrence S. Eagleburger, addressing the
Council on Foreign Relations, 7 January 1993,
New York City

Pax Democratica is a concept, likemindedness the precondition to
realizing the concept, and the Intercontinental Community of Democracies (ICD) a set of structures and working methods to implement the concept.

Pax Democratica denotes a world order strongly influenced and
eventually dominated by the ideals and practices of democracy, both
within countries and among them. In Chapter 6, about 70 democracies exhibiting varying degrees of likemindedness and experience
were proposed as keepers of the peace of democracy. Among these,
a core of around two dozen, enabled by their mature institutions,
developed human and material resources, and long experience in
working together, was suggested to begin building an ICD, the set
of institutions for making *Pax Democratica* operational. In the normal course of events, the other 50 (or so) democracies, at varying
speeds, should be able gradually to assume greater responsibilities
leading to full membership.

Recall the purposes of *Pax Democratica*:

1. Promote and consolidate the spread of democratic ideals and

146

practices, including the protection of human rights and the Rule of Law, among the peoples and nations of the world.

2. Extend the community of democracies, viz., bring all democracies into a common system of mutual help.

3. Oppose inter-state aggression; resist tyranny; help damp down violent conflict within states; reduce the spread of weapons of mass destruction and armaments generally; contain states which are a danger to international order and to their own peoples; make democide impossible; resist international terrorism and crime; and support other measures conducive to international stability, security and world order.

4. Give better form and rules to the global economy, in the process furthering free market systems, unfettered trade, international investment, monetary integration and harmonized economic policies, with the democracies as the core structure, open to all nations as they qualify. Mitigate commercial competition among the democracies, as required, to achieve the community's top priorities of promoting democracy and opposing aggression.

5. Protect the environment, assist economic development, further the broad distribution of prosperity and opportunities the world over, encourage population control, discourage disruptive migration, and otherwise promote the sustainability of the planet.

6. Strengthen the Rule of Law in world affairs; introduce democratic forms and practices into international institutions.

Bearing in mind that the democracies have already pioneered a number of bodies that try to address most of these aims, the architecture of *Pax Democratica*, embodied in an overarching Intercontinental Community of Democracies, is now logically the next agenda item. How could existing structures be re-configured, improved? What new ties, mechanisms and forms of interaction between peoples and nations will be required?

THE INTERCONTINENTAL COMMUNITY OF DEMOCRACIES

The relative paucity of working institutions is often overlooked when discussing international relations. In domestic society, institutions are so prevalent that we take them for granted, but in the global arena, there are really not that many, the United Nations and NATO being the most prominent. Without institutions, it's hard to get work done because all your consultations have to be done bilaterally; with an institution, you create a forum for consultation and can greatly expand cooperation.

James A. Baker, III[1]

Intercontinental Community of Democracies (ICD) is the proposed name for *a beginning, expandable framework agreement* among a number of key democratic *peoples*.

The treaty would state the founders' purposes, pledge members to work *gradually* for these, support important international processes now under way, and devise a set of linked, *integrated* institutions to make possible expeditious *joint planning, decision-making and action*. Some of these structures might begin with Third Phase characteristics, others straight off as Fourth Phase ventures, still others of mixed character. Signatories would commit themselves to the principle that all structures and working patterns would evolve gradually in the direction of Fourth Phase, democratically accountable institutions.

Several terms, italicized above, are cardinal:

A Framework, Beginning Gradually

Beginning and *framework* imply that one would start with essentials and a general agreement by around 70 democracies, then move on to make and implement detailed plans *gradually*. It is unlikely that ICD could, at the present juncture in world history, be created by means of some full-blown 'constitutional convention' at which the powers would at one leap transform their relations from inter-state to supranational. The experience of the American states in 1787, writing an unprecedented federal constitution in one summer, is almost surely not reproducible, even though Clarence Streit in the dark days of 1939–45 and again in the crises of 1947–53 believed that it could be done.[2] In 1940 Winston Churchill proposed union, with common citizenship and a united government, to France, but the offer came too late. In 1951–54, six west European countries tried to form an advanced form of political union embodied in treaties for a European Political Community and a European Defence Community, but even in those crisis years it proved too much for some parliaments. In contrast, the union of the United Kingdom has taken centuries. The Swiss Confederation began in the

13th century as a loose arrangement among three cantons, becoming a multi-ethnic federation only in 1848.

This suggests that a supranational community of the democracies can only develop *gradually*, especially in an environment that is generally (if wrongly) perceived to have few elements of crisis about it that would energize the constituent peoples to take dramatic steps. The ICD will come about through evolution, not through the strokes of a few pens on a finished constitution. Practical politics and the sociology of likemindedness, which requires time and trust to develop, dictate this.

Peoples, not only Nations

Earlier in this book, the importance of thoroughly involving *peoples*, not only governments, has been underscored. Because nation-states and nationalism itself are still strong, there will be resistance from bureaucrats and politicians, many of whom will fear that Fourth Phase measures might disemploy them. But at some advanced stage in the evolution of the ICD, it will become necessary to allow the will of the constituent peoples to supersede that of their governments. This was the profound meaning of the first words of the United States Constitution: 'We, the people, in order to form a more perfect union . . .'. For it is the sovereignty of the *peoples* and not of their parliaments or cabinets or political classes that is ultimately at issue. Observance of this essential principle can safely be left to the future, but it is important not to ignore it, even in the beginning.

Integration

Integration came into general usage in Euro-American politics and diplomacy in the 1950s, to describe the evolutionary process whereby postwar western Europe was to become a whole that would be greater than the sum of its individual constituent states. *Webster's Third New International Dictionary* refers to the process as that of a nation or smaller community 'forming into a more complete, harmonious, or coordinated entity' and among a group of nations, that of 'coming together . . . into a larger unity or group'.[3]

The political scientist Claude Ake explains:

> A political system is integrated to the extent that the minimal units (individual political actors) develop in the course of political interaction a pool of commonly accepted norms regarding political behavior and a commitment to the political behavior patterns legitimized by these norms.

Ake states further that in 'malintegrated political systems the emphasis is on effective rather than on legitimate means for pursuing political goals; in highly integrated political systems the emphasis is on legitimate rather than on effective means'.[4] This is indeed the heart of the matter: Fourth Phase international relations are characterized by the supremacy of legitimacy under law over the 'effectiveness' of Second Phase, balance-of-power international politics. The peoples of western Europe since 1950 have been building a system based on the supremacy of community law over the the traditional European interplay of national interests, the *Realpolitik* system which brought total catastrophe from 1914 to 1945. The United States, from the 1940s, aided and abetted and, in many cases, participated actively in the beginnings of this new, Fourth Phase of relationships based on democratic states which trust each other. In this sense, the foundations of the new ICD have already been well laid.

Community

Integration is the process whereby a multinational group builds a *community*. According to Karl Deutsch, integration is 'the attainment within a territory of a "sense of community" and of institutions and practices strong enough and widespread enough to assure, for a "long" time, dependable expectations of "peaceful change" among its population'. (This elaborates Ake's emphasis on 'legitimate' change as against change based on power relationships.) Deutsch defined 'a sense of community' as the belief that common social problems must and can be resolved through peaceful change; this implies the resolution of common problems normally by institutionalized procedures without resort to large-scale physical violence.[5] Put in yet another way, members of a community share a 'we-feeling'.

Although the 'Atlantic community' was an expression used often from 1948 to the 1960s to characterize the close ties of history, culture, economics and political interests which had evolved among Canadians, Americans and western Europeans, the term became passé. Even when it was fashionable, lower-case 'community' juxtaposed with 'Atlantic' meant something a good deal looser than the 1950 treaty-enshrined term 'Community', which the six original members appropriated for Europe's prodigious Fourth Phase experiment. After 1961, Atlantic 'partnership', rather than 'community', was often employed for discussions of relations between the two sides of the North Atlantic. More recently, this amorphous but strong tie has been dubbed the 'Euro-Atlantic Community'. Now, with the adoption by treaty of 'European *Union'* to supersede 'European Community', the transatlantic confusion is itself passé. But another terminological complication has arisen: in the past ten years or so, American policy makers have come to describe the new, looser, and largely will-o'-the-wisp relationships among the 'Pacific Rim' countries as a 'community'. In 1992 these ties were formally embodied in a treaty creating the 'Asia-Pacific Economic Cooperation' forum (APEC); there is little chance, however, that this will soon be formalized as a 'Pacific Community'. The great disparities among the vast numbers of peoples and nations clustered around the Pacific could hardly lend themselves in our time to such devaluation of 'community'.[6]

Similar caveats might also apply to the links between Western Hemisphere nations; even though the Latin south and the Anglo north have much in common historically, geographically and economically, there is not yet enough connective tissue to justify calling the New World a true 'community'.

To call the proposed ICD ties a 'union' is premature; the system may never progress that far. However, given *Community*'s modern etymology, that term should now be available to describe precisely the kind of Fourth Phase – supranational – relationship which the likeminded democracies ought to build. James Baker once called for a 'new commonwealth of freedom',[7] but this term too is confusing; there is a British 'Commonwealth' which replaced the old Empire and which is now so loose an aggregation as to suggest that the stable democracies would only find such an arrangement a burden. Australia and some American states also bear the formal title of 'Commonwealth'.

Considering alternatives and present usage, *Community* seems the most appropriate term for a Fourth Phase system bringing together the democratic peoples and states. But it should not be used lightly.

Intercontinental

The adjective *Intercontinental* connotes the scope – beyond regions – of the proposed community of democracies. To use instead the term 'International', might suggest including virtually all countries; the ICD is more limited, based on trusting relationships and the likemindedness of members, but regardless of where they may be located. In this age of jet travel and the Internet, distance is no longer the enemy it once was of intimate contacts which characterize a community. Geographical propinquity has much less to do with the operation of a multinational democratic polity than do the factors that make up likemindedness – agreement on democratic principles, shared common interests, comparable and intertwined economic systems, and a great well of the necessary human resources to make a vast community's institutions work.

Joint Planning, Decision-Making and Action

This is the heart of the ICD, Fourth Phase approach and will be discussed at length, beginning on page 171. Without this collective capacity on the part of the most experienced democracies, at the very least, *Pax Democratica* will remain only a slogan.

FIRST STEPS

Architectural proposals follow for an ICD which should have a good chance of being effective, long-lasting and expandable – a 'house' for the democracies to which one can add 'rooms' and new housekeeping systems as the family grows and times change.

But first there should be a crucial preparatory step: the calling together of an *Intergovernmental Commission on the Common Future of the Democracies*. This might consist of a small number of leading statesmen, currently independent of the political fray and drawn from the most important and seasoned democratic countries. Their charge from (say) the G-7 governments could instruct them to review and suggest changes in current multinational arrangements among the democracies (e.g. NATO, OECD, EU); to propose additional institutions and working methods which should be considered; to recommend the elimination or streamlining of some existing bodies; and to provide for expansion. The result should

be a set of long-range concepts and structures to make them operational, for broad discussion in legislatures and other market-
places of ideas.

   If the wisest and most experienced persons, representing not only
politics in the narrow sense but the industrial and academic worlds
as well, were chosen for such a Commission, and given broad scope,
the results could be illuminating. But to give the Commission's work
the likelihood of serious consideration, the constituent governments
will first have to embrace the central argument of this book, i.e.
that the democracies share significant common interests which must
in the future be served by them *jointly* – and in more effective and
expeditious ways than at present, and that it will be up to the five
to ten most experienced and powerful democracies to take the lead
in constructing what will be essentially a new system. Perhaps former
Secretary of State Eagleburger's parting words about strengthening the collective ties of the Western democracies, quoted at the
beginning of this chapter, can serve as a point of departure.

   In the following sections of this chapter, proposals are set forth
in some detail for new architecture and methods which an Intergovernmental Commission and governments might consider. Some
have already been mentioned earlier.

A CAUCUS OF THE DEMOCRACIES AT THE
UNITED NATIONS

> It is a striking fact that there is no organizational forum in which
> the world's democratic governments can meet regularly to dis-
> cuss shared values, common objectives, and peaceful ways and
> means to sustain and advance the development of pluralistic
> democracies.
>
> Irving Brecher, McGill University[8]

Because the Caucus will doubtless be one of the easiest all-democ-
racies organs to form, it could well be first in the new system. One
of the ICD's prime objectives should be to concentrate its members'
energies on the improvement of the United Nations. This might
take the form of a Caucus of the democratic states' delegations to
the UN, buttressed perhaps by periodic attendance of special delegates from their parliaments. The Security Council and General
Assembly probably need the most attention, but a general review

of all the associated agencies would be in order. The Caucus could also serve as a device for concerting policy among as large a group of democratic states as possible, with respect to matters before the UN at any time.

Examples of issues that such a Caucus, if it had existed, might have dealt with:

- In 1990 some democracies might have expressed their concern to the other members of the Caucus about *Rwanda*. The seeds of great internal upheaval were growing obvious; in a timely way, the Caucus of Democracies could have tried to energize the UN – or its own members – into taking steps to head off violence and give political counsel aimed at stable and accountable government, plus enhanced respect for human rights. If the UN were to have taken up the subject at all, prior to the outbreak of the crisis, the concerted views of the Caucus of Democracies might have made a difference. What such undemocratic neighbours of Rwanda as Nigeria and Zaire thought about the consequences of impending catastrophe would have been important, but not nearly so important as what the community of the world's democratic nations saw, understood and was willing to do. When the crisis came, it might have been less tragic, the terms of reference of UN aid and refugee agencies could have been framed or at least bent to reflect a democratic view, and action could have been more effective. Burundi, it seems in hindsight, would also have deserved comparable, timely treatment.

- With respect to *Cambodia*: Although the UN could consider its massive and extended efforts in that war-torn nation, from 1990 to 1994, as at least a qualified success, the mission might have been undertaken earlier and with better effect in establishing democratic government if a Caucus of Democracies had dominated the initiative and provided the human resources pinpointed at long-term civic education.

- With respect to the Security Council and *Bosnia*: The United States, Britain and France, as permanent members, usually led and guided the necessary initiatives, which nevertheless failed in many crucial respects. With guidance and backing from a UN Caucus of Democracies, there might have been pressures for stronger measures than those first taken, plus willingness among a larger number of democracies to help with a concerted effort. It is noteworthy that the despotic government of Nigeria was a member of the Security Council during a good deal of this period; certainly it was in no position to exercise a positive influence on the Bosnia question.

The Democracies' Caucus could also concentrate on the reform of the UN, its eventual 'democratization' and management. It could publish studies and concert the voting of its members on such issues.

Guidelines for participation in the Democracies' Caucus could be based on some sort of weighted formula, suggested in Chapter 6 (likemindedness) and Appendix A, to determine both qualifications for membership and numbers of delegates. Per capita GDP, proven durability of democratic institutions and protection of human rights, population and commitment to common economic and defence institutions of the democracies could all be taken into account. As many as 70 democracies would seem qualified as the century draws to a close.

A PARLIAMENTARY ASSEMBLY OF DEMOCRACIES

Democratization of the common structure of the democracies is surely a linchpin of *Pax Democratica*, if it is to mean anything to the world. During the last half of the 20th century, only the west Europeans made visible progress in the direction of international institutions directly accountable to electorates. Their creation of a European Parliament, alongside the executive and judicial organs of the European Union, was a significant move towards representative democracy on a Europe-wide basis. Since 1979, the Members of the European Parliament (MEPs) have not been appointed by their respective national legislatures but *elected* by the voters of all the EU members, in carefully-drawn constituencies within each country. In the European Parliament the MEPs sit in international party groupings in the assembly hall, not as national delegations, as in other international fora, e.g. the UN or the Council of Europe. Thus, Christian Democrats, Social Democrats, Greens, Liberals and other party members sit with their ideological partners from other EU countries and make common cause with them, rather than with their national colleagues.

The European Parliament (EP) has limited but real powers of its own. It can, for example, reject the annual budget put before it by the European Commission, forcing significant changes in expenditure or in policy. It can also reject appointments to the Commission (EU's executive) proposed by member governments. Finally, the EP debates virtually all important questions and interests that the member countries hold in common, and sometimes (if not always) its deliberations influence what the Council of Ministers or the Commission decide for the entire community. The European Parliament is the first supranational, democratic, representative body in history; so far, its powers are quite limited but so were those of the English Parliament in the days of King John and Magna Carta; EP will probably grow in power and influence.

Several other interparliamentary (but not supranational) bodies also tie democratic countries together; these could perhaps be combined and strengthened to represent more directly the peoples of the coming Intercontinental Community of Democracies. Notable are the parliamentary assembly of the Council of Europe – formed by treaty in 1949 and today including many more countries than the EU – and the North Atlantic Assembly, an extremely useful collection of parliamentarians from the NATO countries and lately still other democracies, which has grown up independently alongside NATO since 1954. In both these bodies, the chief value so far has been the opportunity for national legislators to discuss the common interests of their countries and to learn to know their colleagues from other countries and better understand their perspectives on important questions.

There was no mention of an interparliamentary assembly in the North Atlantic Treaty of 1949, but some enterprising MPs from Canada, Britain and a few other NATO countries went ahead, quite on their own, to create one five years later. In the beginning, the NATO governments took as little notice as possible of the meetings of the 'NATO Parliamentarians Conference', as it was initially called. But gradually, the Conference became an Assembly, it began to deal with affairs beyond those strictly of NATO, and its membership was increased to welcome Associates and Observers from some of the new democracies in eastern Europe and from as far away as Japan and Australia. After all, the latter could hardly ignore the joint defence efforts of the North Atlantic countries when their own broad interests in Pacific defence – and indeed global security – began clearly to intersect with NATO's. Today, the North Atlantic Assembly has acquired quasi-official status. The Secretary General of NATO addresses its plenary meetings annually, with the beginnings of a 'State of NATO' report. The North Atlantic

Assembly's members are selected by their respective parliaments, including the US Congress, so that indirectly there is already a small element of democracy in this body.

The Council of Europe's assembly, which today includes many fledgling democracies from the former Eastern bloc and which sometimes invites members of the US Congress, Canadian Parliament and other democratic legislatures beyond Europe to join in discussions of the future of democracy, can talk about literally any subject. But the assembly has only influence and no powers. The fact that no non-democratic parliaments may send delegates is in itself valuable. The desire of peoples and parliamentarians to be members of a 'democratic club' can be quite powerful, which improves the chances for democracy in 'aspirant' or backsliding countries and helps gradually to strengthen the 'club' itself.

These and other valuable practices of European and Atlantic interparliamentary assemblies should be incorporated in a new *Parliamentary Assembly of the Democracies*, intercontinental in scope.

This, then is a major proposal that the experienced democratic governments and an intergovernmental commission – if they appoint one – should consider: that one 'branch' of the Intercontinental Community of Democracies should be a parliamentary assembly; that its members should initially be chosen by their respective parliaments but at an early date be directly elected by the people; that the Assembly should be able to discuss any subject it considers important and make recommendations to the constituent governments; that the Assembly should receive and debate reports from all the organs of the growing democratic Community (such as the defence and economic unions and other bodies outlined below) and make recommendations to them; that the Assembly's membership be drawn initially from the legislatures of all reasonably well-functioning democracies; and that gradually it should acquire limited but real powers in matters affecting the vital common interests of the world's democracies.

One could envisage a constituent group of, say, 20 to 30 tested democratic parliaments drawing up criteria for further membership and inviting legislators from other democracies to join. Within a year or two, from 50 to 70 democracies could be represented in the Assembly. While some organs of the ICD would initially need to be more restricted in membership (to countries capable of sharing fully all necessary responsibilities and burdens), the proto-legislature of the ICD ought to be the one place where the smallest democracies (such as Barbados or San Marino) and the newer or less stable democracies (such as Ukraine or Brazil) could have a voice. Surely the larger countries would have more parliamentary members and the smaller proportionally fewer or in some cases no more than one; such provisions could be based on the same factors considered in developing membership and voting strengths for the Democracies' Caucus at the UN.

An Assembly of Democracies could prove invaluable for debating such items as the 'carrying capacity' of Planet Earth; the abatement of the drug trade; the economic challenges facing the democracies; the outlines of better common defence and collective security systems; the curbing of human rights abuses and the broader questions of tyranny and democide; the propagation of democracy itself.

The Assembly would be a Third Phase forum with the germ of Fourth Phase characteristics. It would gradually assume more and more prerogatives of its own. Gradualism has been the Western tradition of solid parliamentarism; the Icelandic Althing, the oldest parliament in the world, dates from 930 AD; a few Swiss Cantons in the Middle Ages began settling community matters by annual voting of all male adults; the American colonies in 1775 formed a weak confederal assembly, in 1787 gave it much greater powers in the federal constitution, and today's Congress is much evolved; the British, French and German parliaments started as councils of elders appointed by the monarch and grew erratically but ultimately with sureness and solidity into the modern, representative legislatures they are today. One should begin as modestly as public opinion would require, but not in any way block off scope for long-term evolution towards the combined sovereignty of all the democratic peoples, as the need becomes evident – as it surely will.

The creation of a Parliamentary Assembly of the Democracies might well obviate the need to continue the Council of Europe's and NATO's assemblies (and perhaps others), thus making for economies.

AN ECONOMIC UNION OF THE DEMOCRACIES

The abolition of all obstacles to economic intercourse among the democracies, beginning with those which are most advanced, should be a first order of business for the ICD. Open trade, free invest-

ment flows, a common patent system, full scope for technology transfers, uniform rules of competition, the creation of a common monetary regime and all other freedoms of an open market system should
be near the top of the democracies' agenda. Such measures have
proven over 40 years to be a good thing for Europe's Union; does
not logic and need suggest that the extension of these provisions
to other highly-developed, free economies sharing a high degree
of likemindedness and strong political ties, is a Good Thing...
perhaps even a *Better* Thing? The development of the global economy,
of which the advanced democracies are the heart, already tends in
this direction. But improved structures and common rules are
essential.

Accomplishing such a vast change in the economic order of things
will be extremely complex. There are several models and 'building
blocks' at hand which can be useful: the experience of Europe's
Common Market (now 'single' market) guided by its extranational
Commission; the various regional free trade areas, usually good
first steps towards full economic union; the plans for Europe's central
bank and common currency, now fairly well advanced; the G-5, G-
7 and G-10 informal groupings for charting out broad fiscal and
monetary steps; and the policy coordinating, 'information
clearinghouse', annual reviews of national economies, and consen-
sus-building functions of the Organization for Economic Cooperation and Development. In fact, the latter – the OECD – includes
among its members a logical nucleus of more than 20 nations which
could start a movement towards step-by-step, full economic union.

As in the case of interparliamentary reform, some existing economic bodies and functions could be combined or eliminated to
advantage. The new body could be termed a 'Union' to signify that
commitments made to it would be weighty, involving more than
the words 'Organization' or even 'Community' imply.

A DEFENCE UNION OF THE DEMOCRACIES

NATO and other Alliances as Building Blocks

The North Atlantic Treaty Organization provides a solid base for
a larger intercontinental mutual defence union. There are others:
Canada and the United States have operated NORAD, their own
mutual defence organization, since 1940. The ANZUS Tripartite

Security Treaty of 1952, between the US, Australia and New Zealand; the US–Japan Security Treaty of 1951 (later updated); and Western European Union (1954), bringing a number of European NATO members together for common military purposes, offer yet more building blocks. There are bilateral defence treaties between a number of European countries or the United States with special client states (Saudi Arabia, Egypt, Israel, Malaysia, Singapore, the former French colonies in Africa and others) which ought to be taken into account.

NATO is by far the most important model. It has, over nearly half a century, developed a sophisticated system of political-strategic coordination and decision-making, an integrated system of military infrastructure in Europe, major steps towards standardized weaponry and supplies, and a fully-integrated multinational command, involving joint general staff planning, command and control systems, and forces in being or on call which have constituted a formidable deterrent to war in Europe. With its many political difficulties over the years and suffering the yo-yo of parliamentary credits, plus interminable interallied wrangling over 'burden sharing', NATO has not functioned easily. But it was a major factor in 'winning the Cold War', later (behind-the-scenes) preparing and executing Allied prosecution of the Gulf War, and in the late 1990s undertaking its first (and major) peacemaking/peacekeeping deployment in Bosnia. Perhaps NATO's greatest value is psychological, hard to prove but very real: virtually all the former Soviet satellites in eastern Europe, plus recently liberated Soviet 'republics' such as the Baltic states, want to join NATO. Most of them give NATO membership an even higher priority than joining the European Union, most likely because NATO provides the greatest proof that America, in spite of geography, is indeed a 'European power'. Small nations especially value American political involvement and the protection which NATO implies, and also the association with a solid group of democratic states within whose embrace many of their statesmen believe their own fledgling democracies can best flourish.

It would be immensely constructive for Sweden, Austria, Finland and Switzerland immediately to join NATO and prepare for a wider Defence Union of the Democracies at the same time. The delicate arguments about neutrality of these nations are gone with the winds of the Cold War. All have considerable, well-trained armed forces that would enhance NATO's order of battle at once; also, their economic and human resources would bring proportionally much greater contributions to the NATO burdens/benefits table than will the inclusion of the weaker, fledgling democracies of central Europe. This is no argument for necessarily bringing in the great neutrals more quickly than the ex-Communist states, but the process of including the latter could be smoothed by incorporating the former. The borders of effective and stable democratic rule should be congruent with those of NATO and the wider Defence Union-to-be. There should also be a place for Ireland.

Canada and the United States, geographically parts neither of Europe nor Asia, nevertheless have accepted integral roles in the defence of both continents. East Asian/Pacific defence has offered a good deal more complicated set of equations than has European, but there is no doubt that such stability as the Pacific region has enjoyed after 1945 has been in large part due to US, Canadian, Australian and New Zealand resolution and willingness to commit forces as a backup to maintain the peace. Japan has gradually become part of this process.

The United Nations and the Democracies

As the post-Cold War era evolves, it becomes increasingly clear that security challenges all over the world are of a piece, yet less easy to fit into one clear, aggregate world-view, such as 'defence against the Communist threat' once offered. However, disorder leading to destabilization of key governments in Africa, the Middle East, the Balkans, and east and south Asia is a long-term continuing threat to the positive tasks of global progress in all aspects. The United Nations Security Council has, and sometimes with reasonable success, been able to intervene in conflicts both domestic and international. But many crises are too big or too urgent for the UN.

There is a strong case to be made that the most serious threats to world peace, arising from the spread of biological, chemical or nuclear weaponry and long-range missiles, whether openly or clandestinely; the conduct of rogue nations such as North Korea, Iran, Libya or Iraq; or the major unsettling of regional stability which could come about, for example, if Chinese muscle-flexing towards neighbours appears to become sustained policy, will have to be dealt with collectively by the likeminded and powerful democracies, which know from experience how to deter and if necessary contain serious threats to world peace. More and more, it is less and less possible to separate such threats neatly into regional compartments and expect nearby powers to deal with them; security is globally indivisible. The United Nations usually is already involved in such questions and should be encouraged and empowered by the great democracies to take whatever steps it can, but the essence of *Pax Democratica* commits the democracies to take the lead, make commitments and follow through – all of this collectively – if the UN is unable or unwilling to resolve the issues at hand.

Global Defence and Security Requirements

Halford Mackinder pointed out as the 20th century began[9] that the Eurasian continent – what he called 'the world island' or 'Eurasian heartland' – is where the overwhelming number of wars have taken place over the centuries. The sum of all conflicts that happened in the Western Hemisphere or in Africa by comparison have been mere sideshows. In recent centuries, the maritime powers of North America and western Europe have contained the land powers of Eurasia. In the centre of the world island sits Russia, facing east, west and south – throughout history beleaguered or menacing, depending on one's perspective. If Russia evolves towards full membership in the Intercontinental Community of Democracies, the peace of Eurasia will be immeasurably strengthened.

On the eastern borders of the world island sits China, strong candidate for the next fateful world struggle if there is to be one. To the south lie India and her neighbours, whose precarious situation also requires priority attention by the great democratic powers. Circumscribing the world island, from Vladivostok through the Malacca Straits, past the greatest oil lands, into the Mediterranean and around to the North Cape and Murmansk, the earth's main sea lanes of communication run; this too, in an increasingly seamless and vulnerable global economy, is another striking feature of the strategic pre-eminence of the Eurasian world island.

In all logic, it is today virtually impossible to maintain that 'East is east, and West is west'. European/Atlantic and east Asian/Pacific security are not, if they ever were, divisible. The strategic centres of potential disorder scattered all around the world argue strongly for a NATO that is reconfigured to add, at the very least, members from east Asia and the Pacific Rim and to extend its coverage world-wide. The advanced democracies, gathering new and trusted allies as they proceed, need to build a well-integrated global security 'safety net' to contain major dangers to world peace and political modernization. This does not mean that UN machinery is irrelevant or necessarily powerless, but that it must be backed up squarely and, in some cases, perhaps superseded by the responsible democracies in concert.

Woodrow Wilson prematurely inspired the peoples of the victorious powers after World War I to create the League of Nations, committed to stopping aggression and safeguarding the self-determination of 'nations'.[10] Eventually, the League comprised virtually all important states except the United States, whether they were democracies or not. Wilson's ideals were limited by the temper of the times and the nationalisms and lingering animosities of the late belligerents, but they were not wrong. However, his own country in particular and the traditional practitioners of the balance of power were not ready for so radical a departure – in some respects an early Fourth Phase scheme for international relations. In the end, the despotic powers of the 1930s – Japan, Germany, Italy – defeated the purposes of the League system and brought about its collapse.

As the 21st century begins, the great democratic peoples will be firmly in the ascendancy in the world for the first time. Their economic, political and military power combined is clearly overwhelming. It is now of paramount importance to consolidate and use this combined power to back up the process of community building, global security, the Earth's sustainability, economic progress and free markets, and the gradual, deliberate democratization of the societies and peoples which demonstrably aspire to free regimes. In idealistic terms, but backed up by power, this is the meaning of *Pax Democratica*.

The tasks of mutual defence and the projection of military power cannot be separated today from those of 'peacekeeping', 'peacemaking' and collective security. The two processes must go hand in hand. This comprises the challenge, in the most urgent terms, of assuring the peaceful and democratic incorporation of the former countries and satellites of the Soviet Union into the community of free peoples. This is also the essence of the challenge of helping to organize mutual defence *and* collective security on the littorals of east Asia, and in other continents as well. We democrats should no longer attempt to meet this tremendous global challenge piecemeal or individually, occasionally in concert but often disjointedly. Separate policies, economic and political/security, could prove disastrous.

Designing the Defence Union

Any blueprint for a Defence Union of the Democracies will require at least as much thought and effort as the original twelve
Allies brought to the architecture of NATO in 1949. But some of
the same principles, and a couple of new ones, should obtain:

1. A paper treaty of alliance is not enough; integrated military
commands and a political superstructure to control them are essential.

2. The mutual defence clause – an attack on one is an attack on
all and must be met with combined force – should be as unequivo-
cal as possible. (This was the rock of collective responsibility on
which the United States Senate based its principal opposition to
the League of Nations Treaty in 1919, and for which a later Senate, in 1949, had to find an ingenious form of words that reassured
Allies, but still left an 'out' for American nationalists – an out which
in practice has meant less and less over the decades.)

3. Broad provisions for peacemaking and peacekeeping activities, anywhere, should be included, probably the Defence Union's
most crucial function in the new age. A system of collective security
must be built alongside the mutual defence provisions of NATO
and the future Union.

4. It must be possible, in carefully defined crisis cases, for a
weighted majority of Defence Union members to commit the Alliance
to act. Former US Secretary of State James Baker, who favours
this, calls it a 'super-majority'. At least initially, the United States
probably would not accept a situation in which it could be committed to war against its will; the voting must be carefully calculated.
On the other hand, it should not be possible for Luxembourg or
Portugal, or even France or Britain alone, to immobilize the Alliance in the face of a preponderant majority.

5. Relationships with the United Nations, and especially its Security Council, must be carefully worked out so that Allied arrangements support and not weaken the UN. But neither must the UN
provisions be allowed to hamstring forceful international action which
the UN's large and multifarious character renders it incapable of
taking, as in the former Yugoslavia – for example – in the 1990s.
The Defence Union must retain the power of initiative and be
prepared to act with speed.

6. Fully integrated defence production, armaments standardiza-

tion and logistical capabilities for the joint Defence Union, possibly financed by a common defence supertax to ensure equitable burden-sharing, would be essential. This will entail, among other things, substantial savings for all members.

These are all further steps in the democracies' progression, begun on 26 March 1918 with the appointment of Marshal Ferdinand Foch as head of the Allied high command, to integrate Allied political-military capabilities. The United States, Britain and their Allies created a similar but much stronger joint system in World War II. The present Supreme Headquarters Allied Powers Europe, set up by NATO in 1951 with General Eisenhower heading combined forces and staffs, was a major factor in the successful conclusion of the Cold War. SHAPE still exists. NATO's political Council and civilian secretariat are also important antecedents, all of which could be incorporated in a new Union.

To move fully to a Fourth Phase system of mutual defence and collective security in the 21st century cannot be done with a mere collection of signatures; a process must be started that clearly states long-term goals to be reached by evolutionary steps that match increasing mutual trust and confidence within an expanding membership. And the consultative mechanisms, peacetime staff and forces in being will have to be at least as impressive as those of NATO.

AN EDUCATION UNION FOR DEMOCRACY

If, as proposed, the Intercontinental Community of Democracies accepts as one of its top priorities the strengthening and extension of democracy itself, then a special 'action arm' will be needed. All democracies, seasoned or emergent, could actively participate. The Democracies Planning Group and the Court of Democracies for Human Rights (see page 168, below), plus the Parliamentary Assembly of the ICD, are intimately related.

Since World War II, the experienced democracies, usually led by the United States, have employed a variety of means, almost always bilateral, to help cultivate democracy in politically less developed countries. But these disparate, uncoordinated efforts (see Chapter 5, pages 73–86), even though the majority seem well-intended and helpful, must today be judged as inadequate. The inner core of capable democracies should establish a new joint mechanism for assessing world needs for political modernization, determining the desires of nations for such help (for it is no good trying to assist in educating for democracy if a country and its people do not want it), establishing priorities (for one cannot help everywhere at once) and mounting jointly conceived and administered educational and other supportive programmes that have a fair chance of success.

Haiti, for example, is a country where a long-range effort to support democracy is both needed and wanted. The US and UN intervention in Haiti, the substantial humanitarian and technical effort to give the Haitian economy a chance, the establishment there of an accountable government chosen – however imperfectly – by the popular will, and the endeavour to establish a regime of law and reasonable protection for the population all are but short-term steps – however necessary and helpful – that should be followed with a very long-term programme of across-the-board education. Education in the classic sense of well-established schools and colleges, technical education to undergird a sustainable economy, of instruction for future leaders of business and finance, and health education, but also – above all – of civic education, will be required for years to come. Surveying the situation in 1997, as both the UN and the US gradually withdraw, the most basic task now seems made to order for an Education Union for Democracy.

The world currently lacks a high-level training and research institution directed at democracy-building. An Education Union might consider this, with a glance at the NATO Defense College, established by General Eisenhower in 1951 to provide common staff training for officers of the member countries; it continues to work superbly, and remains virtually unknown.

Promoting democracy, however, is not entirely a question of education; sometimes it can and should be linked to economic aid. It is possible for an ICD, closing ranks, to be hard-headed about extending aid to countries which desperately need it but which will not work to safeguard the human rights of their citizens. Except to alleviate famine or fight disease directly, African or Asian tyrannies – for example – deserve no economy-building aid unless they are willing also to accept assistance in the fundamentals of protecting civil rights and building accountable governments. This educational process would go far beyond the usual monitoring of 'fair elections' which the UN and other bodies often undertake.

Political modernization is an extremely complex process. Promoting it can be costly, but the costs are small compared to the huge effort involved in undertaking a Desert Storm operation or the political and economic impact of incorrigible renegade governments, such as Nigeria's, on their neighbours. If an ICD, with its Education Union for Democracy, could agree on steps to pressure Nigeria but also offer to help her positively to restore and build democracy with carrot – and stick if necessary – the results might be important for Africa and set a global precedent.

The Education Union would of course have to pick and choose among 'targets' for promoting democracy. Second Phase considerations, such as the size, geopolitical and geoeconomic importance of a country (e.g. Saudi Arabia, Algeria, Brazil, Egypt or Jordan), would play an important role in establishing priorities. A wide variety of methods can be considered as the take-off point for substantial, long-range, coordinated efforts. The matter requires great study.

But the improvement of democracy is not just a matter for countries such as Brazil, Russia, India, Ukraine or Paraguay, which struggle to modernize politically against difficult historical and contemporary odds. No so-called 'advanced' democracy, including the United States, Britain or Sweden, has so perfected its political practices that it can justify self-satisfaction. The more-developed democracies could learn a great deal about government and a civil society from one another and sometimes from those peoples emerging freshly from tyranny and striving for a new, free system; Vaclav Havel, for example, has been a great source of inspiration in the democratic West. In short, the methods the experienced democracies use to help the inexperienced might also be applied *among* the 'givers' of democracy-building aid to help *us* better to live up to our own professed ideals. Should not an Educational Union for Democracy begin by establishing a process of Annual Reviews of Democratic Practices, similar to the defence reviews of NATO and the economic reviews of OECD, among its own members?

A final word: history shows that the process of democracy enhances the chances for improved standards of living, but the reverse can also be true, i.e. that economic 'take-off' in a country brings about the growth of a middle class, which in turn clamours for accountability of government, the free choice of leaders by the people, a secure rule of law and the establishment of inalienable rights for minorities and individuals. This is why one of the major goals for *Pax Democratica*, the extension of democracy, should be coupled with the encouragement of free economic systems.

A COURT OF THE DEMOCRACIES FOR HUMAN RIGHTS

Dissatisfied with the UN's Charter of Human Rights (1948) and particularly with its almost nonexistent powers of enforcement, the members of the Council of Europe in 1953 created a European Court and Commission of Human Rights. Citizens of member countries are enabled to appeal against decisions of their national courts for alleged violation of their human rights. Hundreds of cases have been brought before the Court and often the verdicts have gone against governments. Implementation of such decisions depends upon the willingness of signatory governments to accept supranational adjudication for the good of the whole and general advancement of human rights. This in turn requires a high degree of likemindedness and mutual trust.

Alongside the European Court of Human Rights, member governments of the Council of Europe have also adopted a series of conventions regarding such matters as the humane treatment of prisoners, the rights of aliens and the right of compensation for the miscarriage of justice. A further development was the signature of Canada and the United States to a Council of Europe convention to allow persons convicted abroad to serve their sentences in prisons in their own countries. There is therefore a precedent for extra-European involvement in this important but little-noticed institution for protecting human rights in a majestic, no-nonsense, Fourth Phase manner.

What more practical and highly symbolic way could all the democratic nations choose to express the supreme value they place on human rights than by creating such a Court intercontinentally, or perhaps simply by extending the geographic scope and membership of the existing European Court?

FOURTH PHASE ATTENTION TO OTHER MATTERS

So far this book has tried to suggest some new directions and new ways of thinking about the common predicament of the democracies and indeed all the world, and cite a few matters deserving priority attention. But there are still other matters which the democracies have a special responsibility for addressing jointly. In most such cases, they have already been working together and helping the UN and its affiliates to better deal with universal questions. But by bringing problems and efforts such as those suggested below within the ambit of an Intercontinental Community of Democracies and energizing fresh leadership, the chances for a better world can be enhanced.

First, there is the matter of *economic development*. Aid has become a feature of the foreign policy of every well-to-do nation. Rich individuals within every society, and the rich countries within the society of nations, have a duty to the poor – humanitarian assistance *in extremis* and well-calculated technical and financial help to support economic development and independence. This can be especially effective for less developed democracies or those which genuinely aspire to democracy, in preference to non-democracies which usually tend to misuse aid. Disillusionment with 'foreign aid', however, is widespread in some donor countries, out of frustration and a general lack of understanding of the process, and also because until recently economic aid has not been directly linked to political development. Economic aid, coupled with programmes of an Education Union for Democracy, plus the general improvement in coordination which the ICD should bring about, could go far to remedy such disjunctures.

The European Union countries for several decades have been channelling most of their development aid through the Union at the expense of bilateral programmes. In the OECD, the rich democracies have held annual reviews of individual aid policies and their results; a good deal has been learned; some coordination takes place. The World Bank, the IMF and the UN Development Program are important international instruments. The work of such bodies as the US Peace Corps also comes immediately to mind. This multifarious effort might be streamlined; the ICD could try, perhaps through its Democracies Economic Union.

Second, economic and other forms of development cannot be satisfactorily separated from what is now called, '*the sustainability of the planet*'. Population control, environmental protection, the melioration of public health, agricultural improvement, social modernization and improved government all are interrelated. An ICD effort to support the UN's work in these fields and to take direct action for the Community in cases where this is called for, might come under a single heading for strategic consideration.

Third, there is the problem of *migration*, especially the displacement of populations by wars and democide. The UN High Commission for Refugees by and large has done a creditable job for decades, but with limited resources and scope for action. Within regions vital to democracy – and here one might cite especially Europe, North Africa and the Middle East, plus the vast population movements, in the recent past and the probable future, in south and east Asia – the large and powerful democracies of western Europe, North America, Japan and Australasia have a special concern because of the potential for extreme instability.

One might cite three contemporary examples of great danger arising from the mass expulsion of populations: (1) the outflow of about 2 million refugees from the former Yugoslavia into adjacent parts of Europe, and the subsequent effort to resettle them at home or elsewhere; (2) the spillover of several million displaced Afghans into Iran, Pakistan, and other countries during the decade-long civil war in Afghanistan; and (3) the flight of millions of Hutus from Rwanda and Burundi into Zaire, Tanzania and other nearby nations. Such movements have serious political consequences, not to speak of the humanitarian suffering and economic catastrophes. If such dislocations could be foreseen, in some cases they might be averted through timely diplomacy. If not, armed international intervention may be called for; sometimes the democracies must take a lead if universal bodies move too slowly. To some extent the European Union has recently faced these questions and taken joint measures within its region. But North America and Japan, in particular, may need to help Europe to cope with a prospective and menacing influx of vast proportions from Algeria, in particular, or from portions recently liberated from the Soviet empire. Nor should Europe expect to stand aside if deterioration in North Korea eventuates in chaos and mass migration to the South.

Fourth, there is the escalating problem of *international crime*, and specifically its solid link with the *drug trade*. *International terrorism* also comes under this heading. Interpol, with its communication links between the world's police establishments, has proven of great value in combating international crime and terrorism; the European Union recently established an even tighter organization – Europol – to work within its region. An ICD could strengthen such efforts in important ways.

A fifth set of serious questions to which an ICD, by means of coordinating existing bodies or creating a new one, should address itself consists in the continuing opportunities, e.g. for *scientific and technological cooperation*, including the sponsorship of big projects for space, supercolliders, hydrogen power and environmental research which no single nation can any longer afford.

An ICD or its subsidiary bodies could not, of course, try to deal with every important set of international problems. In many cases, the UN is taking an adequate lead and should continue to do so, with the ICD in a supporting role. In other cases, independent organizations, including non-governmental ones, may have a set of problems under control. But the ICD should regularly survey the entire international scene, relate economic to security questions in new ways, find the serious gaps in dealing with truly great or dangerous issues, and then see what its individual members or its own 'democratic system' could or should do to help. Without the well-articulated, strategic attention of the Community of Democracies – and, again, especially the rich, powerful and experienced ones – much that the world requires for its future safety, health and prosperity will remain undone.

THE DEMOCRACIES PLANNING GROUP

For *Pax Democratica* to have a good chance, the ICD must have 'operational hands and feet', a *Democracies Planning Group (DPG)*, with an agenda broad enough to deal with the full range of common challenges and the defence of the common interests of the democracies, yet small enough in membership to make it workable. It will need broad powers, for continuing surveillance of the world situation, information-gathering, strategic goal-setting, joint task formulation, ordering of priorities, assuring fair burden-sharing, overseeing the work of the special Unions outlined earlier and making plans for action to be taken together, when necessary, by some or all of the democracies. In effect, the DPG will be the precursor of a cabinet, where the strands of the various enterprises that make up ICD can be gathered together.

The DPG should be the chief instrument for considering all that must be involved in *Pax Democratica,* and how to bring it about. But to make it work well will be extremely difficult, and will call for extra-national powers. To understand why, we should look again at some first principles, as applied to our current situation.

Kant and Fourth Phase Ideas

Many have puzzled about how best to organize the nations for peace, beginning with Kant and his scheme for 'Perpetual Peace' and continuing into our own century with the ideas of Wilson and others for a League of Nations, of the framers of the United Nations, of the visionary proponents of 'world federal government', of Streit who wanted federal 'Union Now' for the Western democracies, and of Monnet with his plans for a United States of Europe. Statesmen and thinkers have sought a more integral whole, capable of dealing effectively with problems which not even the largest nations could singly manage. It has been a formidable, tortuous and sometimes moderately successful quest, but fraught also with great setbacks and seemingly insoluble obstacles. These efforts and obstacles have characterized our century, as the stakes became ever greater. Now, with the ending of the Cold War and the psychological impetus of a new millennium, perhaps it is time for a fresh start.

The Democracies Planning Group is the indispensable heart of the fresh start, the crucial first step to Fourth Phase order. It should benefit from earlier visions, but also from mistakes and dead ends.

Sorting Through World Order Ideas

What big world order ideas, floated or tried in the past, can we safely set aside in our search? Is there already a good model?

1. The world as a whole cannot accept, or make workable even in the unlikely event it could accept, a world government. A global federation is too much for the political classes or peoples of large, disparate groups of nations to swallow at one gulp. If world government is ever to be brought about, it is many decades – probably centuries – off in the future; in short, unnecessary even to think about. Conclusion: Only democratic, likeminded countries are capable of initiating Fourth Phase systems that can work.

2. The balance of power system, although it may be important for many transitional years, is a dark vision of the future which portends yet more cataclysms along the way. *Realpolitik* depends for even limited and temporary success on tactical geniuses, balancers such as Metternich, Castelreagh, Bismarck or Kissinger. Not many of them come along. Conclusion: As the central organizing principle for a new start, balance of power is a dead end.

3. The world is dissatisfied with its 50-year experiment with the United Nations, a body with which we cannot dispense, but the main inadequacies of which we cannot correct any time soon. Strong supportive measures now can help, but only an eventual replace-

ment will do. Conclusion: The UN is an important piece of the world puzzle, but not the critical one.

4. Among the regions of the world, only western Europe has made a reasonably successful, if still unfinished, Fourth Phase effort to reconcile the realities of the nation-state with the common good of several peoples and the vital tasks with which single governments can no longer cope. This is the *only* successful undertaking of this kind, on any significant scale, in world history. Conclusion: The EU should be considered as the precursor, in the broadest sense, for an ICD, the next important stage in the Fourth Phase.

5. To an important but lesser extent, the Atlantic powers, principally through NATO and OECD, have also developed hybrid Third Phase/Fourth Phase multinational instruments with unprecedented powers to manage their common affairs. Japan and Australasia have figured prominently in this equation for more than three decades; one would not be wrong to speak today of an 'Atlantic–Pacific community' or of an 'extended Atlantic community'. Conclusion: The EU, NATO and OECD, together with the Council of Europe's supranational Court, are already the real beginnings, the solid underpinnings – but only that – for the Intercontinental Community of Democracies.

By elimination, our main hope thus lies in building on Third and Fourth Phase structures developed among the likeminded democracies in the last half-century. If it works, the ICD will eventually comprise a large number of experienced, likeminded, stable democracies. The ICD's spearhead and its main 'hothouse' for experiments in international democracy,[11] which could later be applied generally, is the Democracies Planning Group. The DPG is the focus for preparing a strategy for the 21st century and beyond. *Integrated, joint planning, decision-making, and action* will characterize its methods and structure and, if they work well, should be applied on a much broader basis.

Constructing the DPG, the Spearhead for Fourth Phase World Order

Although a democratically representative executive for the ICD, drawn from a large number of countries, might make a tidy scheme for political scientists to contemplate, it is out of the question at startup time. Until the entire Community can become fully operational on the basis of democratic principles, i.e. representative of the constituent governments and peoples and capable of making binding, Phase Four decisions for several score nations the Democracies Planning Group will have a crucial pioneering role. The initiative must rest with a compact group representing likeminded, powerful and experienced governments, all sharing agreed common interests and goals and used to working together. They must usher in the Fourth Phase as custodians for a more democratic arrangement when the ICD is ready for it.

Five countries – all members of the current G-7 – are the obvious core candidates: France, Germany, Japan, the United States and the United Kingdom. Such a grouping is simply the natural coming together of the democracies which are the largest, the most experienced in international cooperation and the most 'likeminded' They possess the largest pool of sophisticated manpower – governmental and non-governmental – for running international undertakings. They can bring the greatest financial resources to bear together they possess an overwhelming preponderance of military power, and they jointly comprise the huge, sophisticated heart of the global economy. They understand by reason of their long association that they share ineluctably a great number of common interests which none – even the United States – could today successfully hope to manage alone.

The G-7, a rather loose association, is not a good institutional model for the proposed Democracies Planning Group. It is essentially an informal 'club' of the richest democracies which works ad hoc, with the national bureaucracies together planning an agenda for the annual meeting of the seven heads of government plus the President of the European Union Commission. Each year a different member country is host for the next Summit and its bureaucrats coordinate the others. Various cabinet ministers meet occasionally between Summits. G-7's emphasis has been on economics, with crises such as the Gulf challenge in 1990 occasionally elbowing their way on to the agenda. Like the UN, G-7 has been indispensable. However, it would be a mistake to ask the G-7 to accomplish the tasks proposed here for the Democracies Planning Group (DPG).[12] G-7 is a Third Phase body, the DPG is Fourth Phase; this implies that from the outset, the DPG should be prepared to make some decisions by majority, even if these will be 'weighted'. Democratic decision-making will need to evolve, but not too slowly; the political essence of the DPG process is that no single member, not even the United States, should be able to block action by all. That is much for some Americans (and others) presently to swallow, but the principle of integration requires it.

A highly-integrated planning group might involve, at least soon after start-up, a few other nations beyond the five core members. These could include Canada and Italy (already in G-7), plus four smaller but experienced and internationally competent democracies that could bring major assets to the enterprise, viz.:

1. Australia, a highly-developed, fully 'likeminded', responsible democracy which offers human, geographic and other resources virtually equal to those of Canada, and which for the most compelling strategic and geopolitical reasons should not be disregarded. Consider: Australia's huge and resource-laden bulk sits athwart the most strategic sea lanes of communication, whether past its north through the Straits of Malacca around China and on to northeast Asia, or from its western littorals across the Indian Ocean to Africa, or traversing the South Pacific to the Western Hemisphere. Australia is an outpost of the most modern political and economic life which by its contiguity to East Asia has an inordinate effect on those countries; it also enjoys good relations with them. It possesses one of the few substantial military establishments on which Japan, the United States, Canada, South Korea and New Zealand can count in the Pacific. Finally, Australia has a history of defending democracy.

2. Belgium and the Netherlands should also be included. They are smaller in population than the the Big Five (Australia and Canada approximate them), but their economic weight and political attachment to all forms of European, Atlantic and global togetherness has put them at the centre of Fourth Phase internationalism in this century. The were foremost pioneers of the EU. Trusted by virtually all countries, they possess reserves of highly-trained civil servants and other experts which could greatly enhance the workings of a proper DPG.

3. Finally, Spain today, because of its size, location, and rapid – even astounding – evolution into modern democractic and economic life, and because of its increasingly key role in the European Union, could not be omitted if the Low Countries and Italy are to be included.

One needs to start with a workable critical mass; the author favours the larger Eleven; the Big Five governments offer a more compact initial grouping. At some point, the EU might develop sufficient political authority to be represented by a single delegate – rather than three to seven – to the DPG's Council of Governments.

Staffing the DPG

The Democracies Planning Group will require a small but highly-qualified multinational secretariat of, say, two hundred civil servants, military strategists, expert economists and perhaps a sprinkling of innovative people recruited from private industry or thinktanks. These will need staff support, so that the total might number four or five hundred. More would tend to become unwieldy in the manner of all bureaucracies; fewer would not provide the independent capabilities on which the DPG should be able to call.

Independence is a key word for the DPG. Its secretariat would ill-serve the purposes of the ICD and *Pax Democratica* if it were to consist merely of bureaucrats 'seconded' for short periods by member governments according to a quota system. The few top people heading the DPG should recruit their own staff, regardless of nationality. The suggestions of governments should be heeded, but once each has appointed, say, its one member of DPG's directing council, they should leave all other staffing decisions to that group. DPG's terms of reference, laid down by the constituent governments, must be both broad and well defined but, once adopted, left to the directing group to carry out. The DPG will need its own lines of direct communication with agencies of member governments and the various bodies comprising the Intercontinental Community of Democracies, such as the Defence and Economic Unions.

Georges Berthoin, the European Communities' former ambassador to the United Kingdom and European chairman for some years of the Trilateral Commission, in 1995 made an interesting proposal which could bear on the composition and character of the Democracies Planning Group. He recommended a 'truly extra-national institution', along the lines of the Commission of the European Communities, to 'formulate the common interest in an independent fashion, and the mandate to issue specific proposals accordingly'.[13] Following the European Commission analogy, perhaps the DPG's council and members of its staff, once appointed, should pledge not to take instructions from an individual government, but only from the DPG. They would thus work in the common interest, with arm's length independence from constituent governments and their bureaucracies, submitting analyses and proposals to DPG cabinet ministers and heads of governments – and perhaps eventually to the Parliamentary Assembly of the ICD. The DPG heads of governments could of course reject the joint staff's proposals as they wished – perhaps by means of a qualified majority – providing a political 'firebreak' that sometimes could be necessary. Greater independence for the DPG would depend on evolving circumstances; the right of independent and public proposal would be its greatest strength. It might be well for the heads of government to appoint a respected political figure to chair the DPG's directing council and to speak for it.

If something like this Democracies Planning Group could be created, it should still be regarded as an interim solution to the problem of defining and promoting the common interests of the democracies. Practically, it could not be much expanded (i.e. adding more governments) without becoming unworkable. The great democratic powers, probably for some years, would remain in charge of developing broad strategies for the entire Intercontinental Community of Democracies. These could and should be debated in the Democracies' Parliamentary Assembly, with several score countries represented; the Assembly might sometimes on its own initiative offer proposals to the DPG or member governments. More and more, as the weaker democracies become stable and strong and as the characteristics of likemindedness and the habits of working together grow, the membership of the DPG's directors (Commission?) and chairman could be elected democratically from among a larger number of seasoned democracies participating fully in all the activities of the ICD. The work of the Defence, Economic and Education Unions would be overseen, in a broad sense, by the DPG. As the initial steering committee for the Intercontinental Community of Democracies, the DPG should prefigure a common, democratically accountable executive for the ICD.

Practical Applications

Assume that the DPG's planning staff has analysed a crisis situation – economic, political, military or otherwise – that it believes calls for decisive joint action by DPG countries and other democratic partners. Assume that a relevant council of DPG cabinet ministers (for example, foreign and defence secretaries; possibly the new Defence Union's council) has confirmed the DPG's proposals. Then the heads of government will have to decide if and how to act. For example, if the DPG had existed around 1990 and had prepared a joint analysis and recommendations with regard to the deteriorating situation in Yugoslavia, its heads of governments might have been more easily induced to take timely preventive action. The presence of a DPG, continuously monitoring crisis points and offering definitions of the common interest, could conceivably have forestalled the tragic events which later unfolded.

Another example would be a world financial crisis, perhaps occasioned by the failure of the US Congress to raise the 'debt ceiling', thus causing a default on US treasury obligations globally (which nearly happened in 1996). In either situation, an independent chairman of the DPG would be empowered to propose action and to coordinate the execution of decisions, sometimes by the Defence or Economic Unions, if that were appropriate.

In crisis situations, the DPG governments could put into force, if necessary, a 'constitutional' procedure adopted at the Planning Group's inception: if a decision could not be taken unanimously, then it should be made by a 'qualified (weighted) majority', i.e. a voting formula taking into account the size and weight of the member countries. The reservations of, say, two or three countries could be overriden by a substantial majority. There would be no veto on action, as there is in the UN Security Council.

More examples of hard cases for a DPG: In April 1997, two mini-crises loomed for the West, one with respect to Iran, the other concerning China. US policy towards Tehran since the 1979 hostage-taking had been icy, with commercial as well as diplomatic relations virtually nil. But the European powers continued investing and trading with Iran, brushing off its state-sponsored terrorism in the interests of commerce and long-term hopes. In 1997, a Berlin court found Tehran-paid terrorists responsible for the killings of Iranian dissidents in Germany and, in its verdict, cited proof that the terrorists' orders had come directly from Iran's two top leaders, Rafsanjani and Khameni. Germany and most EU governments recalled their ambassadors from Tehran; Iranians rioted at the German embassy; European policy was in disarray.

At virtually the same time, the UN Human Rights Commission met to consider gross violations of human rights around the world. Indonesia and Burma were among the targets for critical resolutions. But China's infractions could not even make it to the Commission's agenda; European powers hoping for Airbus orders from China, plus others who believed that human rights in China were better dealt with 'bilaterally' simply outvoted the United States and a few small European nations who felt that moral considerations should come first.

Neither of these cases is cited to suggest that either approach on the part of the democracies is 'wrong', but that a divided approach could in the end have serious consequences. If a DPG were in place and considering strategic, commercial, political, economic and 'democracy' factors concurrently, the great democracies would have been more likely to have had a *common* policy . . . whatever it was.

The Requirements of Fourth Phase Integration

Fourth Phase integration involves a profound commitment that goes beyond nationalism. It requires a high degree of mutual trust and a belief in the overriding necessity – in some critical cases – for a substantial majority of the democratic nations to be able to outvote the others and enable action. This kind of constitutional provision lies at the heart of Fourth Phase arrangements.

It is highly doubtful that the US Congress in 1998, for example, facing an electorate which does not yet understand the commonness of the dilemma of the democracies and the dangers of *not* moving into Fourth Phase institutions, would approve a voting formula in which all the other DPG members could outvote the United States and force it to take action of which it disapproved. Other large countries might balk as well; it might be necessary initially to allow for 'coalitions of the willing', constituting a preponderant majority, to take action, with reluctant governments 'opting out'. In any case, how to write a treaty that will overcome the defects of previous Third Phase intergovernmental arrangements and provide the opportunities for less-than-unanimous, yet binding, Fourth Phase decisions will no doubt require careful, deliberate attention, and patience. The governance of the NATO forces in Bosnia suggests a model: key NATO members committed themselves, then invited others (including some non-NATO members such as Russia) to join with them. In such a case, the core is solid, the peripherals can be flexible.

PARTNERSHIP COUNCILS

If the democracies of the world were to create an Intercontinental Community of Democracies and the ancillary bodies described in this chapter, concerns could be raised by powers – especially those of substantial size – that they might be left out of important deliberations that could affect them. To meet this concern, and still to retain the potential effectiveness of tight coalitions of the likeminded, a series of partnership councils, comprising key representatives of the established democracies, major 'half-democracies' and major non-democracies, is suggested, in order to discuss major issues and, wherever possible, to coordinate approaches. Membership in such Third Phase partnership councils would vary according to the subject under consideration. For example, a council on trade and monetary affairs might include the DPG countries plus India, Brazil, Russia, China and Indonesia. Other questions suggest some of the same partners. Some council members (such as Russia or India) might find that these exercises in delineating common interests would prepare them for full participation in the Fourth Phase DPG, the economic or defence unions, and so on.

Parenthetically: In view of the involvement of Russia in some G-7 discussions in recent years, questioners might well ask why that great nation would not be included in the DPG from the start? The answer lies in a sober evaluation of Russia's likemindedness qualifications measured against the Big Five or eleven democracies. Such an analysis (see Chapter 6 and Appendix A) must conclude that Russia has far to go in many respects.

PUTTING THE WHOLE COMMUNITY TOGETHER

In this chapter, the creation of several new, interlocking community structures has been proposed, comprising, all together, an *Intercontinental Community of Democracies*:

- An overarching ICD, initially in the form of a framework agreement
- A Caucus of the Democracies at the United Nations
- A Parliamentary Assembly of the Democracies
- An Economic Union of the Democracies
- A Defence Union of the Democracies

- An Education Union for Democracy
- A Court of the Democracies for Human Rights
- A Democracies Planning Group

To prepare the process, a one-time Intergovernmental Commission to make architectural recommendations to democratic governments would be useful. Once the ICD began to work, Partnership Councils, in which key ICD members could counsel with major half-democracies and non-democracies, could also help.

Pax Democratica and the ICD must be comprehensive in scope in order to encompass all vital global challenges. A full range of issues important to all ICD members could be brought up for debate and advisory votes in the Parliamentary Assembly, to which all would belong. With time, the powers of the Assembly in such matters should naturally be strengthened. Critical first steps towards common policy, at least in the early years, should not be hamstrung, however, by the absence of sufficient likemindedness or the inability of some participating democracies to carry full shares of responsibility.

As the 21st century opens, the vital interests of the democracies are – for all practical purposes – virtually congruent. All of them, however, will not understand this in the early years. The most likeminded and experienced democracies and their peoples, used to working together for half a century, are best able to comprehend this crucial requirement of international life straight off, to prepare themselves for a new, better form of unity of purpose and action, and to begin the process of integration. They should be the first to accept collective responsibilities, to give up some freedom of individual action in order to achieve the greater benefits of unity.

The newer, uncertain and less practiced democracies would need to work their way gradually into the frame of thought and the habits of togetherness which will enable them to participate responsibly in the more sophisticated and demanding forms of Fourth Phase community-building. Some ICD enterprises, such as the UN Caucus and the Parliamentary Assembly, can begin under a wide canvas of Third Phase cooperation. Other bodies, such as the Fourth Phase Democracies Planning Group or the Defence Union, will have to start with an inner core of nations, and in some cases initially with only the biggest, richest and most powerful. Starting small and then gradually adding members and increasing powers is potentially a more effective strategy than to begin with a very large but unwieldy group of countries, which might be philosophically compatible but unused to working closely together. It is most important that the initial decision-making bodies – especially the DPG – be workable and durable; they can become gradually more inclusive as others are ready to participate fully.

Jean Monnet once said that he conceived of the European Communities Treaties as an 'escalator'; one would start with less-demanding provisions for decision-making, and move up gradually to tighter forms of integration as participants came to see the growing need and became increasingly used to Fourth Phase working-together. The Intercontinental Community of Democracies' scheme is comparably flexible. It can be modified continuously and adapted to a large membership for some purposes, and to more restricted groups for others. To understand this graphically, it may help to turn to Chart 10, page 214 in Appendix B: the ICD Framework Treaty forms the outer ring of Third Phase cooperation, grouping more than 50 democracies, of whom not too much – initially – is demanded. As a 'peripheral' member increases its participation by moving towards the inner, Fourth Phase concentric rings, more and more would be required of it. Economic and defence unions, for example, are no mean arrangements, lightly entered into. But these would also yield comparable benefits.

The DPG asks for the greatest commitments. Conversely, from the DPG at the centre should grow an increasing and expanding body of knowledge about how to conduct Fourth Phase extra-national relations, i.e. learning so that one could know how best to involve others. The core would work towards the periphery, the periphery would work towards the core. This concept would seem to resolve a key issue for Fourth Phase communities: how to deepen and expand at the same time.

It should be possible for ICD to conduct its work in such a way that it will buttress the larger international order overall, especially the UN and its related bodies, as well as constructive regional arrangements. This can be the case if the ICD's members conceive of its mission as pre-eminently to serve the common interests of the democracies and of democracy itself; if this is so, then its actions in pursuit of that mission will, with virtual certainty, also serve the long-term interests of all the world's peoples. The ICD must be able to formulate and communicate this conviction to its own peoples as well as to those not living under democracy but whose chances for civil rights, political liberties, economic prosperity and quality of life the ICD's members are also committed to serve.

There is very little that will be easy about *Pax Democratica*. The foregoing suggestions are only that; the problems they seek to address and the specific prescriptions for community-building will require study by the democratic world's greatest experts and most experienced leaders. But it is the principles that matter, not the detailed sketch above, which represents simply one carefully-considered way that one might proceed.

9 Afterword

DEMOCRACY. One of the three forms of government; that in which the sovereign power is neither lodged in one man, nor in the nobles, but in the collective body of the people.

Samuel Johnson's Dictionary, 1775

Democracy is the worst form of government . . . except for all the others.

Winston Churchill

Why should we do the things proposed in this book? Why not trust to present forms of international collaboration and, in the last analysis, to the good old nation-state – still, with all its defects, our most solid reality? And why not trust to luck?

Drifting is not good enough. First Phase systems – empires – are definitely passé, but that does not mean some big nation, grossly misapprehending its place in the world scheme of things (China is the glaring candidate), or out of desperation trying to control a world spinning out of order (*Pax Japonica* or *Pax Americana*, under barely conceivable but not impossible circumstances), might not give regional or even world imperium another try. More plausible is a reversion to the Second Phase, 17th century balance-of-power system, which no doubt averted some wars but brought horrendous others when the supply of presiding geniuses ran out at critical moments. The more recent Third Phase intergovernmental system, composed of patchwork coordination among nations and cooperation-but-on-your-own-terms, is an improvement . . . but only just.

FOR THE 21ST CENTURY, OLD SYSTEMS ARE INADEQUATE

When bad men combine, the good must associate; else they will fall one by one, an unpitied sacrifice in a contemptible struggle.

Edmund Burke, 1770

Recent attempts at Fourth Phase institutions, which strictly speaking are not *inter*national but *extra*national or *supra*national, portend a potential quantum leap for humankind. Only a well-

184

thought-out, coherent structure of new links among peoples and their governments, embodying the joint capability for timely, effective action to manage change in ways which serve the common interest, will be able to meet the challenges of a new and probably very difficult century. Democracies can do this; experience suggests that less politically compatible groupings cannot.

The old systems, although we must live with their vestiges and seek to improve them – especially Third Phase intergovernmental cooperation – will simply be insufficient. Why? Here are some reminders:

1. The 20th century brought *democide* by despotic governments to a pitch never before encountered – more than 170,000,000 human lives snuffed out arbitrarily and illegally, quite apart from war deaths. Tyrannies in the 21st century, employing quantum leaps in technology, could readily better this record by several orders of magnitude, disposing of unwanted or hated human beings on a much vaster and more efficient scale. If we give them the chance. To promote democratic government, vigorously, is the best way to ensure that such abominations can be avoided, at least held in check to be eventually overwhelmed by the decent opinions of mankind. And to do this will require that the democracies combine.

2. *Wars in the 20th century* have snuffed out more than 40 million lives, and for the most part needlessly if we look dispassionately at what the nations could have done had they been able to rise above destructive nationalisms and ethnic hatreds within a world governed by law and restrained by strong, common, accountable institutions.

3. *Democracy* has been given third or fourth or last place – and more often no place at all – in the hierarchy of values and goals which animate the foreign policies of the nations, including the great democracies. Nor has democracy been made a leading principle (again with a few notable, recent exceptions in Europe) in the design and operation of international institutions themselves. Yet democracy, in all its exuberant variations and permutations, remains the one set of principles the world can no longer afford to do without. However, there are no common mechanisms for advancing democracy.

4. Prevailing world systems – still based on Second Phase, *Realpolitik* prestidigitation – depend overwhelmingly on *Power*. To a fortunate – yet still woefully inadequate – extent, Second Phase and more recently Third Phase institutions have begun to incorporate

Law which is superior to the nations. Finally, Fourth Phase systems (and more feebly, Third Phase Systems) are showing what a powerful expression of mutual *Love* (*agape*) can do to reorder and improve the conduct of human affairs. Synonyms are Humanitarianism, Benevolence, Charity, Brotherhood, Philanthropy or Magnanimity. The most fundamental factor that has brought about the great sea-change in relations among the peoples of western Europe since 1945, is precisely this impulse of compassion and fellow-feeling, the ultimate expression of likemindedness. The great significance of the European Coal and Steel Community Treaty of 1951 – the first Fourth Phase institution – was that for the first time in history it committed two historic enemies, France and Germany, to a common future based fundamentally on brotherhood: the principle of all for one and one for all.[1] Any new phase in international community-building must be based on this first principle: The antithesis of the 'law' of the jungle, *agape* is the hallmark of modern organized society and gives to all government, and to all human existence, their ultimate justification.

5. It is essential to complete the construction of a *security community* among likeminded nations; otherwise the hard-built foundations could crumble. These underpinnings have already been laid around the rim of the North Atlantic, and among Japan and a few other democracies in the Pacific area. Karl Deutsch gave a very particular meaning to 'security community': an integrated group of nations among which the possibility of intracommunity war has become virtually impossible.[2] If mutual understanding is great, if there is a vast flow of interaction of all kinds among members, if there are many dense and demanding ties – non-governmental as well as intergovernmental – among members, and if there are shared visions of the future . . . then the chances of future violent conflict among the members become inconsequential.

Is it not worth a very great deal for the future of the world to build, and then deepen and widen, such security communities, as a basis for an eventual peaceful and free world order globally? Should we not begin where we can? Is not the ultimate argument for an Intercontinental Community of Democracies this very idea: that only the gradual interlocking of likeminded peoples and nations, under law, within institutions that embrace the extra-national principle, has a fair chance of seeing humankind safely into an era of perpetual peace, with freedom?

WHO CAN HAVE HOPE? WHO TAKES ACTION?

> The death of democracy is not likely to be an assassination from ambush. It will be a slow extinction from apathy, indifference, and undernourishment.
>
> Robert M. Hutchins, *Great Books*, 1954

Men and women, anywhere, who cherish democracy or who, even if they do not enjoy even a semblance of a free way of life but yearn for it, can work to bring about *Pax Democratica.*

The Nigerian student who spent a year at a Norwegian university and tasted freedom; the Chinese scientist who earned his doctorate in the United States and returned home with new perspectives; the North Korean diplomat who represented his country to UN agencies in Geneva, and saw free Swiss society and a nascent rule of law at work among the nations; the Saudi woman who studied modern political science at the Sorbonne but is not allowed to drive an automobile in her own country; and the businessman in Cairo who had the chance to see how free enterprise works in Australia ... all these and thousands more, who have become democrats in their hearts but suffer under unfree regimes, crave the benefits of modern society, their rights as human beings and ways to bring about non-violent change. All such persons have a great stake in *Pax Democratica*, even if they cannot, at the present time, do a great deal to bring it about. They must combine with others and await opportunity. They must believe that eventually they, with the help of those of us in the lucky democracies, can prevail.

As we begin to lay the groundwork for a better free world order – building on good foundations laid down in the dramatic past half-century – we should not insist that it all be done with the stroke of a pen, by some miracle, but understand that we must first develop a long-term vision (*Pax Democratica)* for our Intercontinental Community of Democracies that in turn can evolve gradually (remember Monnet's escalator?) to realize the vision. And although it will be difficult initially, we should ensure that our Community itself unfolds along democratic lines. Eventually ... and not in too long a time-frame at that ... the architecture of the ICD should become an expression of the popular will of the peoples involved, i.e. increasingly less of a loose arrangement among states, whose governments retain the right to opt out when it does not suit them. 'We, the people' of the democratic nations of the world must gradually form our own overarching political community, in which *we* have the final say. Parenthetically, we 'founders' should understand that Fourth Phase arrangements will entail not some derogation from the sovereignty of our states, but a delegation – a pooling – of well-defined functions to achieve sovereign purposes.

All who become involved in this great quest should remember soberly that no set of institutions – not even the ICD – will necessarily bring quick solutions, or in some cases any solutions at all, to the full range of the knotty problems of life, international or domestic. But a better framework for working together can make a major difference in the chances for democracy and a better world.

None of this will come about, or even begin, if the peoples of the practiced democracies – inviting all democrats, everywhere, to join with them – do not exercise the initiative of citizens. Even if most of the heads of government of the proposed Democracies Planning Group or of the larger inner core of some two dozen experienced democracies identified in Chapter 6, or of the fledgling and tiny democracies, were to subscribe to most of the ideas in this book, that will still not be enough to jumpstart such an ambitious enterprise. Presidents and prime ministers have their parliaments and congresses to think about, and the mercurial but still very real 'public opinion' of their electorates to convince. They may, as did Teddy Roosevelt, look on their high offices as 'bully pulpits' and set out to elucidate the requirements of modern life in an interdependent world as they really are . . . but that alone will still not be enough. They will need the ground-plough work of intellectuals, civic leaders, business statesmen, journalists, philanthropists, moral and religious leaders, and educators of every stripe, some of whom themselves will need educating for Fourth Phase citizenship. For if we, the democratic peoples, cannot mutually educate ourselves to the overpowering demands of interdependence, no one else will do it for us.

A final thought: the formation of the United States, and its continued inflow of new citizens from around the world, assumed that all within its ambit assent to the proposition of Jefferson's famous Declaration (1776), that 'all men are created equal, with unalienable rights'. And in 1787, the magicians of the Philadelphia Convention, realizing that to be free and equal was necessary but not sufficient, endowed their fellow Americans with a federal constitution, which showed how democracy must be incarnated in a system that could ensure its perpetuation. In 1789, the French established the Rights of Man, *Liberté, Egalité, et Fraternité.* Such world-embracing principles – and not some spurious new super-nationalism or devotion to a 'civilization' – represent a good enough creed on which to found the 21st century's Intercontinental Community of Democracies.

Much of humankind spent the last half-century locked in a Cold War, a deadly serious contest between ideologies. For many, this was a 'cause' for which sacrifices could be made, lives risked and given. Now that is over, we are in a new era. It is natural that people should ask, 'What should we now strive for? What is worth great sacrifice, great effort?' *Pax Democratica*, this book suggests, merits effort on an even grander scale because – if accomplished and done well – it can provide the best and most feasible long-term framework within which men and women everywhere can work out the problems of existence.

Pax Democratica promises the best chance to individuals for the basic freedoms of which Roosevelt spoke in 1941: freedom of speech and expression, freedom from fear and from want, and freedom to worship in one's own way. Democracy itself is only a framework within which these goods can be pursued; *Pax Democratica* unites the democratic societies so that the pursuit can be continued securely, with eventual freedom for all from the curses of wars, democide and tyranny.

Appendixes

Appendix A:
Some Observations on Likemindedness

Chapter 6 presented the complex question of 'Likemindedness' at some length, discussing criteria developed by the author over many years[1] in trying to understand why some countries and their governments seem to be more ready than others to engage in sophisticated forms of international cooperation and, especially, Fourth Phase supranational integration. As with so many intricate patterns of human and institutional behaviour, it is not too difficult to set up criteria of this kind (although many, depending on perspectives and tastes, could dispute selections). But to apply these to determining which countries are 'in' and which, at least for the time being, are 'out' demonstrates the validity of the contemporary cliché, 'the devil is in the details'. This short Appendix describes the author's methodology and its application in arriving at three levels of readiness for participating in an Intercontinental Community of Democracies: (1) the experienced democracies; (2) democracies which are fairly well developed, but which do not qualify in important respects for the closest forms of integration; and (3) 'aspiring' democracies, still – one way or another – in the throes of modernization and which have cast their lot with the democratic community, but are able to assume only the least onerous responsibilities.

The criteria which define the first, experienced group (extracted from Chapter 6) are repeated below; by extension, democracies in the second and third groups do not meet the criteria fully, or only to minimal degree. Of course, *no* nation on the face of the earth, in this decade at any rate, is without flaws in taking the various measurements. All rankings are relative and based – one hopes – on a relatively consistent methodology and, in as many instances as possible, on objective statistical bases and the systematic analyses of others. In the last analysis, however, the individual and cumulative judgements are subjective, for which the author alone takes responsibility.[2]

States with high degrees of 'likemindedness' might be characterized as follows:

1. *Stable, experienced, advanced, politically democratic regimes*, in which political freedoms and representative government, protection for civil rights and the Rule of Law are essentially unchallenged and the habits of democracy pervade the conduct of civic business.[3]

2. *Advanced economies*, characterized by sophisticated free markets, close monetary cooperation with similar states, substantial overseas investment and aid programmes, open trading and other economic exchanges with likeminded nations, high levels of exporting and importing dependency, comparatively low degrees of business and governmental corruption, and deep involvement in the integration of the globalizing economy.

3. *Knowledge-based socio-economies*, integrating the most modern forms of science, education, communication and high-technology industries.

4. *Modern humane societies*, which accept a high degree of responsibility for the general welfare and quality of life of their citizens, enjoy high standards of living, and embrace and express the ideal of *agape* – the caring society. There is also a high incidence of private initiative working for the good of the community, e.g. voluntarism and foundations, the hallmarks of a civil society.

5. *A deep and widespread understanding that the vital interests of their people are widely shared* with likeminded peoples. Vital common interests of the democracies include: mutual defence, security and the diminution of war, terrorism, civil strife and democide; global economic growth and prosperity embracing free markets and widely accepted rules; the sustainability of Planet Earth – emphasizing development and growth, protection of the environment, mitigation of crime and the drug trade and other destabilizing transnational phenomena; the growth of stable democracy and the indivisibility of human rights.

6. *Proven capability for engaging in joint efforts with likeminded countries* to serve the common interest, expressed through participation in a number of cooperative and integrative schemes – especially in building the foundations of multinational architecture (Chapter 5; Appendix B). This comprises not only adherence to sophisticated treaties pledging mutual aid, but a sustained commitment of political and diplomatic 'muscle' to the service of the common interest and a demonstrated willingness to share burdens fairly.

7. *A substantial body of diplomats, civil servants, military officers, political leaders, academic experts, business leaders and others who are trained, available and oriented towards international cooperative*

work. This denotes a society so rich in human resources that it can – and does – afford to share them with likeminded partners in the ICD's own integrative venture, and – especially – with less fortunate countries needing help in modernizing.

There is an *eighth, very important criterion: the relative economic weight and political-military power* of the various countries. This is important to consider because it fits under the heading of 'what does the nation in question bring to the table?' when the Community is under construction. In a thoroughly advanced Fourth Phase community, which would constitute a limited federation of its members (probably some years off), this question would be less important; in the US federal system, for example, the comparative weight of New York as against that of, say, Delaware or Idaho is much less important than is the relative importance in today's unfinished European Union of Germany's weight as against that of, say, Portugal or Belgium. Within half-built Fourth Phase communities, as well as with respect to those communities' relations with countries and groups outside, composite economic-political heft must still count for a great deal.

The table on pages 196–7 assigns weights for these eight factors – elements of likemindedness, or of preparedness to participate in ICD – to some 52 states. One might have added another twenty or so tiny democracies, but this would complicate the matrix unnecessarily; although they can bring little to the table in a practical sense, the minuscule democracies should be included under the broadest 'tents' cast by ICD. Not to do so would violate ICD's highest reason for existing. We may simply assume their inclusion.

A few comments on the assigning of weights, for which the author assumes complete responsibility; except for the Freedom House calculations on democracy, the slings and arrows will be his alone to receive:

1. *Advanced state of democracy*: Weights are those assigned in Freedom House's *Freedom in the World: Annual Survey of Political Rights and Civil Liberties, 1996–97*, New York, 1997. The Surveys have been published regularly for more than two decades by a reputable non-governmental group. One may quibble with Freedom House's methodology or with its individual marks for democratic performance, but generally its work is thorough, systematic and impartial. One can especially rely on the analysis of several annual editions of *Freedom in the World* to obtain trend lines for various

countries, and for the world as a whole. The author accepts the Survey's work as the best available source in its field. (Note that Russett, op. cit., does not arrive at conclusions substantially different from those of Freedom House.)

2. *Advanced, market-global economy*: After extensive research in tables of current statistics (such as the 1997 *Encyclopaedia Britannica Book of the Year*; the *OECD in Figures: Statistics on the Member Countries*, 1996 edition; World Trade Organization's 'Special Report' on leading exporters and importers in world trade, *Focus 12/96*, 5, and trade in services, op. cit., March–April 1995, 9; competitiveness surveys of the Harvard Institute of Economic Development and others), plus leading periodicals such as *The Economist* and the *International Herald Tribune*, the author has made his own judgements which reflect the degree of openness of an economy, trade practices and policies, the degree of monetary integration with other countries, GDP per head, productivity, and so on.

3. *Knowledge-based economy and society*: users of the Internet, communication volumes, technology bases, educational facilities, developed computer and ancillary industries are indicators.

4. *A modern, humane society*: Weighting is mainly subjective, based on careful reading of press and periodicals from several countries; influenced in part by Freedom House's weightings on civil liberties and Department of State's annual survey of human rights.

5. *Understanding of common vital interests*: Again, mainly subjective but attempting to judge: (a) the extent to which the general population of a particular country comprehends that it is 'in the same boat' with others of the democratic ilk; (b) the same attitudes as reflected in the press; and (c) the actions and pronouncements of governments as indicators. Over the years, the author has also compiled extensive material on opinion polling results, especially in Europe and the United States, regularly surveys press and radio accounts from several countries, worked in the UK, France, Germany, Italy and Belgium for many years, and has made extensive on-site studies of Japan and the Far East.

6. *Proven capability for joint undertakings*: Weightings based primarily on formal memberships (and the quality of participation) in key Third and Fourth Phase organizations composed of democracies – NATO, OECD, EU, Council of Europe, G-7, others.

7. *Substantial core of available leadership for international tasks*: Here the record – over some years – shows which countries, on a volume or per capita basis, provide the most skilled and educated

manpower for cooperative work with other nations. Performance in UN peacekeeping, leadership in the various world and regional economic bodies, contributions of officers and experts to NATO, WEU, OSCE and like organizations, quality of international civil servants seconded to the UN, European communities, and so on. It is evident that this aspect of likemindedness inevitably correlates to some extent with the degree of social modernization, the output of education systems (especially at the graduate level), the wealth and economic dynamism of countries. The weightings, once more, are the author's alone.

8. *Economic weight and power*: This is a fairly simple calculation based on the size and quality of a nation's economic and military share of world power. The G-7 countries, for the most part, lead in this calculation; that is why they are in G-7. Middle-sized, small, tiny and less-developed countries unfortunately come short ... but again, one is measuring capability for participating in the shaping of the world to come.

A further note: As one moves on from the twenty 'core' democracies and 'second tier', to the aspirants, it is evident that the paucity and reliability of data in most cases prevent one from rendering judgements – especially comparative ones – which are as 'accurate' as those developed for fully modern, stable, complex governments and societies. It is, for example, much more difficult to gauge the present and future capabilities of South Africa or Brazil, or to compare them, than it is to make a considered judgement with respect to Germany's or New Zealand's contemporary performance and future prospects.

Table A.1 The Likeminded – Criteria Weightings

Criteria	USA	Germany	France	UK	Canada	Australia	Italy	Japan	Netherlands	Norway	Belgium	Denmark	Sweden	New Zealand	Austria	Finland	Luxembourg	Switzerland	Spain	Iceland	South Korea	Czech Rep.	Portugal	Ireland
1. Advanced democracy	1.0	1.5	1.5	1.5	1.0	1.0	1.5	1.5	1.0	1.0	1.5	1.0	1.0	1.0	1.0	1.0	1.0	1.0	1.5	1.0	2.0	1.5	1.0	1.0
2. Adv mkt/global economy	1.5	1.5	1.5	1.5	1.5	1.5	1.5	1.5	1.5	1.5	1.5	2.0	1.5	2.0	1.5	2.0	1.5	1.0	2.0	2.0	2.5	3.5	3.0	2.5
3. Knowledge based economy	1.0	2.0	2.0	2.5	2.0	2.0	2.5	2.0	2.5	2.0	2.5	2.0	1.5	3.0	2.5	2.0	2.0	2.0	3.0	2.0	2.0	2.5	3.5	2.5
4. Modern, humane society	1.5	1.5	1.5	1.5	1.0	1.0	1.5	2.0	1.0	1.0	1.5	1.0	1.0	1.0	1.0	1.0	1.0	1.5	2.0	1.0	3.0	2.0	2.0	2.0
5. Understand vital interests	1.5	1.0	2.0	2.0	1.0	1.0	1.5	3.0	1.0	1.5	1.0	1.5	2.0	2.0	2.0	2.0	1.0	3.0	2.0	2.0	2.5	2.0	2.0	2.0
6. Cap for joint undertakings	1.0	1.0	1.5	1.0	1.0	1.0	1.5	2.0	1.0	1.0	1.0	1.0	2.5	1.0	2.5	2.5	1.0	3.0	2.0	2.5	4.0	3.0	2.5	3.0
7. Core leaders available	1.0	1.0	1.0	1.0	1.0	1.0	1.5	1.5	1.0	1.0	1.0	1.0	2.0	1.5	2.0	2.0	3.0	2.0	3.0	3.0	4.0	3.0	3.0	3.0
Sub-score	8.5	9.5	11.0	11.0	8.5	8.5	11.5	13.5	9.0	9.0	10.0	9.5	11.5	11.5	12.5	12.5	10.5	13.5	15.5	13.5	20.0	17.5	17.0	16.0
8. Power/economic weight (see Notes 1 & 2 on p. 197)	1.0	3.0	4.0	4.0	7.0	7.5	5.0	3.0	9.0	10.5	10.0	11.0	10.0	11.0	10.0	11.0	13.0	10.0	10.0	14.0	8.5	11.0	12.0	13.0
Total Score	9.5	12.5	15.0	15.0	15.5	16.0	16.5	16.5	18.0	19.5	20.0	20.5	21.5	22.5	22.5	23.5	23.5	23.5	25.5	27.5	28.5	28.5	29.0	29.0
Overall Rank	**1**	**2**	**3**	**3**	**4**	**5**	**6**	**6**	**7**	**8**	**9**	**10**	**11**	**12**	**12**	**13**	**13**	**13**	**14**	**15**	**16**	**16**	**17**	**17**

Criteria	Israel	Taiwan	Poland	Singapore	S. Africa	Greece	Hungary	Thailand	Malaysia	Turkey	Argentina	Slovenia	Uruguay	Chile	Brazil	Philippines	Venezuela	Russia	India	Lithuania	Estonia	Latvia	Bulgaria	Costa Rica	Mexico	Ukraine	Slovakia	Romania
1. Advanced democracy	2.0	2.0	1.5	4.5	1.5	2.0	1.5	3.0	4.5	4.5	2.5	1.5	1.5	2.0	3.0	2.5	2.5	3.5	3.0	1.5	1.5	2.0	2.5	1.5	3.5	3.5	3.0	2.5
2. Adv mkt/global economy	3.5	3.0	4.0	1.5	4.0	3.5	4.5	3.0	3.0	4.0	3.5	3.5	4.0	4.0	4.0	3.5	3.5	4.0	4.5	4.0	4.0	4.0	4.5	4.0	4.5	4.5	4.5	5.0
3. Knowledge based economy	2.0	2.5	3.0	2.0	3.0	4.0	4.0	3.0	3.0	4.5	4.0	4.0	4.0	3.0	5.0	4.0	5.0	5.0	5.0	4.0	4.0	4.0	4.0	4.0	5.0	6.0	5.0	6.0
4. Modern, humane society	2.0	3.0	3.0	2.0	3.5	3.0	3.0	3.5	3.0	4.0	3.0	3.0	3.0	3.0	4.0	4.0	4.0	5.0	5.0	3.0	3.0	3.0	3.0	2.0	4.0	4.0	4.0	5.0
5. Understand vital interests	3.0	2.0	2.5	3.5	2.5	3.0	2.5	3.0	3.0	2.0	3.0	2.5	2.5	3.0	3.5	3.0	4.0	4.0	4.0	3.0	3.0	3.0	3.0	5.0	3.5	4.0	4.0	5.0
6. Cap for joint undertakings	3.0	4.0	3.0	3.0	4.0	3.0	3.0	3.0	3.0	2.0	4.0	4.0	4.0	5.0	4.0	3.0	4.0	4.0	5.0	4.0	4.0	4.0	4.0	5.0	5.0	5.0	5.0	5.0
7. Core leaders available	2.0	3.0	4.0	3.0	5.0	4.0	4.0	4.5	4.0	4.0	5.0	5.0	5.0	5.0	5.0	5.0	4.0	6.0	5.0	6.0	6.0	6.0	6.0	7.0	6.0	6.0	6.0	7.0
Sub-score	17.5	19.5	21.0	19.5	23.5	22.5	22.5	23.0	23.5	25.0	25.0	23.5	24.0	25.0	28.5	25.0	27.0	31.5	31.5	25.5	25.5	26.0	27.0	28.5	31.5	33.0	31.5	35.5
8. Power/economic weight (see Notes 1 & 2 below)	10.0	9.0	10.0	13.0	10.0	12.0	12.0	12.0	12.0	11.0	11.0	13.0	13.0	12.0	9.0	13.0	12.0	8.0	8.0	14.0	14.0	14.0	13.0	13.0	11.0	12.0	14.0	14.0
Total Score	27.5	28.5	31.0	32.5	33.5	34.5	34.5	35.0	35.5	36.0	36.0	36.5	37.0	37.0	37.5	38.0	39.0	39.5	39.5	39.5	39.5	40.0	40.0	41.5	42.5	45.0	45.5	49.5
Overall Rank	15	16	18	19	20	21	21	22	23	24	24	25	26	26	27	28	29	30	30	30	30	31	31	32	33	34	35	36

Notes

1. Rankings on the first seven criteria are on a scale of 1.0 to 7.0, 1.0 representing the highest degree of 'likemindedness' in each category. But the eighth factor (Power/economic weight) has been calculated on a scale of 1.0 to 15.0. This has been done because there is such a vast difference in power and economic weight between the largest and the smallest states. This score has been added into the first calculations for each country after the first seven factors were averaged.

2. Calculations for a few countries have derived identical overall rankings; these are shown with underlining below the rankings.

Appendix B: Selected Organizations

FIFTY YEARS OF EVOLUTION

The following graphics illustrate the growth in membership, since 1947, of intergovernmental and supranational organizations among the democratic nations. These bodies have been devoted to economic, political, military and other tasks for the common good of the members. None of the universal or other 'UN family' intergovernmental organizations are shown; those data can be found elsewhere and, in any case, do not help to tell the specific story of cooperation among democracies.

The author first began to maintain such charts in 1957, when actively engaged in helping to build the European and Atlantic communities. As the years went on, membership of some groups (such as OECD and defence alliances) spread to the Pacific area, and later to central and eastern Europe as the former USSR broke up. By 1997, it had become virtually impossible to show these phenomena in one chart, as there were by this time a plethora of members and organizations, even though a few of the latter had fallen away as they became obsolete. Chart 8 is thus only an approximation of the situation.

Nonetheless, the charts still help to show a central reality of our time: the democracies have progressively institutionalized their cooperation and moved towards integration, realizing that good intentions and ad hoc collaboration are usually not sufficient to safeguard their common interests. Brief texts accompany the charts, explaining how the different bodies came about, how they fit – or in some cases did not fit – together, and how they metamorphosed and evolved. (In Chapters 2, 3 and 5, readers can be reminded of the genesis and functions of these bodies.)

Compared to anything that happened before 1950, this complex of community-building institutions dwarfs anything that nations have ever done together, except fight wars. The democracies have created these interlocking bodies in large measure to avoid fighting wars and to spread liberty.

The *Agreements for the Occupation of Germany* (Chart 1), dating to the end of World War II, provided for an Allied Control Council. This broke down in 1947; the USSR left to run its own zone of Germany; Britain, France and the United States began to create what eventually became the Federal Republic of Germany (1949). From 1949 to 1953, there were Allied agreements and authorities for important economic purposes; the coal and steel arrangements eventually metamorphosed nicely into the European Coal and Steel Community (Chart 3).

The *Dunkirk Treaty* (1947; Chart 1) between France and the United Kingdom, reflecting the bitter experiences of the interwar period, pledged each signatory to 'give all the military and other support in his power' in the event of hostilities with a resurgent Germany. The signers also declared their intention 'to strengthen the economic relations between the two countries to their mutual advantage and in the interests of general prosperity'. These and other provisions were reflected later in the Brussels, Western European Union and North Atlantic Treaties (Chart 2).

Chart 2 also shows:

1. Belgium, the Netherlands and Luxembourg created *Benelux* (1948), an economic union and forerunner of the European Communities. The Communist *putsch in* Czechoslovakia and Berlin airlift (February and May 1948), alarming Europe, led to a comprehensive alliance (the *Brussels Treaty*) between five powers. But the Berlin crisis of Summer 1948 convinced the Europeans and the United States that Europe alone could not match possible Soviet forces, were the latter to advance westward, or to threaten to do so. The Treaty of Washington (1949), creating the *North Atlantic Treaty Organization*, was the result.

2. Meanwhile, western Europe had begun to organize itself economically, with US help under the Marshall Plan. In April 1948, seventeen countries established the *Organization for European Economic Cooperation* to channel US and Canadian aid. OEEC eventually took on many further tasks to strengthen European economic cooperation.

3. The *Council of Europe* came into being in 1949, initially grouping eleven countries in various cooperative enterprises outside economics and the security sphere. Originally, the Council hoped to lead in political unification.

INSTITUTION-BUILDING IN

CHART 1: 1947

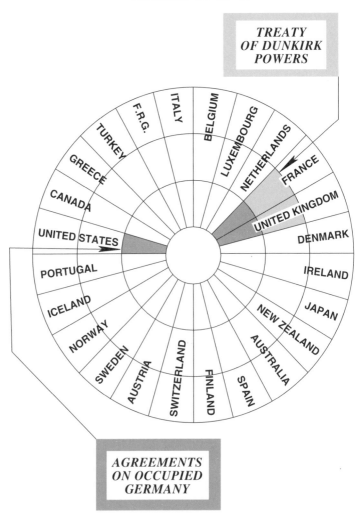

TREATY OF DUNKIRK POWERS

AGREEMENTS ON OCCUPIED GERMANY

©James R. Huntley 1996

THE ATLANTIC / PACIFIC AREA

CHART 2: 1949

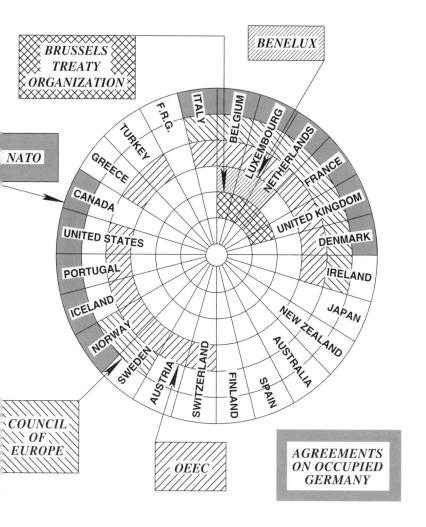

040897   J. Bulger

INSTITUTION-BUILDING IN

CHART 3: 1955

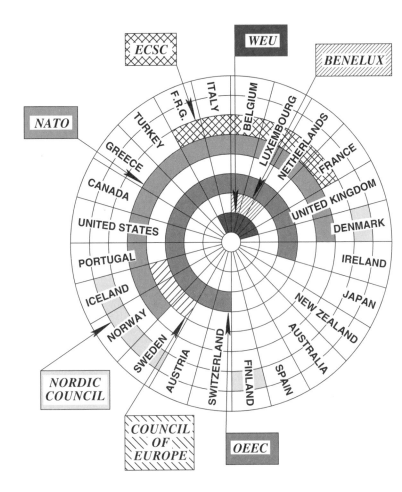

©James R. Huntley 1996

THE ATLANTIC / PACIFIC AREA

CHART 4: 1958

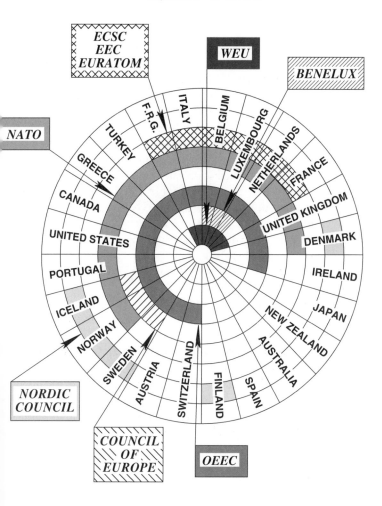

040897   J. Bulger

Efforts to create a supranational European union by means c
the Council of Europe had, by 1950, proven unsuccessful. A smalle
group of six countries, led by France, determined to seek close
ties on their own; the *European Coal and Steel Community* (195:
Chart 3) was the first result. This pooled members' production c
coal and steel under a supranational authority, and was the protc
type for later, larger Communities and the eventual European Unioi

The Korean War (1950–53) energized the members of NATC
which had until this time remained largely a paper alliance. A
attempt was made to form a European Defence Community, wit
its own multinational army, which among other things would hav
permitted arming the Germans – considered essential in face of
worldwide Communist threat. This was to be coupled with an overa
European Political Community. Both projects, however, failed rat
fication by the French Assembly. NATO meanwhile created a mu
tinational military command structure and general staff; membe
nations substantially increased defence spending within a coord
nated plan. A way was found to enable the Federal Republic c
Germany to contribute its share to the NATO forces-in-being, b
enlarging and re-crafting the Brussels Treaty (*Western Europea*
Union, 1954; Chart 3), with checks (appropriate at the time) o
German rearmament which might give that country military indc
pendence. Germany also joined NATO (1955); Greece and Turke
had become members in 1952.

In 1952 three (later five) Scandinavian countries established th
Nordic Council, to harmonize social and other aspects of member
policies.

In Chart 4, the enlargement of the European 'construction'
seen in the addition of two more Communities, the *European Ecor*
omic Community and *Euratom* (1958). The mission of the forme
was to create a European common market, sweeping away all ecoi
omic barriers; Euratom attempted to meld the various efforts c
members to exploit peaceful uses of nuclear energy. The thre
Communities were to use many of the same institutions, amon
them an Investment Bank, a European Parliament and a supra
national European Court.

In 1956, Austria was able to join the Council of Europe, a stat
treaty having freed her from occupation by the four wartime allie

Even before the new European Community treaties entered int
force, the British government proposed a larger 'free trade are:
to link the six EC countries with the rest of western Europe. No

gotiations were pursued, but were ultimately unsuccessful. A group of seven countries, outside the Communities, drew up their own agreement for a *European Free Trade Association* (EFTA, 1960), which dropped many barriers between their economies but gave each control of its own trade relations with nations outside EFTA (Chart 5).

In 1961, the OEEC was transformed into a transatlantic instrument for economic cooperation and the planning of development aid, the *Organization for Economic Cooperation and Development* (OECD). The US and Canada became full members. With the accession of Japan (1964), Australia (1971) and New Zealand (1973), OECD became in effect the common economic organ of the industrialized democracies, in the Pacific as well as Atlantic areas.

Some EFTA countries used their treaty as a device to gain entry to the Communities; Denmark and Britain entered the combined European Communities in January 1973, as did Ireland, which had so far stayed outside both economic and defence arrangements. Chart 6 also shows various changes in membership of the now-numerous organs of European, Atlantic and Atlantic-Pacific cooperation which took place in these years. Some of these had to do with the compelling nature of the organizations – how could one afford to stay out of, say, the Council of Europe which ratified one's democratic credentials? Or even more to the point, could a country afford to remain excluded from serious economic decision-making by the EC or OECD?

In 1965 France withdrew from participation in the joint NATO commands, but said it would remain faithful to the commitments of the Treaty of 1949. For a few years in the 1960s and 1970s, Greece made a similar partial withdrawal during its rule by military dictatorship.

In the face of the Oil Crisis of 1973, key members of OECD created a subsidiary, the *International Energy Agency*, with the critical tasks of assessing world energy needs and supplies, and developing strategies for the industrial consuming countries.

(*Note*: In November 1973, the first 'Economic Summit' of the five top industrial democracies took place; this remained for several years an informal meeting of heads of governments and other ministers. It is not shown until Chart 8; by 1997, institutionalized or not, it had become an accepted – indeed critical – fixture in the democracies' panoply of special-purpose bodies. In 1975, the heads

INSTITUTION-BUILDING IN

CHART 5: 1965

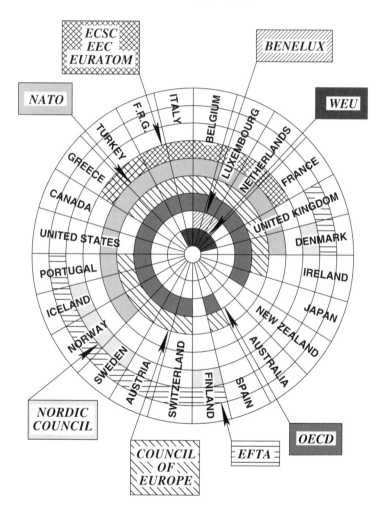

©James R. Huntley 1996

THE ATLANTIC / PACIFIC AREA

CHART 6: 1975

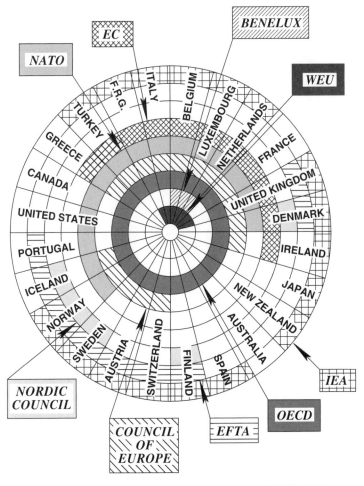

040897   J. Bulger

of government of Canada and Italy, as well as the President of the European Communities Commission, became regular invitees.)

By 1984, Portugal and Spain had once again 'joined Europe', from which they had stood aside for generations – centuries by some historic measures. Now they became members of the Council of Europe (1976 and 1977, respectively); Spain took full part in the new *International Energy Agency* (1975), Portugal later; more involvement would follow, including membership for both in the European Communities (1986). Finland, New Zealand, Switzerland, Sweden, Australia and Greece joined IEA during this period. Spain had special bilateral defence arrangements with the US, which led in 1986 to membership in NATO.

In 1981, Greece became a full member of the EC; Turkey had become an Associate Member of the EC in 1964, but was not – in this or subsequent periods – accepted for full membership.

Chart 7 also shows, within the 'NATO' ring of the organizational 'pie', that Australia, New Zealand and Japan are associated with the Atlantic powers in substantial mutual defence arrangements, through the *Tripartite Security Treaty* (ANZUS, 1952) and the *Japan–US Mutual Security Treaty* (1951; later amended and reinforced). The navies of these three Pacific powers, plus those of the United States and Canada, have participated frequently beginning in the 1980s in the joint RIMPAC and other exercises.

The period 1984–97 saw major changes in Atlantic, European and Atlantic-Pacific organizations; Chart 8 shows most of these, but lack of space does not permit a complete display. The state of affairs in 1997–98 could best be described as 'flux', with memberships and organizational missions both changing rapidly. There were also more organizations, including APEC (Asia Pacific Economic Cooperation forum) and Mercosur in South America; this Chart cannot show them all. The main catalysts for change were the disintegration of the Soviet empire (1991) and global economic modernization.

By Allied/Soviet agreement, Germany was reunified (1990) under a single federal government; this brought East Germany also into EU and NATO.

Ukraine, Hungary, the Czech Republic, Slovenia, Bulgaria, Poland and Slovakia were among those former Communist states which immediately sought membership in various European and Atlantic bodies. The accession of these nations, to such bodies as OECD and the Council of Europe, is indicated in Chart 8. Although Russia

INSTITUTION-BUILDING IN THE ATLANTIC / PACIFIC AREA

CHART 7: 1984

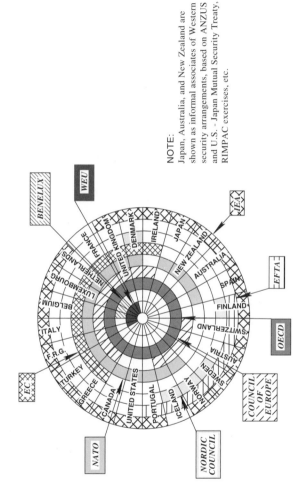

NOTE:
Japan, Australia, and New Zealand are shown as informal associates of Western security arrangements, based on ANZUS and U.S. - Japan Mutual Security Treaty, RIMPAC exercises, etc.

040897 J. Bulger

© James R. Huntley 1996

INSTITUTION BUILDING in the ATLANTIC / PACIFIC AREA

CHART 8: 1997

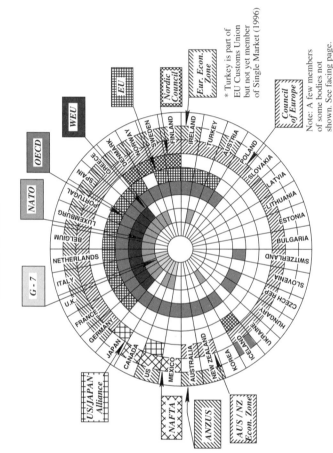

* Turkey is part of
EU Customs Union
but not yet member
of Single Market (1996)

Note: A few members
of some bodies not
shown. See facing page.

040997 J. Bulger

© James R. Huntley 1996

is not shown, she became a member of the Council of Europe (1996) and appeared to be on a short list for OECD membership.

The *European Economic Zone* was a transitional mechanism for candidate countries to the EC/EU.

Many other central and eastern European states sought membership in the EU and NATO. Some were made EU Associates, preparatory to accession. NATO took a different course, beginning with formation of the *North Atlantic Cooperation Council* (1991) and the *Partnership for Peace* (P4P, 1994). Such innovations are enabling NATO to help former Warsaw Pact members, Russia included, to modernize military and civilian defence structures, take part in peacekeeping (Bosnia) and other humanitarian activities. In 1996 Switzerland, surprisingly, also joined P4P, and many other countries became associated, by various devices, with WEU. For some nations, such arrangements may be seen as preparatory to full NATO membership. In 1997, the NATO powers agreed to add the Czech Republic, Hungary and Poland to their ranks as full members, subject to ratification of the amended Treaty. Virtually all states, from the Atlantic to the Urals and beyond, are involved in the *Organization for Security and Cooperation in Europe*, which grew out of the Helsinki conferences (from 1973) and contributed to developments in human rights and mutual trust among the participants. All of this could well presage quite new security structures for Europe and beyond in the years to come.

Other changes, exogenous to the breaking up of the ice in eastern Europe, involved membership for Spain in NATO (1986); Finland, Sweden and Austria into the EU (1995); several more countries joining the WEU; and membership of them all in the new Partnership for Peace.

A quite different Chart from the first eight, Chart 9 attempts to show graphically, but only illustratively, how the degrees of 'likemindedness', plus acknowleged common interests and long involvement in international cooperation of certain countries bring them together naturally.

The three interlocking circles represent (1) strong economic interests which impel certain nations to act together; (2) prime security interests which some share with others; and (3) a vital interest in the development of democracy and the protection of human rights, which countries of that bent deeply share.

At the centre of the interlocking circles are the present G-7 countries (plus an additional seven) which share all these interests and

LIKEMINDEDNESS, SHARED INTERESTS, TREATY LINKS

CHART 9: 1997

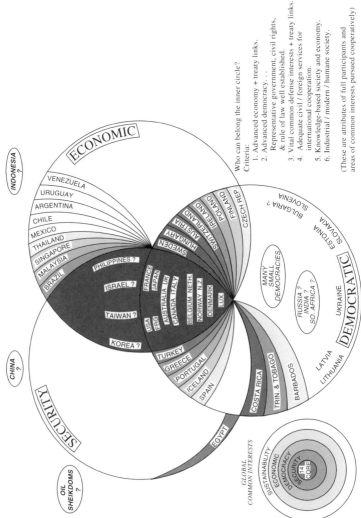

Who can belong the inner circle?
Criteria:
1. Advanced economy + treaty links.
2. Advanced democracy . . .
   Representative government, civil rights,
   & rule of law well established.
3. Vital common defense interests + treaty links.
4. Adequate civil / foreign services for
   international cooperation.
5. Knowledge-based society and economy.
6. Industrial / modern / humane society.

(These are attributes of full participants and
areas of common interests pursued cooperatively)

040997 J. Bulger

© James R. Huntley 1996

ties strongly. Also, all fourteen measure up well to the 'inner circle' criteria noted briefly in the righthand bottom corner of the Chart. (See also Appendix A and Chapter 6.)

Some countries, such as Egypt, are not strongly involved in the global economy or, at this stage at any rate, in promoting the expansion of the community of democracies. Yet Egypt is vitally linked for its survival to the United States and the Western community as a whole. So it is in the Security circle.

Some countries share close economic ties with the Inner Circle, yet they – although perhaps 'aspiring' democracies (e.g. Mexico, Malaysia) – are not much involved in or committed to the spread of democratic values in other parts of the world, nor are they deeply involved in mutual security arrangements. An additional group of countries understand their vital connection in both security and economic terms with the Inner Circle: these include the Philippines, Israel, Taiwan and Korea.

Finally, in the lower ('Democratic') circle are countries which see their future tied to the development of democracy and also share either strong economic ties (e.g. Switzerland, Finland, Ireland) or strong defence ties (e.g. Turkey, Spain), but not both – at least to the same degree – with the Inner Circle.

This schematic, subjective diagram should be taken with large grains of salt; its purpose is (a) to suggest the strong congruence of the interests and the capabilities of a small group of major states which form the core of the present and putative community of democracies, and also (b) to suggest that other nations are already beginning to make common cause with the core and could well, in many cases, become part of a general effort before too long.

Chart 10 is even more speculative than Chart 9, yet it also has a purpose: to give a hint of how the world of inter-democratic organizations might look in the second decade of the 21st century, suggesting which nations might take full part in the various organs of an *Intercontinental Community of Democracies* (see Chapter 8 for full descriptions), which countries might take longer to be involved, and so on. A few highly speculative comments, not meant invidiously for any country left in or out of the whole Chart or of any particular sub-organization, may be in order:

By, say, the year 2015, all 52 nations shown (plus at least twenty or so tiny democracies and one or two whose development might take off meteorically) could be signatories to the *Framework Agreement for ICD*. This would commit them to the values and practices

CHART 10. THE INTERCONTINENTAL COMMUNITY OF DEMOCRACIES – 2015

(AN OPTIMISTIC VIEW)

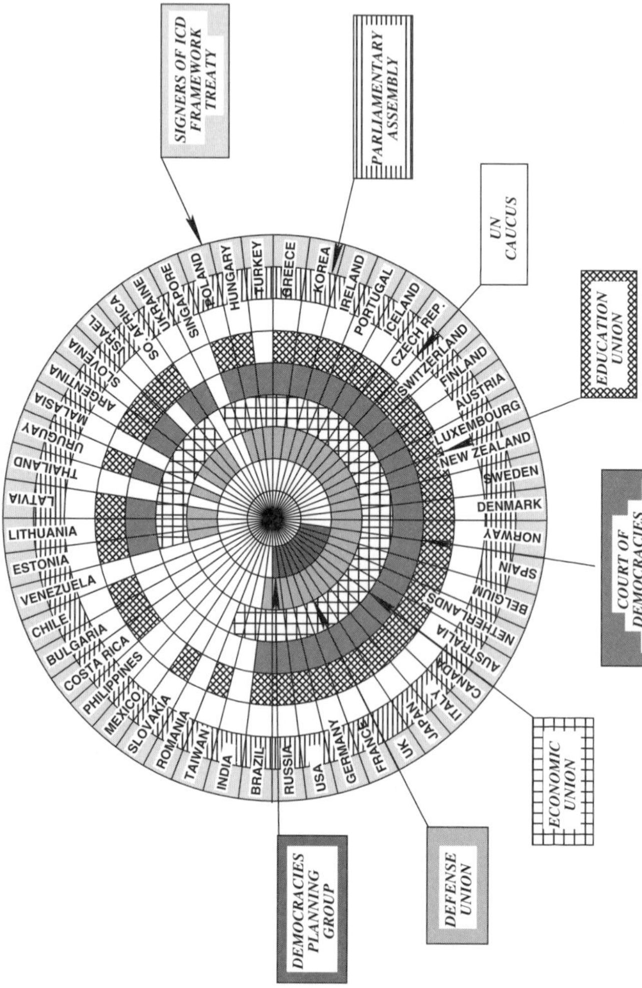

SIGNERS OF ICD FRAMEWORK TREATY

PARLIAMENTARY ASSEMBLY

UN CAUCUS

EDUCATION UNION

COURT OF DEMOCRACIES FOR HUMAN RIGHTS

ECONOMIC UNION

DEFENSE UNION

DEMOCRACIES PLANNING GROUP

GREECE, KOREA, IRELAND, PORTUGAL, ICELAND, CZECH REP., SWITZERLAND, FINLAND, AUSTRIA, LUXEMBOURG, NEW ZEALAND, SWEDEN, DENMARK, NORWAY, SPAIN, BELGIUM, NETHERLANDS, AUSTRALIA, CANADA, ITALY, JAPAN, FRANCE, UK, GERMANY, USA, RUSSIA, BRAZIL, INDIA, TAIWAN, ROMANIA, SLOVAKIA, MEXICO, PHILIPPINES, COSTA RICA, BULGARIA, CHILE, VENEZUELA, ESTONIA, LITHUANIA, LATVIA, THAILAND, URUGUAY, MALASIA, ARGENTINA, SLOVENIA, ISRAEL, SO. AFRICA, UKRAINE, SINGAPORE, POLAND, HUNGARY, TURKEY

040997 J. Bulger

of democracy and open doors to them, as they wished and as they qualified, to take part in the various sub-organs.

Virtually all subscribers to the Framework Agreement would probably wish immediately to become members of both the *Parliamentary Assembly of the Democracies* and the *Caucus of the Democracies at the United Nations.* In this way, every democratic nation would have a voice in both fora; larger nations would probably have more than one seat in the Assembly.

Belonging, however, to either the *Defence Union* or the *Economic Union* would not, at least by 2015, be for all. The membership obligations of both bodies would presumably be formidable, involving mutual defence commitments of a global nature and substantial expenditures in the one, and the lowering of economic barriers and the concerting of economic policies along lines of the European Union's example, in the other. These kinds of commitments could not be undertaken lightly; the broad suggestions as to which countries might, by 2015, be ready for one or the other or both, are – again – meant only to be illustrative. Actual membership-constellations in twenty years would probably look quite different.

Membership in the *Education Union for Democracy* is another matter; presumably any signer of the Framework Agreement could be eligible; the main qualification would be a desire to help spread democratic institutions and practices. Yet the founders of the Union would be wise to attach obligations to membership which every aspirant might not feel able to discharge. For example, members would presumably offer educational resources to the effort; not all might be able, at least initially, to do so. Also, such a Union might do well to start small and learn by experience how to do its difficult job.

The *Court of Democracies for Human Rights* is a most delicate matter; countries accepting its supranational jurisdiction would undertake most serious obligations, i.e. to allow their nationals to appeal to it and then, as governments, to abide by its decisions. Given the vagaries of politics and the difficulties of creating sound judicial systems, especially in new democracies, these are not commitments which all will be prepared to accept initially.

Finally, the *Democracies Planning Group* is probably the most sensitive and crucial ICD body. For reasons outlined in Chapter 8, there needs to be a small executive body to act for other members of the Community, appraising the international scene and formulating plans. By the third or fourth decade of the next century, it should be possible to begin to change the composition of the DPG, from representatives of certain governments to individuals chosen more democratically by organs of the entire Community. The evolution of the European Commission can be studied here usefully. Note that in Chart 10, however, only one country-member, Russia, has been added notionally to DPG. This assumes (a very big assumption) that political and economic development in Russia both proceed at a rapid pace in the next few years, adding to its domestic stability and its capabilities for Fourth Phase integration. The Russians, already clamouring to join the present G-7, would be keen to belong to DPG were it to be constituted. Two other countries, India and Brazil, would also seem to be likely candidates; much would depend in their cases, too, on the pace and quality of their political and economic evolution and on the extent to which they could begin to identify themselves with the global common interests of major democracies. Note (Appendix A) that the three countries rank low on the 'likemindedness' indices, and political development can be slower in very large and populous nations.

Some decades later (by, say, 2050), DPG would presumably disappear from this kind of chart and become an elected, collective executive of some sort – a kind of cabinet for the democracies – responsible either to the Parliamentary Assembly or to a broad electorate. But, in the increasingly speculative mode of this discourse, such notions remain quite theoretical. The ruminations of others can, perhaps, help define the process and its maturation.

(*Note*: The tiny democracies which might also be members of ICD by 2015 are not shown in Chart 10, for want of space. Most would probably be involved in no more than the parliamentary and UN caucus bodies, but could well have special arrangements with the Economic Union. These countries might include: Andorra, Barbados, Belize, Cyprus, Kiribati, Liechtenstein, Malta, Marshall Is, Micronesia, San Marino, Tuvalu, Bahamas, Cape Verde, Dominica, Grenada, Mauritius, Monaco, Palau, St Vincent, St Lucia, Solomon Is, Trinidad & Tobago, Nauru and St Kitts-Nevis.)

Notes

PREFACE

1. From a letter written to the League to Enforce Peace, an American citizens' organization which from 1912 to 1919 promoted the idea that eventually became the League of Nations. Quoted in Ruhl J. Bartlett, *The League to Enforce Peace*, University of North Carolina Press, Chapel Hill, 1944, 204.

1 WAR, DEMOGRAPHIC CLEANSING AND DEMOCRACY

1. Harcourt, Brace, New York, 1940.
2. Transaction Publishers, New Brunswick, NJ and London, 1994.
3. Op. cit.; Rummel comprehensively defines democide, 36ff.
4. Charles Scribner's Sons, New York, 1993, 7–18.
5. Sir John Weston, UK Permanent Representative to the United Nations, speaking in London, 10 April 1997.
6. See for example Bruce Russett, *Grasping the Democratic Peace*, Princeton University Press, Princeton, NJ, 1993; Francis Fukuyama, *The End of History and the Last Man*, The Free Press, New York, 1992, 262–4; Dean V. Babst, 'A Force for Peace', *Industrial Research* 14 (April 1972), 55–8; Z'ev Maoz and Nasrin Abdolali, 'Regime Types and International Conflict, 1816–1976', *Journal of Conflict Resolution* 33 (March 1989), 3–35; and R. J. Rummel, 'Libertarianism and International Violence', *Journal of Conflict Resolution* 27 (March 1983), 27–71. Some writers question the assertion that democracies do not make war on one another; see e.g. William Pfaff, 'No, Democracies and Their Citizens are not Immune to War Fevers', *International Herald Tribune*, 23 January 1995. But usually the critics look back in history to half-democracies (such as Wilhelmine Germany) or bypass the essential point that *democracies tend not to make war on other democracies* and instead focus on the readiness of democracies to war on non-democracies when survival is at stake. Russett and his colleagues seem to have the most definitive – and positive – conclusion: '[Democracies] rarely fight each other even at low levels of lethal violence, and never (or almost never) to war against each other' (119).
7. Edward D. Mansfield and Jack Snyder ('Democratization and the Danger of War', *International Security*, Summer 1995, Cambridge, Massachusetts) point out that *democratizing* states (as opposed to established democracies) are often likely to go to war because of their inability to manage change. Finding ways to help such emerging democracies to minimize the risks that accompany liberalization should be a top priority for the United States and its democratic allies.
8. Related, but somewhat different concepts for world order have recently

been published by Jean-Marie Guéhenno, *The End of the Nation-State*, University of Minnesota Press, Minneapolis, 1995, and by Alfredo G. A. Valladão, *The Twenty-first Century will be American*, Verso, New York and London, 1996. Both argue that future world order should no longer be conceived in hierarchical terms, but as a wheel, with spokes emanating from a centre. Guéhenno argues that the old 'nation-state democracies' cannot form the basis for a new order, but that 'new communities' enabled by communications technology and new economic values might. Valladão believes that the United States has taken a commanding lead in creating a 'World-America' and that this will be characterized by democratic values and institutions.

9. Drawn in part from Alan Bullock and Oliver Stalleybrass (eds), *Harper Dictionary of Modern Thought*, Harper and Row, New York, 1977, 161. Other terms are used to typify democracy; Karl Popper, for example, preferred 'the open society'. See *The Open Society and its Enemies*, 1945, and Russett, op. cit., 14–16.

10. See the annual survey, *Freedom in the World*, published by Freedom House, of New York, since the early 1970s. In the 1996–97 edition, 79 countries enjoy an excellent or good rating as practising democracies. About a third of these are tiny (e.g. Liechtenstein, Marshall Islands, Cape Verde, or Malta) and of little weight in the world. Nonetheless they and their bigger democratic partners represent together a significant number of the world's peoples, but still not a majority.

11. For another, widely-debated view, see Samuel Huntington, *The Clash of Civilizations*, Simon and Schuster, New York, 1996. Huntington believes that several distinct 'civilizations' persist in the world, that democracy is peculiar to Western civilization, and that the next great conflicts will be of civilizations, not ideologies.

12. 'A security community is one in which there is real assurance that the members of that community will not fight each other physically, but will settle their disputes in some other way.' This term was coined by R. W. Van Wagenen and Karl Deutsch and colleagues in their pioneering study, *Political Community and the North Atlantic Area: International Organization in the Light of Historical Experience*, Princeton University Press, Princeton, NJ, 1957, 5–6.

2 HOW THE DEMOCRACIES SAVED DEMOCRACY: 1940–90

1. Adams wrote to a friend: 'We have got to support France against Germany and fortify the Atlantic System beyond attack; for if Germany breaks down England or France, she becomes the center of a military world and we are lost.' Quoted in Forrest Davis, *The Atlantic System: The Story of Anglo-American Control of the Seas*, Reynal and Hitchock, New York, 1941, 197. Davis also cites Walter Lippmann, writing in the *New Republic* on 17 February 1917: '. . . on the two shores of the Atlantic Ocean there has grown up a profound web of interest which joins together the western world . . . if that community were destroyed we should know what we had lost' (Davis, 241).

2. Karl Kaiser, director of the German Society for Foreign Affairs, epitomized the transformation in security terms: 'A new German military class that grew up under democratic principles cooperated within the NATO institutions, numerous contacts developed and partners became friends, making war among them unthinkable. They were cooperating for a common purpose' (*NATO Review*, July 1995, 5).

3. For a slightly different historical view, see G. John Ikenberry, 'The Myth of Post-Cold War Chaos', *Foreign Affairs*, New York, May–June 1996, 79–91. He avers that some of the most important, and mainly economic, organs of international cooperation – such as the IMF, World Bank and GATT, were launched on earlier (1945) and more broadly internationalist grounds than the essentially Cold War bodies, such as NATO, which followed them into existence shortly. This is correct, but does not invalidate the importance of the Cold War Damocles sword in impelling Western nations and peoples, through the new European and Atlantic institutions of the time, to sacrifice some independence of action in return for perceived security. Both institutional developments were complementary.

4. See pages 16, 26–7 for a discussion of the contributions of Andrew Carnegie, Henry Adams and others to the early development of the Anglo-American de facto alliance and the international rule of law. (Also, Forrest Davis, op. cit., 68–9, 92–3, and elsewhere; this synergism is also discussed by Solomon P. Bloom, *Europe and America: The Western World in Modern Times*, Harcourt, Brace & World, New York, 1961, 481.)

5. In 1996, ASEAN (Association of Southeast Asian Nations) members were Brunei, Indonesia, Malaysia, Philippines, Singapore, Thailand and Vietnam; Cambodia, Laos, and Burma were in various stages of near-membership.

6. A full account of such regional bodies can be found in the annual *Political Handbook of the World*, Arthur S. Banks (ed.), CSA Publications, State University of New York at Binghamton. The Organization of American States, whose origins pre-dated the European communities, is worthy of special note. Modelled on the European example, the Mercosur free-trade agreement of 1995 between Argentina, Brazil, Uruguay, Bolivia, Chile and Paraguay had brought forth in less than a year a veritable flood of exports and imports. ('As Trade Soars, So Do Language Lessons', *Christian Science Monitor*, 20 March 1996, 6.)

3 THE LONG SEARCH FOR INTERNATIONAL ORDER

1. Will Durant, *The Life of Greece* (*The Story of Civilization: vol. 3*), Simon and Schuster, New York, 1939, 444.

2. William C. Olson and A. J. R. Groom, *International Relations Then and Now: Origins and Trends in Interpretations*, HarperCollins Academic, London, 1991, 8–9. See also Henry Kissinger, *Diplomacy*, Simon and Schuster, New York, 1994, 21, 27, 65. For a general review of the concept see, 'Balance of Power,' *Dictionary of the History of Ideas*, Charles Scribner's Sons, New York, 1973, vol. 1, 179–88.

3. Kissinger, op. cit., *in extenso.* Machiavelli and Hobbes were Kissinger's early forerunners. For the students of Kissinger's generation, Hans Morgenthau (*Politics Among Nations: The Struggle for Power and Peace,* 2nd edition, Alfred A. Knopf, New York, 1955) was the leading proponent of the 'neo-realist' school. He acknowledged the need for some stronger form of international governance, but argued that the best the United States (and by inference all other states) could hope to do is to define its interests and live within the system. In Morgenthau's revised 6th edition (1985), he defined even more carefully the requirements of a 'world state', but also made it seem exceedingly difficult to realize. In the 1990s, a proponent of the Richelieu-Morgenthau-Kissinger school, John Mearsheimer, can still characterize the international system 'as a brutal arena where states look for opportunities to take advantage of each other; daily life is essentially a struggle for power'. (Quoted by Jim Hoagland, 'America Battles Over Beans and Loses its Worldview', *International Herald Tribune,* 4–5 March 1995.)
4. W. T. R. and Annette Fox have described it: 'The balance of power may be thought of as inherent in any political process; the world political process at any moment registers the equilibrium established by the amount and direction of pressure that each participant is applying. It may be thought of as a policy pursued by a leading participant to make that equilibrium stable' (*International Encyclopedia of the Social Sciences,* Macmillan, New York, 1968, vol. 8, 58).
5. This treaty was based on the Convention de l'Octroi of 1804, by Napoleon and the Holy Roman Emperor.
6. Ruhl J. Bartlett, op. cit., 6.
7. 'By 1914 more than 200 treaties of arbitration had been ratified.' Ibid., 6.
8. Larry L. Fabian, *Andrew Carnegie's Peace Endowment: The Tycoon, The President, and Their Bargain of 1910,* Carnegie Endowment for International Peace, Washington, DC, 1985, 22. Contains a fascinating synopsis of currents of peace thought in the United States in the early 20th century.
9. Bartlett, op. cit., 26.
10. Ibid., 55–6.
11. The story of the extensive popular movement in the United States, and the subsequent demise of both the movement and of the League treaties, is described at length in Bartlett, op. cit. The British Union for Democratic Control was a major force in the UK, where Parliament adopted the League concept.
12. It is interesting that while Kissinger (in *Diplomacy,* op. cit.) singles out Theodore Roosevelt as virtually the only US President (aside from Nixon) who conducted foreign affairs on the basis of 'geopolitical realism' rather than 'high minded altruism' (42), he makes no mention of the inner conflicts and contradictory public statements surrounding arbitration and a league to enforce peace that bedevilled TR from 1910 to 1919. Kissinger alludes to TR's receipt of the Nobel Peace Prize (42), for example, but says nothing about his clearly idealistic and forward-looking acceptance speech.
13. 'Union of the Free Inevitable', first published in *Look* magazine;

republished in *Freedom and Union*, December 1952, 22 (Federal Union Inc., Washington, DC).

4. In the Cold War era, the Security Council was effectively immobilized by Soviet or Chinese vetoes from dealing decisively with major threats to world peace. An important exception was the Security Council decision to intervene in Korea (1950), when the Soviets were boycotting the Council's sessions and when the Chiang Kai-Shek regime was still representing 'China'.

5. China is virtually the only holdover. For a powerful history of that empire, down to the present day, see W. J. F. Jenner, *The Tyranny of History: The Roots of China's Crisis*, Penguin Books, London, 1994.

6. *International Encyclopedia of the Social Sciences*, Macmillan and The Free Press, New York, 1968, v. 11, 35. Compare with J. Moceri's view, above.

7. *Power Politics*, 2nd edn, Frederick A. Praeger, New York, 1954, 48–50.

8. Paul Nitze, *The Recovery of Ethics*, Council on Religion and International Affairs, New York, 1960, 16.

9. There is much debate about this thesis (see my note 6, to Chapter 1), but Francis Fukuyama (*The End of History and the Last Man*, The Free Press, New York, 1992) has summed up the case persuasively (262–3). A nation which formally declares itself a 'democracy' or a 'republic' does not necessarily deserve the full title, but for those with a good track record in, say, the past century, for upholding the rule of law, consent of the governed, a free press, broad enforceable civil rights and other hallmarks of democratic government, the dictum seems to hold. At times, some countries may have maintained some elements of such a system (as Germany, pre-1914) but still made war on their neighbours. However, there are no proven cases in this century of stable full democracies going to war with other stable mature democracies.

10. Kant's ideas on peace are reviewed extensively in Philip P. Wiener (ed.), *Dictionary of the History of Ideas*, Charles Scribner's Sons, New York, 1973, v. III, 442–5.

11. This claim may be debatable, but consider these factors: (a) only a few Swiss cantons, some Dutch provinces and England could lay claim to possessing elements of democratic government in 1775/87, but these did not incorporate the checks and balances of the new American system, balancing the powers of the executive and the popular legislature by a strong judiciary; (b) no other democracy has enshrined its powers in a constitution for as long, or as long a period unbroken to this day, as has the United States; (c) the civil rights protecting Americans from their government, in contradistinction to those of other early democracies, were fully and constitutionally protected, and remain so.

12. François Duchêne, one of Monnet's long-time collaborators, tells the story well in his book, *Jean Monnet: The First Statesman of Interdependence*, W. W. Norton, New York, 1994. Although Monnet is well known as the father of modern European unity, his advocacy of wider schemes is hardly appreciated. See Duchêne, 187–9, 327, 345, and also Éric Roussel, *Jean Monnet: 1888–1979*, Fayard, Paris, 1996, who links Monnet's early ideas with those of Clarence Streit and British progenitors of Atlantic Union, 226, 265, 378–9.

23. *The Saturday Evening Post,* 15 February 1930.
24. Robert W. Merry, *Taking on the World: Joseph and Stewart Alsop Guardians of the American Century*, Viking, New York, 132.
25. First published simultaneously by Jonathan Cape, London and Harp« & Brothers, New York, 1939. Many later versions were published, sor in languages other than English. After the fall of France, Streit r vised his text extensively to concentrate on the US–UK vestige of once-larger democratic world (*Union Now with Britain*, Harper & Brot ers, New York, 1941). For several years following World War II, Str« was to issue frequent revisions and to inspire many others to write (the subject.
26. Freymond recounts how Monick and Monnet convinced Churchill offer federation to France. (See *Western Europe Since the War: A Sh« Political History,* Frederick A. Praeger, New York and London, 196 6–8.) The diaries of Sir John Colville, Churchill's private secreta during the War, provide further details of events leading up to t! offer of union; *The Fringes of Power: 10 Downing Street Diaries, 1939–!* W. W. Norton, New York and London, 1985, 158–63.
27. Op. cit., 161.
28. George Allen & Unwin, Ltd., London, 2nd rev. edition 1950.
29. For a comprehensive account of the intellectual development of Briti federalism, see Richard Mayne and John Pinder, *Federal Union: T. Pioneers*, Macmillan, London, 1990.
30. At least two important lessons can be derived from the European mod (1) the need for patience and a long-term vision; and (2) the need start with a narrow focus – understandable to ordinary people a productive of results. In Chapter 8, new 'architecture' for the dem« racies is proposed, embodying a long-term vision and institutions serve the vision; the Democracies Planning Group (pages 171ff.) wou constitute the initial, sharp focus.

4 THE CHALLENGE AHEAD

1. 'Pivotal States and US Strategy', *Foreign Affairs*, January–February 19« 34. To the authors' 'American interests' I would add 'and those their democratic allies'.
2. *Webster's Third New International Dictionary*, Encyclopædia Britannic Chicago, 1966, v. 1, 537–8; *The Compact Edition of the Oxford Engli Dictionary*, Clarendon Press, Oxford, v. 1, 1178. See also 'Crisis' *International Encyclopedia of the Social Sciences*, Macmillan and T! Free Press, London, 1968, v. 3, 510–15.
3. Op. cit., *Webster's*, v. 1, 375.
4. Stephen H. Dunphy, *The Seattle Times*, 12 March 1995, quoting *Harva Business Review*.
5. Roy Denman, 'Dancing on the Grave is Foolhardy Exercise', *Inte national Herald Tribune*, 5 August 1993, 7.
6. R. N. Cooper, 'A Monetary System for the Future', *Foreign Affai. Fall 1984, 177.

7. 'No excuses, few regrets for worldly weapons dealer', *The Seattle Times,* 3 March 1996, A10.
8. February 1994, 44–77.
9. Op. cit., 54.
10. For just a single manifestation of this kind of phenomenon, see 'Youth Gangs Without Borders: An International Threat', *International Herald Tribune,* 30 August 1995, 2, in which the author describes the transplantation of Los Angeles street gangs to war-torn El Salvador.
11. Rummel, op. cit., 4.
12. He defines democide as 'murder by government agents acting authoritatively . . . the intentional government killing of an unarmed person or people' (36). He points out that democide is committed overwhelmingly by governments exercising unbridled power; the 'cross-pressures' and the 'associated political *culture*' of modern democracies makes their ability to commit democide negligible, if it is done at all (22–3). In the 20th Century, the USSR, Germany, Poland and Yugoslavia, China, Japan and other Far Eastern and Asian powers were the preponderant perpetrators of democide (4), but it is quite likely that with the gathering chaos, plus dictatorial organization and more modern methods of extinguishing life, sub-Saharan Africa could amass an eye-opening record for democide in the 21st Century.
13. Winston Churchill, *The World Crisis,* Thornton Butterworth Ltd. (London) and Scribner's (New York), abridged and revised edition, 1931, esp. 27–9, 38–40.
14. For a detailed account of the failure of Allied diplomacy between the wars, see Richard Lamb, *The Drift to War: 1922–39,* Bloomsbury Publishing Ltd., London, 1991. See also Donald Kagan, *On the Origins of War and the Preservation of Peace,* Anchor Books, New York, 1995, 281–413.
15. For an alternative – and more standard – view of this problem, see Paul Kennedy, *The Rise and Fall of the Great Powers,* Random House, New York, 1987. Like Kissinger, Morgenthau, and Machiavelli, Kennedy believes that international political history will be projected into the future substantially as it has unfolded in recent centuries and that, for example, the United States will eventually be supplanted as the greatest of great powers by another superpower. At Kennedy's reading, a precise candidate was difficult to discern, but assuredly there would be a successor. This writer believes that in the 21st century, a continuing plenitude of candidates – none able to exercise hegemony globally – would be much more likely, and that the great challenge for the democracies is to ensure that chaos will not eventuate . . . that the great development to come will be *Pax Democratica* instead.

THE DEMOCRACIES' UNFINISHED BUSINESS

1. Quoted by Dan Shor, Public Broadasting System, 'Weekend Edition', 4 February 1995.
2. This is not to denigrate important Asian milestones of the law, such

as the Code of Hammurabi or laws of the ancient Chinese or Indian
but the idea that no man is above the law – including the ruler, tha
all men have rights enshrined in law, and that ultimately rulers mak
laws and rule with the consent of the governed came from the We
and was first implemented in Western practice.

3. For the great majority, order is vastly preferable to disorder. The *Di*
   tionary of the History of Ideas, in its article on 'The Concept of Law
   (Charles Scribner's Sons, New York, 1973, v. II) opines that '. . . th
   security and relative satisfaction of desires guaranteed by a legal sy
   tem are to be preferred to the constant conflict of an anarchic soc
   ety, where even the strongest cannot expect peace'. Philip Selznick, i
   the *International Encyclopedia of the Social Sciences*, Macmillan, Ne
   York, 1965, says that '"law" is the enterprise of subjecting huma
   conduct to the governance of rules', but goes on to insist that 'th
   key word in the discussion of law is *authority*, not coercion. . . . [L]egali
   presumes the emergence of authoritative norms whose status as suc
   is guaranteeed by evidence of other, consensually validated norm
   (v. 9, 51–2). In other words, power enforces by sheer coercion, law l
   authority and – in free societies – consent and legitimacy.

4. *Webster's Third New International Dictionary, Encyclopædia Britannic*
   Chicago, 1966, v. 1, 39. If *agape* were a word commonly used in Englis
   I would use it. But it is not, so I shall not.

5. Modern blood banks, in which volunteers donate their blood to t
   given later to persons unknown to them, are a prime example of th
   kind of unselfish love for others.

6. *Oxford English Dictionary*, Compact edition, Oxford, 1971, v. 1, 1669, 107

7. Op. cit., 'Theologians distinguish between the *love of complacenc*
   which implies approval of qualities in the object [individual man c
   woman, or perhaps other members of one's class or ethnic group?
   and the *love of benevolence*, which is bestowed irrespective of the cha
   acter of the object.' v. 1, 1669.

8. Cited by Assistant Secretary of State Winston Lord, speech to th
   World Affairs Council of Seattle, 17 October 1995.

9. See the annual publication *Freedom in the World* (op. cit.) for a rut
   ning tally of the democratic 'performance' of the governments of a
   nations and colonial territories. Such a survey, relying often on sketct
   and unreliable data, cannot always be 'right' in its judgements, bt
   over the years it is perhaps the most useful basis for compariso
   between countries and the changes that time brings to their variot
   practices of democracy.

10. See Francis Fukuyama, *The End of History and the Last Man*, Th
    Free Press, New York, 1992, for a thoughtful and optimistic view c
    the prospects for democracy around the world. His work has bee
    much criticized for too-rosy a perspective, but there is a great deal t
    be said for his analysis and the general trend he postulates.

11. Perhaps the best account is by Peter Coleman, *The Liberal Conspirac*
    The Congress for Cultural Freedom, The Free Press-Macmillan, Ne
    York, 1989.

12. *Freedom in the World: The Annual Survey of Political Rights and Libertie*

1993–94, Freedom House, New York, 1994, 289–91; and private correspondence with William Roach, one of the British government's chief advisers in Guyana in the decolonization period, 1994. Jagan died in 1997.

3. A. H. Robertson, *European Institutions: Cooperation, Integration, Unification*, 3rd edition, Stevens & Sons Ltd., London, 1973, 220.

4. The term was used in a pioneering study to describe 'the ways in which political elites make decisions, their norms and attitudes, as well as the norms and attitudes of the ordinary citizen, his relations to government and to his fellow citizens' (Gabriel A. Almond and Sidney Verba, *The Civic Culture; Political Attitudes and Democracy in Five Nations*, Princeton University Press, Princeton, NJ, 1963, 5).

5. This is not to denigrate the substantial efforts made by Western governments and private groups to help Russia modernize its political culture, but these have not in the aggregate constituted enough to have made a major difference, nor have they been as much as the West could have done.

6. Readers may ask why Italy is not listed as a 'great power' of NATO; the answer is that because of the continued constitutional uncertainty and political turmoil of *fin de siècle* Italy it is currently impossible for that country to play its full role as a large and prosperous nation in the counsels of the major community organs of the West. Given Italy's monumental importance to the history of the West and of democracy in particular, this is regrettable. But it is a fact, even as one hopes for change.

7. The sceptic may say, with some reason (but not too much): 'But what about the Swiss cantons and the American colonies; both became unions voluntarily?' True. However, none of the constituents were, in a modern sense, 'nation-states'. In the Swiss case union was accomplished gradually over centuries; the components were a few small city-states and several wooded and inaccessible counties in mountain valleys. The individual cantons were never recognized as international actors by the great powers of the 13th to 19th centuries; by the conclusion of the Napoleonic Wars 'Switzerland' had become a recognized nation. Its modern federal constitution was not in place until 1848. In the American case, the 13 original colonies were all British dependencies which individually exercised none of the prerogatives of a state, as defined in the 18th century. Only after 1776 did France and the Netherlands, and later other great powers, recognize the new American confederation as – collectively – a nation-state. The provinces of the Netherlands, too, in fighting to break away from Spain and the Habsburgs, came together voluntarily and eventually became a nation. But none of these cases is analogous to the mid-20th century free union of six (more recently, 15) modern states; to weld together such proud and powerful nations as Britain, France, Germany and Italy – and equally proud smaller but distinct nation-states – into one large proto-federation is the political accomplishment of our age, perhaps of the entire millennium just closing.

8. In 1997, these comprised: Australia, Austria, Belgium, Canada, the

Czech Republic, Denmark, Finland, France, Germany, Greece, Hun‚
gary, Iceland, Ireland, Italy, Japan, Republic of Korea, Luxembourg‚
Mexico, Netherlands, New Zealand, Norway, Poland, Portugal, Spain‚
Sweden, Switzerland, Turkey, the United Kingdom and the Unite‚
States. The Commission of the European Communities participate‚
in a limited way; until the OECD voided the Associate Membershi‚
of Yugoslavia in 1992, that fractured nation was also a limited pa‚
ticipant. Argentina, Brazil, Slovakia and Slovenia have all reported‚
made overtures. The OECD also signed a special cooperation agree‚
ment with Russia, in 1994.

19. Members: Albania, Austria, Belgium, Bulgaria, Croatia, Cyprus, Czec‚
Republic, Denmark, Estonia, Finland, France, Germany, Greece‚
Hungary, Iceland, Ireland, Italy, Latvia, Liechtenstein, Lithuania, Lu‚
embourg, FYR Macedonia, Malta, Moldava, Netherlands, Norwa‚
Poland, Portugal, Romania, Russia, San Marino, Slovakia, Sloveni‚
Spain, Sweden, Switzerland, Turkey, Ukraine, United Kingdom. 'Speci‚
Guests of the Parliamentary Assembly': Belarus, Bosnia-Herzogovin‚
Armenia, Azerbaijan and Georgia. (Yugoslavia's guest status was voide‚
in 1992.)

20. A good account of the origins and early development of the G-7 ‚
contained in Robert D. Putnam and Nicholas Bayne, *Hanging Togethe*‚
The Seven-Power Summits, Heinemann, London, 1984, from which th‚
Giscard quote is taken (15).

21. Op. cit., 17.

22. This Japanese attitude changed dramatically during the prime mini‚
tership of Yasuhiro Nakasone (1982–89), but asserted itself again und‚
his successors. Kenneth Pyle (*The Japanese Question: Power and Pu‚*
pose in a New Era, AEI Press, Washington, DC, 1992) discusses th‚
(85–105) and other questions related to Japan's international engag‚
ment in great detail.

6 LIKEMINDEDNESS AND THE DEMOCRATIC PEOPLES

1. 'The Myth of Post-Cold War Chaos', *Foreign Affairs*, New York, Ma‚
June 1996, 87.

2. See page 7 for a working definition of democracy. For an extensiv‚
and reasoned political categorization of all the countries and coloni‚
dependencies of the world, see the annual *Freedom in the World*, op. c‚

3. Calculating relative economic weights of nations is not a simple ma‚
ter. In recent years some experts have begun to substitute 'PP‚
(purchasing power parity), which compares prices paid for univers‚
'market baskets' of goods, for the more traditional per capita Gro‚
Domestic Product (GDP). A good example of PPP is *The Economist*‚
tongue-in-cheek 'Big Mac Standard'. Per capita measurements favo‚
highly-developed countries; PPP gives undue weight (according to son‚
economists) to large population/low income countries, such as Ind‚
or China. Endowment in natural resources is also considered by son‚
as important in such rankings, but there is less and less correlation ‚

today's world between, say, a nation's supplies of coal or oil and its economic growth or power-political importance. (See Jeffrey Sachs and Andrew Warner, 'Natural Resource Abundance and Economic Growth', Harvard Institute for International Development, Cambridge, MA, October 1995, and related article in *The Economist*, 5 January 1996, 87–9).

4. 'Culture Gulf Blamed for Stalled Hong Kong Talks,' *International Herald Tribune*, 8–9 April 1995.

5. See Appendix A, on likemindedness.

6. See Appendix B for 'who belongs to what'.

7. Op. cit., *Freedom in the World, 1994–95*. The survey's ratings can be subject to question when one surveys groups of countries adjudged 'free' and 'partly free', for example, and assigned numerical categories within these broader designations. But for the most part, *Freedom in the World*, if compared and combined with similar if not as extensive analyses as the annual ratings on human rights of the Department of State, or the continuous monitoring of human rights by bodies such as Amnesty International, is a valuable and unique tool. I am greatly indebted to the inventor of Freedom House's annual survey, Raymond D. Gastil, for many observations over the years that have explained its methodology and helped materially to refine my own assessments in these matters.

8. The *Encyclopædia Britannica Book of the Year* provides extensive statistics which can serve as indicators of social and economic progress. The 25 members of the OECD are analysed regularly and in even greater detail by the Organization's economists and statisticians; annual economic and social reviews of each member are undertaken. These may be obtained from OECD, 2, rue André Pascal, 75016 Paris. One might also note an important study which correlated economic growth with economic freedom: James Gwartney, Robert Lawson and Walter Block; co-published by Fraser Institute (Vancouver, BC), Cato Institute (Washington, DC) and Institute of Economic Affairs, London, 1995.

9. *The Economist*, 1 July 1995, 'Survey', 15.

10. One way of doing this is suggested by the present G-7 practice, since 1992, of inviting Russia to a portion of its annual meetings, for 'G-8' consultations that recognize Russia's singular importance to the world economy, but also take into account its present inability to play a full role. Should not India and Brazil, for example, also be included in arrangements of this kind?

11. Each year, *Freedom in the World* lists all countries in a compendium of 'Combined Average Ratings', which averages the scores allotted to the records of each in the exercise of political liberties and the protection of civil rights. The editors start with combined ratings of '1.0' (the very highest, the same as allotted for example to Sweden, Austria, Canada, the USA), of '1.5', and of '2.0'. I have perused *Freedom in the World* listings for the decade 1985–95 and have included in this list of small and tiny democracies only those which consistently were rated with at least a 2.0 (the same ranking as given, for example, to

Japan, Chile and Israel). See, for example, *Freedom in the World: The Annual Survey of Political Rights and Civil Liberties, 1993–94* (op. cit.) 682.

12. A condition of including Cyprus in the ICD should be a settlement and new relationship between the Greek and Turkish Cypriot republics

7 THE VISION AND ITS CRITICS

1. In August 1996, for example, the Indian government found it impossible to join other powers in the Nuclear Test Ban Treaty, and thus blocked the enterprise.

2. Recent 'elections' organized at village and town level in China may be a harbinger of better things, but so far it appears that these, like 'elections' in so many other Communist countries in the past, are contests between candidates selected by the Party, rather than between leaders arising through a popular political process.

3. The author recalls well a long conversation in 1961 with the distinguished historian Arnold Toynbee, who believed that if the NATO/OECD powers were to visibly consolidate their nascent community it would inevitably be seen by the entire Third World as an effort to 'gang up' on them. Western Third and Fourth Phase forms of democratic interaction proceeded, despite his reservations, and the results now, three and a half decades later, seem to have overcome most of his objections. Toynbee's point of view was set forth in *The World and the West*, Oxford University Press, 1953.

4. It is to my intense chagrin that I note the position of my own country, the United States, over the past two decades in this annual 'aid sweepstakes' calculation, viz., at the very bottom of the giving scale in percentage of GDP terms among the rich countries.

5. Asia-Pacific Economic Cooperation forum, established in 1989; 18 members (1997) include Australia, Brunei, Canada, Chile, China, Hong Kong, Indonesia, Japan, Republic of Korea, Malaysia, Mexico, New Zealand, Papua New Guinea, Philippines, Singapore, Taiwan, Thailand, United States. Russia, Vietnam and Peru are to join in 1998.

6. For a fuller quotation by Mr Ibrahim, see page 72.

7. *The Clash of Civilizations and the Remaking of World Order*, Simon and Schuster, New York, 1996; and 'The West: Unique, not Universal', *Foreign Affairs*, November/December 1996.

8. In *Deutsche Bank Research* (Frankfurt, 28 December 1995, 3), Norbert Walter attributed 'recurring currency shocks, disappointed export expectations, a vulnerable economy and the loss of thousands of jobs' in Europe to 'the status quo in monetary policy' and urged that European Monetary Union proceed.

9. Richard N. Cooper suggested this (*Foreign Affairs*, New York, Fall 1984, 166–84), viz.: 'an alternative scheme for the next century: *the creation of a common currency for all of the industrial democracies, with a common monetary policy and a joint Bank of Issue to determine that monetary policy*' (emphasis in original).

10. Monnet's biographer, François Duchêne, confirms this: 'Monnet thought of a European coal and steel authority as a source of peace. . . . All five clauses of the preamble to the Schuman treaty deal with peace in one form or another, and only two turn on economics.' Op. cit., *Jean Monnet: First Statesman of Interdependence*, 224.
11. Op. cit., 54.
12. Ronald Steel, *Temptations of a Superpower*, Harvard University Press, Cambridge, 1995. He advocates US policies that are compatible with the country's supposedly reduced circumstances and minimize the risks of involvement in quarrels (including those of the Balkans) 'in which it has no direct interest, and over causes it will often misunderstand'. It is an instructive and up-to-date statement of the Second Phase balance-of-power theorists, who generally refuse to acknowledge the lengths to which the United States and the other experienced democracies have already moved into Fourth Phase international relations.
13. At the time of writing, it is not at all certain that the US or any of the other powers essential to the NATO peacemaking operation in Bosnia (1995–) will have the political staying power and the financial generosity to bring a durable peace to the Balkans, but there has been progress.
14. From October to December 1995, when President Clinton was making his decision on Bosnia and persuading a reluctant Congress to go along, numerous articles appeared in the press on both sides of the issue. The argument for intervention was cogently put, *inter alia*, by William E. Odom, 'Endgame in Bosnia', *San Diego Union-Tribune*, 15 October 1995, and David Gompert, 'Chicken Little Goes to Bosnia', *Los Angeles Times*, 24 November 1995. A far gloomier view was taken by Nicholas von Hoffman ('Like It or Not, We're an Empire', *Washington Post*, 13 December 1995), who made the case that the United States, for some years, has been an '*imperium*' and ought to accept world housekeeping chores – such as Bosnia – just as the British or the Romans or other empire-builders did, as the price of keeping order. Whether or not von Hoffman's tongue was in his cheek, there is a strong element of truth in his arguments; I believe, however, that the great majority of Americans never had the stomach for *imperium* and will have even less in the future. This is a principal reason why I have argued in this book for a *Pax Democratica*.
15. *The Road Ahead*, Viking Penguin, New York, 1995, 253.
16. *Kiplinger Washington Letter*, 15 March 1996, 4. The *Letter* states that this is 'part of a basic shift in our economy to the Information Age, leaving the Industrial Age'.
17. 'The Slow Growth Mystery: Can We Cure the Cancer?', *Foreign Affairs*, New York, January-February 1996, 146–52. Lawrence reviews a recent book by Jeffrey G. Madrick (*The End of Affluence: The Causes and Consequences of America's Economic Dilemma*, Random House, New York, 1995) and concludes that while much of Madrick's analysis is useful, he overlooks in his conclusions clear evidence that it is productivity growth and the problems of measuring it in America's (and other developed countries') *service* industries, and not in

manufacturing which lie at the root of the sharp decline in economic growth rates. See also Niels Thygesen, Yutaka Kosai and Robert Z. Lawrence, *Globalization and Trilateral Labor Markets: Evidence and Implications*, the Trilateral Commission/Brookings Institution, Washington, DC, 1996.

18. For example, Harvard economist and former Undersecretary of State Richard N. Cooper provides a classic formulation: 'The basic economic rationale for relatively free trade is that it permits each country to concentrate its production on those goods which it can produce relatively efficiently, and to exchange its surplus production for goods which it produces relatively inefficiently.' *The Economics of Interdependence: Economic Policy in the Atlantic Community*, McGraw-Hill Book Company, New York, 1968, 76.

19. Lawrence, op. cit., 151.

20. In a provocative book, Clive Jenkins and Barrie Jenkins argued, ' . . . there really is no alternative to phasing out the distinctions between work and leisure' (*The Leisure Shock*, Eyre Methuen, London, 1981, 177).

21. George Soros, the financier, proposed precisely this in a controversial article in *The Atlantic Monthly* ('The Capitalist Threat', January 1997, 45–58).

22. See, e.g., *International Encyclopædia of the Social Sciences*, Macmillan, New York, 1968, vol. 15, 77–80.

23. See Morita's article, 'Toward a New World Economic Order', *The Atlantic Monthly*, June 1993, 88–98, in which he proposed to the leaders of the G-7 countries 'that we begin to seek the ways and means of lowering *all* economic barriers between North America, Europe, and Japan – trade, investment, legal, and so forth – in order to begin creating the nucleus of a new world economic order that would include a harmonized world business system with agreed rules and procedures that transcend national boundaries'. (88)

24. Op. cit., Kissinger, *Diplomacy*. He asserts the novelty of the present situation: ' . . . none of the most important countries which must build a new world order have had any experience with the multistate system that is emerging'. (26) But he also falls back on the – for him – tested methods: ' . . . the rise and fall of previous world orders based on many states . . . is the only experience on which one can draw in trying to understand the challenges facing contemporary statesmen'. (27) Near the end of his book, Kissinger makes clear his preference: 'If a Wilsonian system based on legitimacy [and democracy] is not possible, America will have to learn to operate in a balance-of-power system, however uncongenial it may find such a course.' (835) Nowhere in *Diplomacy* does Kissinger mention such tools of American diplomacy as the US Information Agency, foreign student exchanges, the Fulbright Act, the Agency for International Development, or the Voice of America. Only glancingly does he refer to the European Community, the European Coal and Steel Community, the European Economic Community or Euratom, the European Defence Community, or even Jean Monnet, father of it all. To Kissinger, these are

minor episodes in the sweep of post-1945 American diplomacy, not the heights of innovation and achievement in transatlantic order-building that I and others believe them to be.

8   THE ARCHITECTURE OF *PAX DEMOCRATICA*

1. *The Politics of Diplomacy: Revolution, War and Peace, 1989–92*, G. P. Putnam's Sons, New York, 1995, 45.
2. Op. cit., Clarence K. Streit, *Union Now*, 1939 and successive, revised editions through 1949. He came close, on at least one occasion (1962) to realizing his dream of a constitutional convention of the democracies, but it was a meeting without powers and – most important – without members of the US Congress, who ironically had authorized, and paid for, the conclave.
3. Encyclopædia Britannica, Inc., Chicago, 1966, v. II, 1174.
4. *A Theory of Political Integration*, Homewood, Illinois, Dorsey Press, 1967, 3.
5. Op. cit., Karl W. Deutsch, R. Van Wagenen et al., 5.
6. In an interesting speech to the World Affairs Council of Seattle (October 1995), Professor Donald Hellmann of the University of Washington, and director of the National APEC Center, told listeners that APEC, while of great potential value, was at this stage in history much like the 1928 Kellogg-Briand Pact outlawing war, 'all declaration and good intentions, but no teeth or bite'.
7. Address in Berlin, 18 June 1991; reprinted in *Dispatch*, Department of State, Washington, DC, v. 2, No. 25, 24 June 1992, 439–44. The idea was elaborated in an article by William Pfaff, 'Baker's Commonwealth of Democracies', *International Herald Tribune*, 26 June 1991.
8. *Statement Presented to the Special Joint Committee of the Senate and House of Commons on Canada's International Relations*, Ottawa, 12 March 1986, 12.
9. Sir Halford John Mackinder's Asian heartland theory was first set forth in a paper read to the Royal Geographical Society in 1904. His extended views were set out in a short book while the Versailles conference was still in session: *Democratic Ideals and Reality*, 1919 (W. W. Norton, New York, rev. edition, 1962).
10. Wilson's espousal of the unfortunate, flawed concept that all 'nations' were entitled to 'self-determination' led to the breakup of natural economic regions and to a plethora of unviable small states.
11. François Duchêne, biographer of Monnet, used this term in a letter to the author, to characterize the decision-making processes of the European Commission and other EU supranational bodies, which are based on the international rule of law accepted by all members.
12. Richard Burt, former assistant secretary of state and ambassador to Germany, argued strongly for such a transformation of the G-7 in the *New York Times*, 14 May 1993, op. ed. page. This might be feasible, but would encounter great bureaucratic inertia.
13. 'Together We Need Balanced Counsel to Guide Our Sovereignties', *International Herald Tribune*, 19 December 1995.

9 AFTERWORD

1. The reader should not assume that, starry-eyed, I believe that thence-forth all Frenchmen and all Germans have loved one another unre-servedly and had no room in their minds or hearts for all the other human impulses of envy, greed, fear, mistrust, and so on. But a good society, by preventing – through law and accepted mores – bad im-pulses and naked power from overpowering it, rests on paramount feelings of brotherhood – or love in its pure sense, reinforced by law. When contemplating the startling evolution of Franco–German relations in the past half-century, the reader should call up a famous picture of French President François Mitterand and German Chancellor Helmut Kohl, standing with hands clasped on the battlefield of Verdun in 1986, on the 70th anniversary of their bloodiest battle, which cost 1 million common dead.
2. Op. cit., Deutsch et al., 6, 30. The work of Deutsch and his colleagues strongly suggests that what they termed 'pluralistic security-communities', i.e. groups of nations that were, in my terms, strongly likeminded, were the least likely to break down into internecine warfare – even more than some security-communities which had been 'amalgamated' (often by force) into the same formal state.

APPENDIX A

1. See, for example, Huntley, *Uniting the Democracies*, New York Univer-sity Press, New York, 1980, Chapter 2, and esp. pp. 24–6.
2. See Russett, op. cit., for an attempt at mathematical analysis of factors which influence democratic development (72–98); Russett and his col-laborators do not seem to arrive at conclusions substantially different from those of this author or Freedom House.
3. See page 7 for a working definition of democracy. For an extensive and reasoned political categorization of all the countries and colonial dependencies of the world, see the annual *Freedom in the World*, op. cit.

Bibliography

Those wishing to probe the subject of this book may wish to consult the following list, which consists of principal works (minus ephemera) referred to in the foregoing text, but also includes additional basic texts which, in the author's judgement, provide essential background to a serious study of the idea of *Pax Democratica*. The trails in history, philosophy, political and economic theory are virtually limitless; this Bibliography contains some of the fundamentals, but represents only a beginning.

Ake, Claude, *A Theory of Political Integration* (Homewood, IL: Dorsey Press, 1967).

Albrecht-Carrié, *One Europe: The Historical Background of European Unity* (Garden City, NY: Doubleday, 1965).

Almond, Gabriel A. and Verba, Sidney, *The Civic Culture: Political Attitudes and Democracy in Five Nations* (Princeton, NJ: Princeton University Press, 1963).

Baker, James A. III, Speech in Berlin, 18 June 1991, *Despatch*, Washington, DC: Department of State, 24 June 1991, 439–44.

Baker, James A. III, *The Politics of Diplomacy: Revolution, War and Peace, 1989–92* (New York: G. P. Putnam's Sons, 1995).

Banks, Arthur S. (ed.), *Political Handbook of the World* (Binghamton, NY: CSA Publications, State University of New York, 1995; published annually since 1927).

Bartlett, Ruhl J., *The League to Enforce Peace* (Chapel Hill, NC: University of North Carolina Press, 1944).

Bloom, Solomon P., *Europe and America: The Western World in Modern Times* (New York: Harcourt, Brace and World, 1961).

Brecher, Irving, *Statement Presented to the Special Joint Committee of the Senate and House of Commons on Canada's International Relations*, Ottawa, 12 March 1986.

Brinton, Crane, *From Many One: The Process of Political Integration, The Problem of World Government* (Westport, CT: Greenwood Press, 1948).

Brzezinski, Zbigniew, *Out of Control: Global Turmoil on the Eve of the 21st Century* (New York: Charles Scribner's Sons, 1993).

Brzezinski, Zbigniew, *The Grand Chessboard: American Primacy and its Geostrategic Imperatives* (New York: Basic Books, 1997).

Churchill, Winston, *The World Crisis: 1911–1918* (London: Thornton Butterworth Ltd, abridged and rev. edn, 1931).

Coleman, Peter, *The Liberal Conspiracy: The Congress for Cultural Freedom* (New York: The Free Press-Macmillan, 1989).

Cooper, R. N., *The Economics of Interdependence: Economic Policy in the Atlantic Community* (New York: McGraw-Hill, 1968).

Cooper, R. N., 'A Monetary System for the Future', *Foreign Affairs* (Fall 1984).

233

Curtis, Lionel, *Civitas Dei* (London: George Allen & Unwin Ltd., 3 vols, 2nd rev. edn, 1950).

Davis, Forrest, *The Atlantic System: The Story of Anglo-American Control of the Seas* (New York: Reynal and Hitchcock, 1941).

Deutsch, Karl W. and Van Wagenen, R. W., *Political Community and the North Atlantic Area: International Organization in the Light of Historical Experience* (Princeton, NJ: Princeton University Press, 1957).

Deutsch, Karl W., art. in James N. Rosenau (ed.), *International Politics and Foreign Policy* (Glencoe, IL: Free Press, 1961), 98–105.

Duchêne, François, *Jean Monnet: The First Statesman of Interdependence* (New York: W. W. Norton, 1994).

Durant, Will, *The Life of Greece (The Story of Civilization, vol. 3)*, (New York, 1939).

Eagleburger, Lawrence S., Speech on 7 January 1993, *Despatch*, Washington, DC: Department of State, 11 January 1993, 19.

Fabian, Larry L., *Andrew Carnegie's Peace Endowment: The Tycoon, the President, and Their Bargain of 1910* (Washington, DC: Carnegie Endowment for International Peace, 1985).

Freedom House, *Freedom in the World* (New York, published annually since 1973, in book form since 1978).

Fukuyama, Francis, *The End of History and the Last Man* (New York: The Free Press, 1992).

Gates, William, *The Road Ahead* (New York: Viking Penguin, 1995).

Goodman, Elliott R., *The Fate of the Atlantic Community* (New York: Frederick A. Praeger, 1966).

Goodrich, Leland M. and Hambro, Edvard, *The Charter of the United Nations: Commentary and Documents* (Boston: The World Peace Foundation, 1949).

Guéhenno, Jean-Marie, *The End of the Nation-State* (Minneapolis: University of Minnesota Press, 1995).

Halle, Louis J., *The Cold War as History* (London: Chatto and Windus, 1971).

Harned, Joseph and Mally, Gerhard, *Atlantic Assembly: Proposals and Prospects* (London: The Hansard Society, 1965).

Hemleben, Sylvester John, *Plans for World Peace Through Six Centuries* (Chicago: University of Chicago Press, 1943).

Hovey, J. Allan, *The Superparliaments: Interparliamentary Consultation and Atlantic Cooperation* (New York: Frederick A. Praeger, 1966).

Huntington, Samuel P., *The Clash of Civilizations and the Remaking of World Order* (New York: Simon and Schuster, 1996).

Huntington, Samuel P., 'The West: Unique, not Universal', *Foreign Affairs*, November–December 1996.

Huntley, James Robert, *Uniting the Democracies: Institutions of the Emerging Atlantic-Pacific System* (New York and London: New York University Press, 1980).

Ikenberry, G. John, 'The Myth of Post-Cold War Chaos', *Foreign Affairs*, May–June 1996.

Jenkins, Clive and Jenkins, Barrie, *The Leisure Shock* (London: Eyre Methuen, 1981).

Jenner, W. J. F., *The Tyranny of History: The Roots of China's Crisis* (London: Penguin Books, 1994).

Kagan, Donald, *On the Origins of War and the Preservation of Peace* (New York: Doubleday/Anchor Books, 1995).

Kant, Emmanuel, *Essay on Perpetual Peace (Zum ewigen Frieden)* (1795).

Kaplan, Robert, 'The Coming Anarchy', *The Atlantic Monthly*, February 1994, 44–77.

Kennedy, Paul, *The Rise and Fall of the Great Powers: Economic Change and Military Conflict from 1500 to 2000* (New York: Random House, 1987).

Kissinger, Henry, *Diplomacy* (New York: Simon and Schuster, 1994).

Kohn, Hans, *The Idea of Nationalism: A Study in its Origins and Background* (New York: Macmillan, 1951).

Lamb, Richard, *The Drift to War: 1922–39* (London: Bloomsbury, 1991).

Lawrence, Robert A., 'The Slow Growth Mystery: Can We Cure the Cancer?', *Foreign Affairs*, January–February 1996, 146–52.

Lawrence, Robert A. and others, *Globalization and Trilateral Labor Markets: Evidence and Implications* (Washington, DC: Brookings and Trilateral Commission, 1996).

Lipson, Leslie, *The Democratic Civilization* (New York: Oxford University Press, 1964).

MacKinder, Halford John, *Democratic Ideals and Reality* (New York: W. W. Norton, rev. edn, 1962).

Manchester, William, *The Last Lion: Winston Spencer Churchill*, (Boston: Little, Brown, 2 vols., 1983 and 1988).

Mayne, Richard and Pinder, John, *Federal Union: The Pioneers* (London: Macmillan, 1990).

Merry, Robert W., *Taking on the World: Joseph and Stewart Alsop – Guardians of the American Century* (New York: Viking, 1996).

Modelski, George and Perry, Gardner, 'Democratization in Long Perspective', *Technological Forecasting and Social Change*, Vol. 39, Nos 1–2, March–April 1991, 23–34.

Monnet, Jean, *Memoirs* (Garden City, NY: Doubleday, 1978).

Morgenthau, Hans, *Politics Among Nations: The Struggle for Power and Peace* (New York: Alfred A. Knopf, 2nd edn, 1955; rev. 6th edn, 1985).

Morita, Akio, 'Toward a New World Economic Order', *The Atlantic Monthly*, June 1993, 88–98.

Morrow, Anne, *The Wave of the Future* (New York: Harcourt, Brace, 1940).

Munk, Frank, *Atlantic Dilemma: Partnership or Community?* (Dobbs Ferry, NY: Oceana Publications, 1964).

Nitze, Paul, *The Recovery of Ethics* (New York: Council on Religion and International Affairs, 1960).

Northrop, F. S. C., *The Taming of the Nations: A Study of the Cultural Basis of International Policy* (New York: Macmillan, 1954).

Olson, William C. and A. J. R. Groom, *International Relations Then and Now: Origins and Trends in Interpretations* (London: HarperCollins Academic, 1991).

Popper, Karl, *The Open Society and its Enemies* (London: 1945).

Putnam, Robert D. and Bayne, Nicholas, *Hanging Together: The Seven-Power Summits* (London: Heinemann, 1984).

Pyle, Kenneth, *The Japanese Question: Power and Purpose in a New Era* (Washington, DC: AEI Press, 1992).

Righter, Rosemary, *Utopia Lost: The United Nations and World Order* (New York: The Twentieth Century Fund, 1995).

Robertson, A. H., *European Institutions: Cooperation, Integration, Unification* (London: Stevens and Sons Ltd., 3rd edn, 1973).

Rosenau, James, article on National Interest, *International Encyclopedia of the Social Sciences*, Vol. 11, 35–9 (New York: Macmillan and The Free Press, 1968).

Rummel, R. J., *Death by Government* (New Brunswick, NJ and London: Transaction Publishers, 1994).

Russett, Bruce (with others), *Grasping the Democratic Peace* (Princeton, NJ: Princeton University Press, 1993).

Sansom, G. B., *The Western World and Japan* (New York: Alfred A. Knopf, 1950).

Schwarzenberger, Georg, *Power Politics* (New York: Frederick A. Praeger, 1954, 2nd edn).

Sohn, Louis B., *Cases and Other Materials on World Law: The Interpretation and Application of the Charter of the United Nations and the Constitutions of Other Agencies of the World Community* (Brooklyn: The Foundation Press Inc., 1950).

Stein, Eric and Hay, Peter, *Law and Institutions in the Atlantic Area: Readings, Cases, and Problems* (Indianapolis: Bobbs-Merrill, 1967).

Storry, Richard, *A History of Modern Japan* (Harmondsworth: Penguin Books, 1960, rev. 1972).

Strausz-Hupé, Robert, *The Zone of Indifference* (New York: G. P. Putnam's Sons, 1952).

Strausz-Hupé, Robert, *Democracy and American Foreign Policy: Reflections on the Legacy of Alexis de Toqueville* (New Brunswick, NJ: Transaction Publishers, 1995).

Streit, Clarence K., *Union Now* (simultaneous versions, London: Jonathan Cape; New York: Harper & Brothers; 1939; reprinted many times, various versions and editions).

Toynbee, Arnold, 'Union of the Free Inevitable', *Look*, New York, 1952 (reprinted in *Freedom and Union*, Federal Union Inc., Washington, DC, December 1952, 22).

Toynbee, Arnold, *The World and the West* (Oxford: Oxford University Press, 1953).

Valladão, Alfredo G. A., *The Twenty-First Century will be American* (New York and London: Verso, 1996).

Wooley, Wesley T., *Alternatives to Anarchy: American Supranationism Since World War II* (Bloomington and Indianapolis, IN: Indiana University Press, 1988).

Index

237